Medical Billing 101

Michelle M. Rimmer, CBCS

Instructor, Medical Billing and
Health Claims Assistance Programs
Ocean County College, Toms River, New Jersey
Owner, Shore Medical Billing and
Shore Health Claims Assistance

DELMAR
CENGAGE Learning™

Australia • Brazil • Japan • Korea • Mexico • Singapore • Spain • United Kingdom • United States

DELMAR
CENGAGE Learning

Medical Billing 101
By Michelle M. Rimmer, CBCS

Vice President, Health Care Business Unit:
 William Brottmiller

Director of Learning Solutions: Matthew Kane

Managing Editor: Marah Bellegarde

Senior Acquisitions Editor: Rhonda Dearborn

Product Manager: Jadin Babin-Kavanaugh

Editorial Assistant: Laura Pye

Marketing Director: Jennifer McAvey

Senior Marketing Manager: Lynn Henn

Marketing Manager: Michele McTighe

Marketing Coordinator: Andrea Eobstel

Technology Director: Laurie Davis

Technology Product Manager:
 Mary Colleen Liburdi

Technology Project Manager II: Carolyn Fox

Production Director: Carolyn Miller

Content Project Manager: David Buddle

Senior Art Director: Jack Pendleton

Print Buyer: Michelle Reeves

For product information and technology assistance, contact us at
Cengage Learning Customer & Sales Support, 1-800-354-9706

For permission to use material from this text or product,
submit all requests online at **www.cengage.com/permissions**
Further permissions questions can be emailed to
permissionrequest@cengage.com

Library of Congress Control Number: 2007013250

ISBN-13: 978-1-4180-3975-2

ISBN-10: 1-4180-3975-6

Current Procedural Terminology (CPT) is copyright © 2006 American Medical Association. All rights reserved. No fee schedules, basic units, relative values, or related listings are included in CPT. The AMA assumes no liability for the data contained herein. Applicable FARS/DFARS restrictions apply to government use. *CPT®* is a trademark of the American Medical Association

Delmar
Executive Woods
5 Maxwell Drive
Clifton Park, NY 12065-2919

Cengage Learning is a leading provider of customized learning solutions with office locations around the globe, including Singapore, the United Kingdom, Australia, Mexico, Brazil, and Japan. Locate your local office at: **international .cengage.com/region**

Cengage Learning products are represented in Canada by Nelson Education, Ltd.

For your lifelong learning solutions, visit **delmar.cengage.com**
Visit our corporate website at **cengage.com**

Notice to the Reader

Publisher does not warrant or guarantee any of the products described herein or perform any independent analysis in connection with any of the product information contained herein. Publisher does not assume, and expressly disclaims, any obligation to obtain and include information other than that provided to it by the manufacturer.

The reader is expressly warned to consider and adopt all safety precautions that might be indicated by the activities described herein and to avoid all potential hazards. By following the instructions contained herein, the reader willingly assumes all risks in connection with such instructions.

The publisher makes no representations or warranties of any kind, including, but not limited to, the warranties of fitness for particular purpose or merchantability, nor are any such representations implied with respect to the material set forth herein, and the publisher takes no responsibility with respect to such material. The publisher shall not be liable for any special, consequential, or exemplary damages resulting, in whole or part, from the reader's use of, or reliance upon, this material.

Printed in the United States of America
8 9 10 11 XXX 13 12 11

This book is dedicated to my past, present, and future students. It is for you that I write and because of you that I am able to live my passion to teach.

Contents

PREFACE ix

ACKNOWLEDGMENTS xi

ABOUT THE AUTHOR xiii

REVIEWERS xv

USING THE STUDENT PRACTICE SOFTWARE TO ACCOMPANY MEDICAL BILLING 101 xvii

HOW TO USE THE ENCODER PRO 30-DAY FREE TRIAL CD-ROM xxi

CHAPTER 1   YOUR JOB AS A PHYSICIAN-BASED MEDICAL BILLER 1

What Is a Medical Biller?   1
In the Office or Not   1
Got Certification?   2
Membership in an Organization   2
Maintaining Certification Status   4

CHAPTER 2   HEALTH INSURANCE AND THE IDENTIFICATION CARD 7

A Bit of History   7
Health Insurance   8
The Identification Card   8
Types of Health Insurance Plans   9
Types of Coverage   15
Medical Discount Cards   15

CHAPTER 3   THE CODES (CPT, HCPCS LEVEL II, ICD-9, AND MODIFIERS)   21

Learning a New Language   21
Healthcare Common Procedure Coding System (HCPCS)   21
Modifiers   22
ICD-9-CM Codes   25

CHAPTER 4   THE FORMS (PATIENT REGISTRATION, SUPERBILL, AND HOSPITAL SHEET)   35

Patient Registration Form   35
The Superbill   37
Hospital Billing Sheet   38
Nursing Home Visits   40
Home Visits   40
Frequency of Billing   40

CHAPTER 5   THE HEART OF MEDICAL BILLING: THE CMS-1500 FORM   45

Introduction   45
Claim Filing Instructions   47

CHAPTER 6   BILLING FOR OFFICE SERVICES AND PROCEDURES   61

Gathering Data   61
Determining Modifier Usage   63

CHAPTER 7   BILLING FOR INPATIENT AND NURSING FACILITY SERVICES   73

Inpatient Billing for Physician Services   73
Billing for Nursing Facility Services   76

CHAPTER 8   ELECTRONIC CLAIMS SUBMISSIONS AND CLEARINGHOUSES   87

Billing Via "Snail Mail"   87
Electronic Claims Submission   87
The Role of a Clearinghouse   88
Electronic Data Interchange   88
Benefits of Electronic Claims Submission   88
Medical Billing Via the World Wide Web   90

CHAPTER 9   EOBs AND PAYMENTS   93

Deciphering the Explanation of Benefits   93
Payment of the Claim   95
Insurance Adjustments   95

CHAPTER 10   DENIALS AND APPEALS   105

The Rejected Claim   105
The Denied Claim   105

CHAPTER 11   MAINTAINING ACCOUNTS RECEIVABLE, AGING REPORTS, AND REBILLING   115

The Aging Process   115
Rebilling   117
Follow-Up   117
Maintaining the Accounts Receivable   118

CHAPTER 12   COLLECTIONS AND THE STATE INSURANCE COMMISSIONER   121

The Need to Collect   121
Insurance Companies Beware   126

APPENDIX I   CASE STUDIES FOR THE CMS-1500 FORM   137

APPENDIX II   FORMS   163

Blank CMS-1500 Form   165
E&M CodeBuilder   166
Evaluation and Management Codes   168
Advance Beneficiary Notice (ABN) Form   169
Notice of Exclusions from Medicare Benefits (NEMB) Form   170
CMS Overpayment/Refund Form   171
Request for Opinion/Consult   172
Refusal to Authorize Payment   173
Informed Refusal   174
Code of Conduct   175
UB-04 Form   179

APPENDIX III   COMMONLY USED ACRONYMS IN MEDICAL BILLING AND CODING   181

APPENDIX IV   MEDICARE PART B CARRIERS BY STATE   185

APPENDIX V   INSURANCE COMMISSIONERS BY STATE   195

GLOSSARY   203

INDEX   211

Preface

Medical billing is an important function of a physician's office. If billing is not performed accurately, reimbursement can be negatively affected. *Medical Billing 101* provides step-by-step instructions for the job of the medical biller. The material presented in this text is on an introductory level, intended to be easily comprehended even by those students with no prior allied health courses.

Frequently, billing texts contain information on many subject areas, leaving students feeling overwhelmed or overloaded. *Medical Billing 101* maintains its focus on billing only so as not to confuse the beginning biller early on in the learning process.

This text is designed for the allied health student who is enrolled in a medical billing, medical coding, medical office specialist, or medical assisting program. While it can be used as a stand-alone text for a medical billing program, it can also be used to supplement other required texts in other allied health programs. It can also serve as a reference guide for medical billers on the job, both in physicians' offices and in medical billing companies.

ORGANIZATION OF TEXT

The chapter order and flow of this text are designed to outline the job duties of a medical biller in the order they are performed in the physician's office setting. Chapter 1 discusses the duties required of the medical biller and the importance of maintaining certification. Chapter 2 through 5 introduce the student to the health insurance identification card, the code sets, and the various forms used to gather the data necessary for completing the medical billing function. Chapter 6 through 8 describe the types of billing the physician-based biller will be performing, and Chapter 9 through 12 guide the student through the processes that occur once medical claims have been submitted.

Features of the Text

- Each chapter starts off with learning objectives and key terms to help orient students to the material.
- A marginal glossary defines key terms on the spot.
- There are many examples of real-world forms, such as EOBs, aging reports, and denied claims.
- An end-of-chapter summary provides an opportunity to assess learning before moving on to the next chapter.
- Chapter review questions provide an opportunity to test learning.

- Case studies written to be completed on the CMS-1500 form allow students to practice billing for different physician service situations, including office visits and inpatient physician services.
- Space is provided in the text for answers, and blank CMS-1500 forms are included for practice.
- Appendix I contains 25 additional case studies for CMS-1500 form completion; these cases are also located on the CD-ROM, so they can be completed electronically or manually.
- Appendix II contains examples of several real-world forms necessary to and commonly used in the billing world, including the UB-04.
- Appendices III, IV, and V contain reference information that may come in handy, both on the job and in the classroom.

SUPPLEMENTS

The following supplements are available to enhance the use of *Medical Billing 101.*

Student Resources

- Free CD-ROM contains 25 case studies designed to help students practice and understand how to complete the CMS-1500 form. These cases provide billing practice for different physician service situations, including office visits and inpatient physician services.
- Free trial CD-ROM of EncoderPro, Ingenix's powerful coding software.

Instructor Supplements

The following supplements are available for instructors.

Instructor's Manual

The Instructor's Manual (ISBN 978-1-4180-3976-4) contains lesson plans, sample syllabi, and answer keys to chapter review questions and to the CD-ROM case studies in Appendix I.

Electronic Classroom Manager

The Electronic Classroom Manager on CD-ROM (ISBN 978-1-4180-3977-2) provides many aids to help the instructor plan and implement a medical billing course. The CD-ROM includes the following items:

- Computerized test bank with more than 500 questions
- Microsoft PowerPoint presentation with more than 300 slides
- An electronic version of the Instructor's Manual

FEEDBACK

Michelle Rimmer can be contacted at MRCMRS05@Yahoo.com

Acknowledgments

I would like to thank the following people:

Kathy Caro, Administrator of Nursing and Allied Health CPE department at Ocean County College, Toms River, New Jersey, for always believing in me and providing me with wisdom I will carry with me always.

Irene Malfitano, my typist, without whom this book would not have been possible.

Valerie Mardsen-Gray, for her computer expertise and assistance with this entire project.

Mike, my husband, for taking the kids and giving me Sundays to write.

My girls, Chelsea, Alyssa, and Megan, for your patience when Mom was busy.

My mother, Peggy, and sister, Annick, for their encouragement from the beginning.

Rhonda Dearborn, senior acquisitions editor, who took a chance on me from an email two and a half years ago.

Jadin Babin-Kavanaugh, product manager, for her advice and expertise on the development of this book.

About the Author

Michelle M. Rimmer has more than 17 years' experience in the medical billing and health insurance reimbursement industry. As a medical biller, she has worked in various physician offices, a medical billing company, and a large university hospital. Most recently, Michelle has worked as the coordinator and instructor of the Medical Billing Certificate program and as an instructor in the Medical Office Specialist and Health Claims Assistance programs in the Allied Health Department of CPE at Ocean County College, Toms River, New Jersey.

Since 1997, she has owned and operated Shore Medical Billing, and most recently started an additional home-based business, Shore Health Claims Assistance. Michelle is nationally certified as a Medical Reimbursement Specialist and a Billing and Coding Specialist and is a member of the American Medical Billing Association and the National Health Career Association.

Reviewers

GENERAL REVIEWERS

Richard A. Durling, CMA, BS, CPC, PMCI
Director, Medical Assisting Program
Linn Benton Community College
Corvallis, Oregon

Norma Mercado, MAHS, RHIA
Department Chair, Medical Coding Program
Austin Community College
Austin, Texas

Pat Gallagher Moeck, PhD, MBA, CMA
Director, Medical Assisting Program
El Centro College
Dallas, Texas

Heather Skow, CPC, CHCT, CCP, CMBS, RHE
Medical Department Faculty Member/Chief Compliance Officer
Spencerian College
Louisville, Kentucky

Gwendolyn Tibbets-Sandoval, BSHA (Bachelor of Science
  in Healthcare Administration)
Senior Electronic Medical Record Consultant
Crosby, North Dakota

TECHNICAL REVIEWERS

Teena Gregory, MS, CMRS, CPC
Medical Reimbursement Program Coordinator/Instructor
Career Learning Center of the Black Hills
Rapid City, South Dakota

June M. Petillo, MBA, RMC
Healthcare Consultant and Coding Specialist
Clinical Trials Director, Women's Health USA
Avon, Connecticut

Autumn Plank, RHIT
Coder 5
State University of New York
Alfred, New York

Using the Student Practice Software to Accompany Medical Billing 101

The Student Practice Software, found on the CD-ROM inside the back cover of the textbook, is designed to help you practice completing CMS-1500 claims. Tutorials for using the blank form, study, and test modes are located on the CD. They can be viewed on your computer screen or printed. Brief instructions to get you started using the software follow. Install the program using the CD-ROM included with this textbook.

COMPLETING CASE STUDY CLAIMS

You can use the Student Practice Software to:

- Print blank CMS-1500 and UB-04 claims for manual completion (handwritten or typewritten).
- View Case Studies 1 through 25.
- Complete Case Studies 1 through 25 (Appendix I of the textbook) in the blank form mode, where no feedback is provided and completed claims can be printed.

GENERAL HINTS

1. Press the Caps Lock key on your keyboard each time you use the Student Practice Software because the CMS-1500 will only accept capital letters.
2. Proofread each CMS-1500 block entry before moving to the next block.
3. Follow Optical Scanning Guidelines when entering data.
4. Enter the provider's complete name and credentials in Block 31.
5. When you use the numeric keypad on your keyboard to enter numbers, press the Num Lock key on your keyboard.

PRINTING A BLANK CMS-1500 CLAIM

1. At the main menu of the Student Practice Software, click the **Blank CMS-1500** tab to open that page. Click the **Blank CMS-1500** button.
2. Click **CMS-1500 Form**.
3. Click **Print**.
4. On the Printing Options dialog box, click **OK** to print the form. (The Print CMS-1500 Form option contains an X as the default.)

KEYSTROKES FOR MOVING AROUND THE CMS-1500 CLAIM

Go to a specific block number	Ctrl-G (and enter the block number)
Go to next block	Ctrl-N
Go to previous block	Ctrl-P
Go to top of claim	Ctrl-T

If you forget these shortcuts, click **View** in the menu bar, and select the action you want.

OPTICAL SCANNING GUIDELINES

The following guidelines must be followed when entering CMS-1500 claims data:

- Properly align CMS-1500 claims in the printer.
- Do not enter a zero for the alpha character O.
- Enter all alpha characters in uppercase (capital letters).
- Do not enter the dollar sign ($) for any charge, payment, or balance due.
- Enter a space instead of any of the following:
  - Decimal points for charges, payments, or balances
  - Decimal point in a diagnosis code number
  - Dash in front of a procedure code modifier or a telephone number
  - Parentheses for telephone area code (parentheses are printed on the form).
- Do not use periods within a name. Use commas to separate the last name, first name, and middle initial. A hyphen can be used in a compound name, but only as printed on the insurance ID card.
- Leave one blank space between the patient/policy holder's last name, first name, and middle initial.
- Do not enter a patient/policy holder's title or other designations (e.g., Sr., Jr., II, or III) on a claim unless they appear on the patient's insurance ID card. For example:

  Insurance ID card states: William F. Goodpatient IV

  Entry on CMS-1500: Goodpatient IV, William F

Exception: TRICARE claims require entry of active duty sponsor rank/grade after the name.

- Enter two zeros (00) in the cents column when a fee or a monetary total can be expressed as whole dollars. For example, $6.00 is written as 6 00

- All dates should be entered using eight digits with spaces between the digits representing the month, day, and year (MM DD YYYY), **except** in Blocks 24A (MMDDYY), 24B (MMDDYY), and 31 (MMDDYYY), where no spaces are entered. Months are expressed as two-digit numbers, as follows:

January	01
February	02
March	03
April	04
May	05
June	06
July	07
August	08
September	09
October	10
November	11
December	12

- Enter Social Security numbers and employee identification numbers **without** hyphens or spaces.

- In Block 31, enter the provider's complete name and credentials.

- Proofread the claim to be sure all blocks that are to contain an X within a box are completed properly.

STUDY MODE FEEDBACK

Use the Tab key on your keyboard to move out of a block and to be presented with the "Sorry, that is not the expected answer" display. Click **Retry** to return to the block, and re-enter claims data. Click **Study** to be presented with Block Help (at the bottom of the screen), and re-enter claims data. Click **Solve** to have the block completed for you.

SAVING A CMS-1500 CLAIM

The Student Practice Software saves completed blank form and study mode CMS-1500 claims to the My Documents folder on your hard drive when you click **Main Menu** and **Yes** when the Save? window is displayed. CMS-1500 claims completed using the blank form, study, and test modes can be manually saved to a different folder on the hard drive or to an external source, such as a CD or flash drive.

1. When you are ready to save your work, click **File**, then **Save As**. . . (located at the top of your computer screen).
2. In the Save As dialog box, click the down arrow in the Save in box to select the drive and/or folder.
3. Enter a file name in the File Name edit box. The file name should correspond to the case study it represents (e.g., Case1.uhi).
4. Click **OK**.

FILENAMING CONVENTION

Label each file saved so it corresponds to the case study represented (e.g., Case1.uhi). The file name can include hyphen (-) and underscore (_) characters, but it cannot include most other symbols.

PRINTING A COMPLETED CMS-1500 CLAIM

1. Once you have completed a CMS-1500 claim in the blank form, study, or test mode, click **Print** (located on the left side of the program window) or click **File**, **Print** (located at the top of your computer screen).
2. Once the Printing Options window displays, click **OK** to print the CMS-1500 Form, Summary Report With Justifications, and Case Study.

NOTE: Default printing functions can be deactivated on the Printing Options dialog box by clicking any box that contains an X (to remove the X). For example, if you want to print just the completed CMS-1500 claim, click on the Summary Report, With Justifications, and Case Study to remove the X in each box.

How to Use the Encoder Pro 30-Day Free Trial CD-ROM

The Encoder Pro software included in the back cover of this textbook is a 30-day free trial of Ingenix's powerful medical coding solution that allows you to lookup ICD-9-CM, CPT, and HCPCS Level II codes quickly and accurately. This software can be used to assign codes to any of the exercises in the textbook. Be sure to check with your instructor before installing the Encoder Pro software because the CD-ROM bundled with your book expires 30 days after installation.

MENUS AND TOOLBARS

- Encoder Pro contains a menu that expands to allow you to easily navigate the software. Click on a menu heading to select one of its options, such as View or Code Book Sections. Encoder Pro contains a toolbar with dropdown menus that allow you to select the ICD-9-CM, CPT, or HCPCS Level II coding system and new, revised, or deleted codes and code book sections.

- Use the coding system dropdown menu on the far left to select a coding system. Then, enter a condition (e.g., diabetes) or procedure/service in the Search box. Click the Search button to view Tabular Results, which can be expanded, or click See Index Listing to use the alphabetic index to locate a code.

- Use the dropdown list on the far right of the black toolbar to quickly access New Codes, Revised Codes, Deleted Codes, and Code Book sections. Make a selection and click the View button to access the dialog boxes.

- Encoder Pro's toolbar with clickable buttons allows you to use its unique features. Simply mouse over a button to view its title, and a brief description of the button will also appear in the status bar on the bottom left of the screen. Click on the button to use its function.

FEATURES AND BENEFITS OF ENCODER PRO

Encoder Pro is the essential code look-up software for CPT, ICD-9-CM, and HCPCS code sets. It gives users fast searching capabilities across all code sets. Encoder Pro can greatly reduce the time it takes to build or review a claim and helps improve overall coding accuracy. If you decide to subscribe to the full version of Encoder Pro, the following tools will be available to you:

- **Powerful Ingenix CodeLogic™ search engine.** Improve productivity by eliminating time-consuming code lookup in outdated code books. Search all three code sets simultaneously using lay terms, acronyms, abbreviations, and even misspelled words.
- **Lay descriptions for thousands of CPT codes.** Enhance your understanding of procedures with easy-to-understand descriptions.
- **Color-coded edits.** Understand whether a code carries an age or sex edit, is covered by Medicare, or contains bundled procedures.
- **Quarterly update service.** Rest assured you are always using accurate codes. You can code confidently throughout the year with free code updates.
- **Great value.** Get the content from over 20 code and reference books in one powerful solution.

For more information about Encoder Pro software, click on the Help menu from inside the free trial version, then select Features by Product, or go to **www.ingenixonline.com.**

Chapter 1
Your Job as a Physician-Based Medical Biller

KEY TERMS

accounts receivable	CHP	medical biller
CAP	CHRS	medical billing company
CBCS	CMRS	outsource
certification	continuing education unit (CEU)	physician-based

OBJECTIVES

Upon completion of this chapter, the student should be able to:

- Explain the job duties of a medical biller.
- Describe the concept of outsourcing.
- Discuss the importance of certification and maintaining CEUs.
- Define key terms.

WHAT IS A MEDICAL BILLER?

Aside from patient care, high on the list of a physician's priorities is getting paid! In the medical office, the person responsible for meeting this objective is the medical biller.

medical biller the person responsible for submitting a provider's charges to the appropriate party.

The role of the medical biller is of utmost importance. If the job is not accurately performed, the physician's income is directly affected. If the physician's income is negatively affected by inaccurate billing methods, a domino effect of other problems can occur. These problems can include an inability to meet the cost of office expenses, malpractice insurance, and payroll.

Duties of a medical biller often include more than simply submitting a provider's charges. These duties can include posting insurance and patient payments and maintaining the physician's accounts receivable.

accounts receivable monies owed to a physician for his or her services.

IN THE OFFICE OR NOT

physician-based pertaining only to a physician.

outsource send work offsite.

medical billing company an offsite company hired to process medical bills for the physician.

Although this text uses the term **physician-based** to describe the medical biller's employment situation, the job opportunities are not limited to those in a physician's office. Some practices **outsource** their billing to a **medical billing company**. These companies solicit physicians as clients. With the number of new medical billing companies constantly increasing, it is quite possible to land a job as a physician-based medical biller at such a company. Regardless of the location, the guidelines for billing are the same.

1

GOT CERTIFICATION?

certification
a professional status or level earned by successful completion of an examination; a person who is certified may subsequently list the designated credentials after her or his name.

Obtaining a certification demonstrates dedication, skills, and achievement of the medical biller. When certification status is obtained, the medical biller is considered a step above those not certified. Having credentials designates the biller as a true professional!

Imagine an employer who has two resumes on the desk. Both candidates have similar experience as medical billers. During interviews, the employer found both comparable. However, one is certified and the other is not. Which candidate do you think the employer will hire? Certification can be *the* deciding factor in being offered the position over a noncertified competitor.

To become certified, one must successfully pass an examination given by a sponsoring organization. Some exams are offered online; others must be taken at an exam site determined by the organization. Some organizations provide study guides for use prior to taking the exam. Some exams require the use of the CPT-4 and ICD-9 coding books, an insurance handbook, and a medical dictionary. Notification will be given, in advance, of any books required to take the exam.

MEMBERSHIP IN AN ORGANIZATION

Before a person takes the exam to become certified, he or she is usually required to become a member of the sponsoring organization. When visiting an organization's Web site, search sections on membership application, benefits, and cost to join. These organizations offer a wealth of information. Some have monthly newsletters, helpful hints, and bulletin boards to keep the medical biller abreast of upcoming changes in the industry. You can network with others in your field, and some sites even offer job listings in your local area. Take advantage of the information from these organizations, as the rules and regulations regarding medical billing and insurance are constantly changing.

Certified Medical Reimbursement Specialist

CMRS
Certified Medical Reimbursement Specialist; a certification offered by the American Medical Billing Association.

The Certified Medical Reimbursement Specialist (CMRS) exam is offered through the American Medical Billing Association. This online exam consists of approximately 750 questions. Because it is an open-book exam, you may use any material needed to research your answers. You are provided with a study guide to use during the exam, and it is recommended that you also have available a medical dictionary, a CPT-4 code book, an ICD-9 code book, and a health insurance handbook. There is a 45-day limit for completing this exam. Sections included in the exam are:

- Medical Terminology
- Anatomy and Physiology
- CPT Coding
- ICD-9 Coding
- Clearinghouses
- CMS 1500 Form
- Compliance
- Fraud and Abuse
- Insurance

Online
Open book
750 questions
45 day limit

- Managed Care
- Insurance Carriers
- Web Technology
- Information Technology
- Acronyms
- General
- Case Studies

After successfully passing the exam with a grade of 85% or better, the student is issued a certificate with the CMRS credential.

Certified Healthcare Reimbursement Specialist

[handwritten: open book 200 questions]

CHRS
Certified Healthcare Reimbursement Specialist; a certification offered by the National Electronic Billers Alliance.

The Certified Healthcare Reimbursement Specialist (**CHRS**) exam is offered through the National Electronic Billers Alliance (NEBA). This open-book exam consists of approximately 200 questions regarding various medical billing issues. Students are encouraged to use the Internet when researching their answers to the exam questions. Upon successful completion of this exam, students may use the designation CHRS and are issued a certificate from NEBA.

Certified Billing and Coding Specialist

[handwritten: 100 multiple choice no books 2½ hr]

CBCS
Certified Billing and Coding Specialist; a certification offered by the National Healthcareer Association.

The Certified Billing and Coding Specialist (**CBCS**) exam is offered through the National Healthcareer Association (NHA). NHA is a leader in health care certification. The exam consists of 100 multiple-choice questions. A study guide is provided, as is a sample test. Students are *not* allowed to use any books or outside materials during the exam. This proctored exam is given at a predetermined testing site, and the sponsor allows two and one-half hours for completion of the exam. Upon receiving a passing grade of 70% or above, the student is issued an NHA certification card with the CBCS credential.

Certified in Healthcare Privacy

CHP
Certified in Healthcare Privacy; a certification offered by the American Health Information Management Association.

The Certified in Healthcare Privacy (**CHP**) exam is offered through the American Health Information Management Association (AHIMA). AHIMA is a leader in medical coding certification. Although the CHP certification is not intended specifically for medical billers, it is an excellent additional certification to obtain. With this certification, the CHP specialist demonstrates knowledge about health care privacy issues in the medical facility setting. This person might be the compliance officer or the person responsible for training new employees about HIPAA regulations (rules under the Health Insurance Portability and Accountability Act of 1996). Check the AHIMA Web site for exam locations and dates in your area.

Claims Assistance Professional

CAP
Claims Assistance Professional; a title used by members of the Alliance of Claims Assistance Professionals.

One need not take an exam to become a claims assistance professional (**CAP**). This title is associated with membership in the Alliance of Claims Assistance Professionals (ACAP). To become a CAP, one must apply for membership and pay the $75 membership fee. To be considered, the application must be submitted with three reference letters. On the application is a question relating to the applicant's experience or history in the health claims field. The CAP may work for a doctor's office as a consultant, or may work primarily as a home-based business owner who assists the public with claims filing, denials, and appeals.

MAINTAINING CERTIFICATION STATUS

After you become certified, you will want to *stay* certified! To do so, you will have to pay an annual membership fee to the certifying organization of which you are a member. Most likely, you will also be required to complete annual **continuing education units (CEUs)**. Each organization will have available the required amount of CEUs needed to maintain certification status. There will also be a list of what CEUs are accepted by the organization. One can earn CEUs through online billing courses, attending seminars, and reading books and industry-related magazines. The costs of CEUs vary. Refer to your individual organization to see specifically which CEUs are offered and the related expenses.

continuing education unit (CEU)
a level of measurement of noncredited education.

SUMMARY

There are many job opportunities for the physician-based medical biller. A person in this position may be physically located in a physician's office, or may work for a medical billing company. It is important to understand all that the job entails and how crucial it is to the physician's practice that the job be performed accurately.

To increase the opportunity for advancement in this field, certification is recommended. Obtaining certification shows dedication and professionalism to prospective employers. It also places the medical biller a step above those who are not certified.

REVIEW QUESTIONS

1. What is the primary job duty of a medical biller?

   submitting provider's charges to appropriate party

2. List three possible job duties of a medical biller.

   posting insurance pmts
   posting patient pmts
   maintenance of A/R

3. *Physician-based billing* refers to:
   a. durable medical equipment billing
   b. hospital room charges
   c. charges for a physician's services
   d. none of the above

4. Explain the importance of accuracy in the job of a medical biller.

   directly affects physicians income

5. Define the following terms:
   a. outsource

   Send work offsite

   b. medical billing company

   Offsite company hired to process medical bills for physician

   c. accounts receivable

   monies owed to a physician for his/her services

6. What is the advantage to the medical biller of obtaining certification?

   sets you apart from others

7. Which exam is offered through NEBA?
   a. CHP
   b. CHS
   c. CHRS   _Certified Healthcare Reimbursement Specialist_
   d. CHMS

8. Which exam is an online exam?
   a. CHRS
   b. CHP
   c. CMRS   _Certified Medical Reimbursement Specialist_
   d. none of the above

9. What does the acronym CEU stand for?
   a. continuous education understanding
   b. comprehensive evaluation unit
   c. critical evaluation understanding
   d. continuing education unit

10. Which designation is not based on passing an examination?
    a. CAP   _Claims Assistant Professional_
    b. CHP
    c. CMRS
    d. none of the above

Chapter 2
Health Insurance and the Identification Card

KEY TERMS

allowed amount
beneficiary
capitated
capitated rate
capitation check
capitation list
carrier
Centers for Medicare and Medicaid Services (CMS)
co-insurance
commercial
contract
co-payment
coverage
deductible
dependents
disability insurance
discount
eligibility category
emergency room visits
employee
employee/significant other (E/S) coverage
family coverage
fee for service

fee schedule
fiscal agent
government plan
group number
health insurance
health insurance identification card
health maintenance organization (HMO)
husband/wife (H/W) coverage
identification number
indemnity plan
indigent
individual
in network
insured
managed care plan
Medicaid
medical discount card
Medicare
Medicare Advantage
Medigap
military treatment facility (MTF)
Original Medicare
out of network

out of pocket
outpatient
parent/child coverage
participates
plan type
point-of-service (POS) plan
policyholder
preferred provider network (PPN)
preferred provider organization (PPO)
prescription drugs
primary
primary care provider (PCP)
referral
secondary
self-pay
sickness insurance
specialist
subscriber
supplemental
traditional
Tricare Extra
Tricare Prime
Tricare Standard

OBJECTIVES

Upon completion of this chapter, the student should be able to:

- Describe the different types of health insurance and the identification cards associated with these plans.
- Explain the difference between co-insurance and co-payments.
- Discuss how health insurance differs from a medical discount card.
- Define key terms.

A BIT OF HISTORY

The state of medicine prior to 1920 was very basic; when a doctor's services were required, most patients were treated in their homes. As a result, medical expenditures were very low, which resulted in a low demand for health insurance at that time.

Complaints during this time period were not related to the costs of medical care, but rather to the wages lost from the inability to work while one was sick. As a result, it was common for people to purchase **sickness insurance**, similar to today's **disability insurance**, to provide income when they lost wages because of sickness.

Progression in the twentieth century led to several changes, including a change in the locus of medical care: instead of visiting homes, practitioners shifted to performing most treatments in hospitals or medical offices. This shift caused an increase in the cost of medical care and hence a need for what today is known as **health insurance**.

HEALTH INSURANCE

Most patients who are seen in the physician's office have health insurance, which covers the majority of the cost for medical care. When the patient checks in at the front desk, the patient is asked to present a **health insurance identification card**. This card provides valuable information for the front-desk staff and the medical biller. This information is discussed in detail in the following sections of this chapter. The patient who has no health insurance and must pay for the entire visit with his own money is known as a **self-pay**.

The first insurance that is billed for the patient's care is called the **primary** insurance. Once the primary insurance pays on the claim, if there is still a balance, the claim is then submitted to the patient's **secondary** or **supplemental** insurance (called **Medigap** for patients whose primary insurance is Medicare). Claims that are denied by the primary insurance are also sent to the patient's secondary insurance. If there is a question as to which insurance is primary for a patient who presents two cards upon registration, be sure to call both insurance companies to verify. This should not occur frequently, as patients are usually well informed regarding the order (priority) of their insurance and the benefits of each. One rule of thumb to remember is that if a patient has insurance through an employer and is also covered through a spouse's employer, the *patient's* insurance is *always* primary.

Need to send paperwork on how primary ins paid to generate claim - EOB

THE IDENTIFICATION CARD

The health insurance identification card will list the name and address of the insurance company. It is important to ask a patient this information when the appointment is made to ensure that the office for which you are billing **participates** with this insurance. The medical biller needs to observe the following on the identification card:

- **identification number**
- **group number**
- **plan type**
- **policyholder**, also known as **subscriber**, **insured**, or **beneficiary**
- **co-payment**
- **co-insurance**
- **deductible**

Margin glossary

sickness insurance
insurance purchased in the early 1900s to provide income replacement in the event of illness.

disability insurance
insurance providing income to a policyholder who is disabled and cannot work.

health insurance
a contract between the subscriber and the insurance company to pay for medical care and preventive services.

health insurance identification card
card given to subscriber as proof of insurance.

self-pay
a patient with no health insurance who must pay out of pocket for medical care.

Part B ←

primary
the insurance plan that is billed first for medical services.

secondary
the insurance plan that is billed after the primary has paid or denied payment.

supplemental
another name for secondary insurance. A supplemental plan usually picks up the patient's deductible and/or co-insurance.

Medigap
supplemental insurance for patients with Medicare as their primary. These plans may pick up the Medicare deductible and co-insurance.

participates
the physician has signed a contract with the insurance company.

Guarantor - person responsible for balance of acct.

identification number
the number listed on the identification card that identifies the patient to the insurance company.

group number
the number on the identification card that identifies the patient's employer group health plan.

plan type
a specific name assigned by the insurance company designating a specific plan for that type of insurance. For example, Oxford has a "liberty" plan.

policyholder
the person who has (carries) the health insurance.

subscriber
another term for policyholder.

insured
another term for policyholder or subscriber.

beneficiary
term used for a patient who has Medicare coverage.

co-payment
a flat fee the patient pays each time for medical services. This is associated with managed care plans.

co-insurance
a percentage the patient is responsible to pay of the cost of medical services. This is associated with indemnity, traditional, and commercial health insurance plans.

deductible
the amount the patient is responsible to pay before any reimbursement is issued by the insurance company. This is usually associated with indemnity, traditional, or commercial plans.

indemnity plan
a type of insurance plan in which reimbursement is made at 80 percent of the allowed amount, and the patient pays the remaining 20 percent.

Make sure that the front-desk staff copies *both* the front and back of the health insurance identification card. Because a single insurance company may have many different addresses, it cannot be assumed that because two patients have health insurance with the same company, the claims for both patients will be going to the same address.

Contract btwn sub + insco

TYPES OF HEALTH INSURANCE PLANS

3rd party payers: patient, insurance co, provider

There are many different types of health insurance plans. It is not the *most* important job duty of a medical biller to memorize these types of plans; however, it is important to become familiar with the different types to make sure that the front-desk staff in the medical office collects the correct co-payment or co-insurance amounts at the time of a visit. Following is a basic introduction to these plans and the health insurance terms relating to them.

Indemnity Plan

An **indemnity plan** is a type of health insurance plan in which the insurance company usually pays 80 percent of the **allowed amount** of that insurance company's **fee schedule**; the patient is responsible for paying the remaining 20 percent. These monies are paid only after the patient's deductible has been met. The 20 percent the patient is responsible to pay is called *co-insurance*. In the field of medical billing and health insurance, you might also hear this type of plan referred to as a **traditional** or **commercial** health insurance plan. See Figure 2-1.

Government Plan

A **government plan** is a health insurance plan that is funded by the federal or state government. These plans are regulated by the **Centers for Medicare and Medicaid Services (CMS)**. Two types of plans that fall into this category are **Medicare** and **Medicaid**.

CMS

RIMMER

[CUSTOMER NAME]
[CUSTOMER NAME]

ID W1234 56789   GRP: 123456-810-001   BIN#18534   RX
01   JOHN SAMPLE
02   JANE SAMPLE
03   JACK SAMPLE
04   JILL SAMPLE
05   JOHN SAMPLE

MEMBER SERVICES   1-800-123-4567

PAYOR NUMBER 60054

Figure 2-1 Sample indemnity card.

allowed amount
the dollar amount an insurance company deems fair for a specific service or procedure.

fee schedule
a list of allowed amounts for all services and procedures payable by the insurance company.

traditional
another term for indemnity or commercial health insurance plans.

commercial
another term for indemnity or traditional health insurance plans.

government plan
a health insurance plan funded by the government.

Centers for Medicare and Medicaid Services (CMS)
a government agency that oversees the Medicare and Medicaid programs.

Medicare
a government health insurance plan primarily covering persons aged 65 and older.

Medicaid
a government plan for financially indigent people.

outpatient
services performed at a facility where the patient stays less than 24 hours and is not admitted to the facility; also, the term for the patient receiving such services.

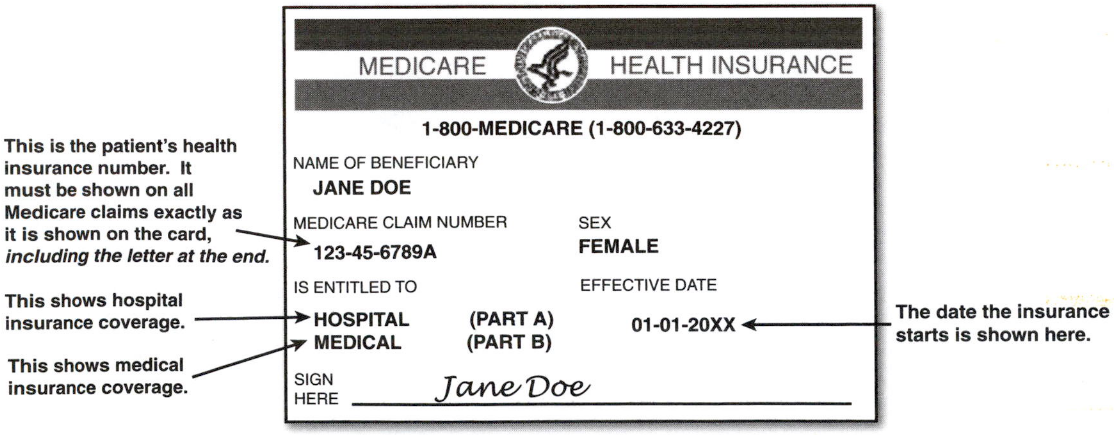

Medicare

The Medicare health insurance coverage referred to in this text is Medicare Part B. This coverage is for physician and **outpatient** services. A person who has Medicare coverage is always referred to as a *beneficiary*. A person may become eligible for Medicare in several ways. Some include:

- Patient is 65 years of age or older
- Patient is disabled
- Patient has end-stage renal disease
- Patient has Medicare through spouse

[handwritten: • US Citizen • 10 yr Contribution (work)]
[handwritten: — death benefit]

The reason why a person has Medicare coverage is not important for the medical biller. What is important is an understanding of the rules and regulations regarding submission of these claims. These rules are covered in detail in Chapter 5. There is more than one type of Medicare plan; the plan discussed in this section is called **Original Medicare**. Because CMS contracts with various **carriers** to pay Part B claims, the address to which these claims are submitted is different for each state. See Figure 2-2.

[handwritten: CMS regulates]

Medicaid

[handwritten: each state different]

Medicaid is for the patient who is financially **indigent**. This type of insurance is funded by both the federal government and state governments. Medicaid claims are paid through a **fiscal agent**. Again, the mailing address for submission of Medicaid claims differs by state. To become eligible for Medicaid, a person must fall into an **eligibility category**. Each state has its own guidelines, so be sure to research the rules of the state in which the patient lives to familiarize yourself with these guidelines. Some states require that an eligible person register with a Medicaid **managed care plan**.

Managed Care Plans

Managed care plans are among the most common types of health insurance plans you will come across as a medical biller. With these types of health insurance plans, the patient is responsible for paying a co-payment at each physician encounter.

This is the patient's health insurance number. It must be shown on all Medicare claims exactly as it is shown on the card, *including the letter at the end.*

This shows hospital insurance coverage.

This shows medical insurance coverage.

MEDICARE   HEALTH INSURANCE

1-800-MEDICARE (1-800-633-4227)

NAME OF BENEFICIARY
JANE DOE

MEDICARE CLAIM NUMBER   SEX
123-45-6789A   **FEMALE**

IS ENTITLED TO   EFFECTIVE DATE
HOSPITAL (PART A)   01-01-20XX
MEDICAL (PART B)

SIGN HERE _____ *Jane Doe* _____

The date the insurance starts is shown here.

Figure 2-2 Sample Medicare card.

Original Medicare
the Medicare plan in which reimbursement for most services and procedures is paid at 80 percent of the allowed amount.

carrier
a company that has contracted with CMS to pay Part B claims.

indigent
impoverished; needy.

fiscal agent
a company that contracts with CMS to pay Medicaid claims.

eligibility category
a category listing requirements for a person to be covered by a specific plan.

managed care plan
a health insurance plan that includes financing, management, and delivery of health care services.

primary care provider (PCP)
a physician (or other health care provider) who is responsible for a patient's main health care.

specialist
a physician who specializes in a particular area of medicine.

prescription drugs
medications prescribed by a physician (or other licensed prescriber).

emergency room visits
an encounter in the emergency room.

health maintenance organization (HMO)
a prepaid medical service plan that provides services to plan members.

in network
medical care sought from participating providers within a managed care plan.

out of network
medical care sought from nonparticipating providers; those providers who have not contracted with specific managed care plans.

Co-payment amounts vary within an insurance plan depending on the type of service that is provided. There is a co-payment for a **primary care provider (PCP)**, a **specialist**, **prescription drugs**, **emergency room visits**, and other various procedures, treatments, and testing that may be done. Co-payment amounts may increase at the beginning of a calendar year. If this happens, the patient will be sent a replacement health insurance identification card that lists the new co-payment amounts.

The number and types of managed care plans can be overwhelming and confusing. To keep it simple, this text covers the basic managed care plans you will encounter throughout your career. These five plans are:

- health maintenance organization (HMO)
- preferred provider organization (PPO)
- point-of-service (POS) plan
- Medicare managed care plan
- Medicaid managed care plan

The HMO

With a managed care plan through a **health maintenance organization (HMO)**, the patient must stay in network for services to be covered. If the patient goes **out of network** to receive medical care, the patient is responsible to pay the entire cost of the services rendered. When the physician has a **contract** with an HMO plan, the physician is considered **capitated** with that plan. Being capitated means that the physician will receive a monthly **capitation check** from the insurance company with an attached **capitation list**, regardless if a patient on the list was seen or not. The physician might see a patient three times in one month, but the **capitated rate** the physician receives for that patient remains the same. If the physician does not see that patient at all that month, the capitated rate is still the same. The advantage of capitation to the physician is that if the physician sees no patients on the list in a given month, he makes money without rendering any services. The disadvantage of capitation is that if the physician sees every patient on the capitation list in a given month, the same amount of money shows up in the capitation check. If the physician were paid a **fee for service** for seeing all of those patients on the list in that given month, he would have made more money on the services provided. Regardless, many physicians join these plans hoping that patients will choose them as the primary care provider, which will in turn increase the monthly capitation check received from the insurance company. See Figure 2-3.

fixed income

The PPO

The **preferred provider organization (PPO)** is a group of physicians, hospitals, and providers that offer price discounts to insurance-company clients in exchange for more members. For example, you work for ABC Company. The ALTA insurance company wants ABC as a client. ALTA is willing to reduce the premiums ABC will have to pay for its employees' health insurance coverage, *if* a large number of ABC employees will choose this plan and the preferred providers in it. The co-payment amount the patient pays is minimal. If the patient goes out of network, reimbursement by the insurance company is at a lower rate; therefore, going out-of-network increases the patient's **out-of-pocket** cost.

ABC Insurance Company
123 Any Street
Anytown, NJ 01234
Capitation List for: October 1–31, 2005

John Smith, MD
456 Any Avenue
Anycity, NJ 01235

Member Name	Date of Birth	Insurance ID #	Capitation Rate	Date Enrolled	Term Date	Adjustment
Aubrey, L.	02/02/1957	XX4587	$8.56	01/01/2005		
Ander, K.	01/06/1952	XZ3356	$7.22	01/01/2004		
Attis, S.	04/02/1967	XO1199	$9.53	01/01/2002		
Barns, P.	03/28/1975	XA5523	$8.56	01/01/2005		
Carney, S.	02/21/1970	XZ2214	$7.96	01/01/2003	08/31/2005	$ 7.96
Zullo, J.	08/30/1959	XO2247	$8.42	01/01/2004		
Totals						
6 Members			$50.25			$7.96

Figure 2-3 Sample capitation list.

contract

an agreement between two or more parties.

capitated

system in which a physician is prepaid monthly for members enrolled in an HMO with which the physician has contracted. The payment is made to the physician regardless of whether the physician sees no patients or all the patients in this plan.

capitation check

a monthly check the physician receives from the HMO plan.

capitation list

a list of patients enrolled in a particular HMO plan with which the physician is capitated.

capitated rate

a rate determined by the HMO for reimbursement for medical services when the physician is capitated with that plan.

fee for service

a payment system in which the physician is paid a specific amount for each service performed.

preferred provider organization (PPO)

this type of plan offers discounts to insurance company clients in exchange for more members.

The POS Plan

The **point-of-service (POS) plan** is one in which a member can choose to stay in network and pay the designated co-payment amount, or go out of network and pay a deductible and co-insurance for the services rendered. If the patient goes out of network in a POS plan, reimbursement to the provider is still very good, and the patient's co-insurance amount is usually between 20 to 30 percent. Many employees choose this type of plan, if offered by their employer, because of its flexibility.

Medicare Managed Care Plans

When a person becomes eligible for Medicare benefits, she has an option to choose a Medicare managed care plan, known as **Medicare Advantage**. This type of Medicare is referred to as *Medicare Part C*. Medicare managed care plans are offered by the same insurance companies that offer managed care plans to non-Medicare patients. When a person chooses this plan, she is still responsible for the monthly Medicare Part B premiums. If chosen, the Medicare managed care plan is the patient's primary insurance. Original Medicare is not billed at all if a patient opts for a Medicare managed care plan. The patient will still carry a Medicare health insurance card, but need not present it to the front-desk staff when asked for the health insurance identification card. If a patient insists that she does have both Original Medicare and a Medicare managed care plan, simply instruct the front-desk staff not to argue with the patient and take both cards for copying. An astute medical biller will know that the patient does not in fact have two plans, and will bill the patient's health insurance claims to the Medicare managed care plan.

The advantages of these plans vary. Some do not charge their members monthly premiums. Some do not require the patient to obtain a referral to see a specialist or to have certain testing or procedures done. With this kind of plan, the patient does not pay a 20 percent co-insurance of the allowed amount, as required with Original Medicare, but does pay a flat co-payment for each medical encounter. This is financially beneficial to the patient who may have several procedures or services done in the office during a single visit. See Figure 2-4.

out of pocket
the patient's share of the cost of health care services. This can include co-payment, co-insurance, or a deductible.

point-of-service (POS) plan
a health insurance plan in which the patient pays a co-payment when staying in network.

Medicare Advantage
a plan offered by managed care companies to replace Original Medicare as the patient's health insurance.

referral
permission from the primary care physician to seek services from a specialist for an evaluation, testing, and/or treatment. Managed care plans require this.

BlueCross® BlueShield®

CHRIS B. HALL   MEDICARE ADVANTAGE | PPO

Subscriber No.
XYZ123456789123

Group No.   BS Plan   BC Plan
70125   740   240

07/04
Date Issued

Indicates this is a Medicare PPO

Figure 2-4 Sample Medicare managed care plan card.

Medicaid Managed Care Plan   *Health New England — Stay Healthy*

Because Medicaid guidelines vary by state, refer to your state's rules and regulations regarding a Medicaid managed care plan. If your state requires eligible Medicaid recipients to choose from a variety of managed care plans, then your state's Medicaid Web site will list the managed care plans to choose from. The income guidelines determining monthly premiums and co-payment amounts will be listed as well.

Tricare

Tricare is the name of health insurance provided for retired military personnel, active military personnel, and their dependents. There are three Tricare regions throughout the United States: West, North, and South. Tricare-eligible beneficiaries have the opportunity to choose from three Tricare plans:

- Tricare Prime
- Tricare Standard
- Tricare Extra

Tricare Prime

Tricare Prime
the only Tricare plan offering coverage for active-duty service members. Retired members may also select this plan.

military treatment facility (MTF)
a place where Tricare members receive medical treatment.

preferred provider network (PPN)
a group of civilian medical providers that has contracted with Tricare.

With the **Tricare Prime** plan, active-duty service members are not required to pay an enrollment fee. Medical services for this plan are given at a **military treatment facility (MTF)**. Members receive treatment at these facilities from a Tricare-contracted civilian medical provider that is a **preferred provider network (PPN)**. Tricare Prime members also have a POS option, as described earlier in the managed care section. If members use the POS option under this plan, there is a deductible to meet and additional charges may apply.

Tricare Prime advantages include:

- No enrollment fee for active-duty service members or their families
- Small co-payment for visit to civilian providers and no fee for active-duty service members
- Guaranteed appointments
- Away-from-home emergency coverage
- POS option

Tricare Prime disadvantages include:

- Enrollment fee for retirees and their families
- Limited provider choice
- Specialty care by referral only
- Not universally available *— only in military bases.*

Tricare Standard

The Tricare Standard plan is available only to retired military service members and their families. This plan option is considered the most flexible of the three plans. It is a fee-for-service plan that gives beneficiaries the opportunity to see any Tricare-authorized provider. The Standard plan covers most of the costs of medical care received from civilian providers when care from an MTF is unavailable.

Tricare Standard advantages include:

- Broadest choice of providers
- Wide availability
- No enrollment fee
- Members may also use Tricare Extra

Tricare Standard disadvantages include:

- No primary care provider
- Members must pay a deductible and 25 percent of the allowed charges for service
- If provider is nonparticipating, members may pay an additional 15 percent of fees if the bill exceeds the allowed charges
- Members may have to file their own health insurance claims

Tricare Extra

Like the Standard plan, the Tricare Extra plan is also available only to retired military service members and their families. The deductible and cost-sharing rules are similar to those of the Tricare Standard plan. Tricare Extra, however, is not available overseas. This plan may also be used on a case-by-case basis by Tricare Standard members.

Tricare Extra advantages include:

- Co-payment is 5 percent less than that of Tricare Standard
- No enrollment fee
- No deductible when using a retail pharmacy network
- No form to file
- Members may also use Tricare Standard

Tricare Extra disadvantages include:

- No primary care provider
- Limited provider choice
- Patient pays deductible and co-payment
- Not universally available

TYPES OF COVERAGE

Regardless of whether a patient has health insurance through a job or has to pay out of pocket for health insurance premiums, the **coverage** falls into one of four types:

- Individual or employee coverage
- Husband/wife or employee/significant other coverage
- Parent/child coverage
- Family coverage

Individual or Employee Coverage

Individual or employee coverage is usually for a single person. The person may or may not have a child, but if she does, and the child is not covered under the plan, then the coverage is **individual** or **employee** coverage. The individual is the only person covered under the plan.

Husband/Wife or Employee/Significant Other Coverage

When an individual has health insurance that covers himself and his spouse, or himself and a significant other, the coverage is called **husband/wife (H/W)** or **employee/significant other (E/S) coverage**. The latter term is fairly new to the insurance industry, as some employers now offer health insurance coverage for the domestic partner of an employee. *varies by state, but most now.*

Parent/Child Coverage

The single parent who insures both herself and her children through a health insurance plan has **parent/child coverage**. This coverage is very common for men who are divorced and required by the divorce decree to carry insurance coverage for their children.

Family Coverage

Family coverage is health insurance that covers the individual employee, the employee's spouse, and the employee's children. For the most part, health insurance premiums will remain the same regardless of how many children are covered or added to the policy. The only time this may not be true is in a Medicaid managed care plan. Depending on the state and the size of the family, premiums may increase as the family size increases. Most family coverage plans now include adopted children and stepchildren. Persons covered under the policyholder's plan are called **dependents**.

MEDICAL DISCOUNT CARDS

A **medical discount card** is *not* a health insurance identification card. These cards can be very deceiving and often are mistaken for health insurance identification cards.

This is how discount cards work. For a monthly premium, the cardholder becomes eligible to receive a **discount** for medical services from participating

Sidebar definitions

coverage
existence and scope of existing health insurance.

individual
the one and only person covered under a health insurance plan.

employee
a person employed who is covered under an employer's group health plan.

husband/wife (H/W) coverage
health insurance covering both the husband and wife.

employee/significant other (E/S) coverage
health insurance covering the employee and the employee's significant other.

parent/child coverage
health insurance coverage for a parent and child.

family coverage
health insurance coverage for the individual employee, the employee's spouse, and the employee's children.

dependents
persons covered under the policyholder's plan.

medical discount card
a card listing the patient's name and verifying that the patient can receive a discount on services, if the provider's office participates.

discount
a reduced fee.

providers. When the patient is finished with the examination and the superbill is coded, a member of the front-desk staff calls the toll-free telephone number listed on the card. A customer service representative at the company will ask for the CPT/ HCPCS codes for the services the patient received. This representative then gives the front-desk staff member an amount from the company's fee schedule, which is the dollar amount the patient should pay. It is entirely up to the provider whether to accept this dollar amount or not.

These cards are for people who have no health insurance through their jobs and cannot afford the cost of health insurance premiums on their own. It is for the self-pay person. It is wise for the physician and front-desk staff to agree with the patient, before services are rendered, whether to accept these types of discount cards. A physician who feels bad for a patient may agree to accept the medical discount card, knowing the financial hardship an uninsured patient may incur for the cost of several procedures or services in one given office visit. For example, the normal fee a physician would charge for a CPT code 99213 is $75. The XYZ medical discount company's fee schedule shows a fair amount for code 99213 to be $48. If the physician agrees, the cardholder will pay $48, and will have saved $27 off the physician's usual charge. See Figure 2-5.

What information is on my card?

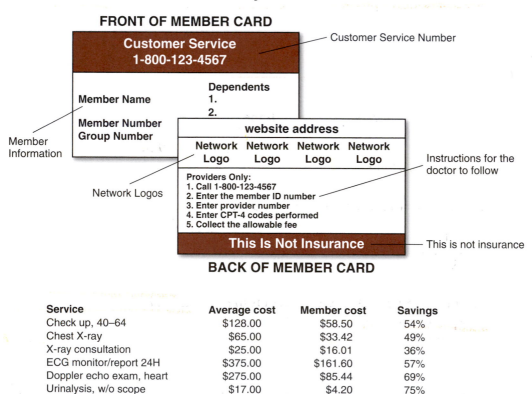

Service	Average cost	Member cost	Savings
Check up, 40–64	$128.00	$58.50	54%
Chest X-ray	$65.00	$33.42	49%
X-ray consultation	$25.00	$16.01	36%
ECG monitor/report 24H	$375.00	$161.60	57%
Doppler echo exam, heart	$275.00	$85.44	69%
Urinalysis, w/o scope	$17.00	$4.20	75%

Figure 2-5 Sample medical discount card and savings chart.

SUMMARY

The health insurance identification card is the patient's proof of health insurance coverage. When the health insurance identification card is presented, make sure to copy both the front and back of the card. This step will alleviate unnecessary stress and reduce the amount of work for the medical biller when it is time to submit the health insurance claims.

Because there are so many different types of health insurance plans, you are not expected to memorize all of them. What is expected is that you know the difference between indemnity, government, and managed care plans. It is important to know the difference between co-insurance and co-payment. A co-payment is a flat fee the patient pays for each physician encounter. Co-payments are used in managed care plans. Co-insurance is defined as a percentage the patient is responsible for paying at each physician encounter. Co-insurance relates to indemnity plans and Original Medicare. Medicaid is for the indigent patient. Depending on the state in which a patient lives, Medicaid may require the patient to use a managed care plan. Active and retired military personnel have health insurance through Tricare. Three types of Tricare plans are offered; eligibility depends on the patient's status as active or retired military, and on family coverage.

It is important not to confuse health insurance identification cards with medical discount cards. It is wise for the physician to determine in advance whether to accept discount cards.

REVIEW QUESTIONS

1. Why is it important to copy both the front and back of the health insurance identification card?

   to obtain correct insurance address on back of card + front – both sides

2. A patient who has no health insurance is called a/an:
   a. self-referral
   b. indigent
   c. dependent
   d. self-pay

3. The insurance that is billed first for the patient is called:
   a. principal
   b. primary
   c. presenting
   d. none of the above

4. Another name for secondary insurance is:
   a. duplicate
   b. supplemental
   c. co-insurance
   d. primary

5. List three synonyms for the term *policyholder*.

   subscriber

   insured

   beneficiary

6. Describe the difference between co-payment and co-insurance.

   co-payment — flat fee

   co-insurance — percentage patients responsibility

7. A nongovernmental plan that usually pays 80 percent and makes the patient responsible for 20 percent is called an _indemnity_ plan.

8. The amount that must be met before any monies are paid by the insurance company is called the _deductible_

p9   9. CMS stands for:
   a. Centers for Medical Supervisors
   b. Centers for Medical Services
   c. Centers for Medicare and Medicaid Services
   d. none of the above

p9   10. Two plans regulated by CMS are _Medicare_ and _Medicaid_.

p10   11. CMS contracts with a _carrier_ to pay Part B claims.

12. List three types of medical care plans that require a patient to pay a co-payment.

   Family   Specialist   PCP provider

   PPO   ER

   POS   RX

p.11   13. List five types of managed care plans.

   HMO - Health maintenance organization

   PPO - Preferred provider organization

   POS - point-of-service plan

   Medicare managed care plan

   Medicaid managed care plan

p11   14. Describe the difference between in network and out of network.

   In - medical care from participating providers

   out - medical care from non-participating "
   w/o contract

p11   15. Describe what *capitation* means and list an advantage and disadvantage of capitation.

   Physician has contract w/ a plan
   Advantage - Dr recvs monthly chk from ins
   from capitation list. Disadv - if Dr sees
   every patient on list, he gets same amt.

p12   16. Describe fee-for-service arrangements.

   a pmt system in which physician is paid
   a specific amt for each service performed.

p12   **17.** Some plans require that a patient obtain a _referral_ to see a specialist.

18. Name three types of Tricare plans.

p13

Tricare   Prime

Tricare   Standard

Tricare   Extra

19. Which two Tricare plans are available _only_ to retired service members and their families?

p14

Tricare   Standard

Tricare   Extra

20. Two health plans that refer to their members as _beneficiaries_ are medicare and tricare .

p.10

21. Give an example of new health insurance coverage that some insurance companies and employers now offer.

p15

Employee / significant other (E/S) coverage

22. Which health insurance plan premiums increase as the family size increases?

p.15

Medicaid managed care plan

23. Describe what a medical discount card is and how it differs from the health insurance identification card.

p16

Card listing patient's name + verifying patient can rcv discount if providers office participates.

Staff calls tel# to get for CPT/HCPCS codes + to get amt from company's fee schedule.

Cord holder pays monthy fee for people w/ no job.

Not insurance related

Insurance card is proof of health ins.

Chapter 3

The Codes (CPT, HCPCS Level II, ICD-9, and Modifiers)

KEY TERMS

audit	diagnosis (plural: diagnoses)	HCPCS national codes
codes	E codes	ICD-9-CM
CPT	HCPCS	modifier
CPT modifier	HCPCS modifier	V codes

OBJECTIVES

Upon completion of this chapter, the student should be able to:

- Differentiate between a CPT and a HCPCS national code.
- Explain modifier usage.
- Recognize an ICD-9 code.
- Define key terms.

LEARNING A NEW LANGUAGE

Understanding the terms associated with medical billing is similar to learning a new language. A huge part of medical billing lingo is comprised primarily of numbers and letters called **codes**. These codes represent descriptions of:

- Procedures
- Services
- Supplies
- Medicine
- Durable medical equipment (DME)
- Diagnoses

Fluency in any language requires practice; medical billing is no different.

codes assigned letters, numbers, or a combination of both used to report procedures, services, supplies, durable medical equipment, and diagnoses.

HEALTHCARE COMMON PROCEDURE CODING SYSTEM (HCPCS)

The Healthcare Common Procedure Coding System or **HCPCS** (pronounced "hickpicks") is a procedure-based coding system used by

 WHAT

HCPCS a coding system used to report procedures, services, supplies, medicine, and durable medical equipment. Comprised of CPT (level I) and national (level II) codes.

WHAT

physicians to document (what) was done *to* and *for* a patient. This coding system has two levels:

- Level I—CPT codes
- Level II—national codes

Current Procedural Terminology (CPT) Codes

CPT codes used to report services and procedures. These are level I codes under HCPCS.

Current Procedural Terminology or **CPT codes**, also known as *level I codes*, are five-digit numeric codes that are assigned for the following services and procedures:

- Evaluation and Management (E/M) (99201–99499)
- Anesthesia (00100–01999, 99100–99140)
- Surgery (10021–69990)
- Radiology (70010–79999)
- Pathology and Laboratory (80048–89356)
- Medicine (90281–99199, 99500–99602)

The CPT manual containing these codes is updated and published yearly by the American Medical Association.

HCPCS National Codes

HCPCS national codes alphanumeric codes used to identify categories not included in HCPCS level I codes. These codes are considered level II codes.

HCPCS national codes, or *level II codes*, are five-digit alphanumeric codes. The codes always begin with a letter followed by four numbers. Level II codes cover:

- Supplies
- Durable medical equipment
- Materials
- Injections/drugs
- Services

See Table 3-1 for a sample of HCPCS level II DME codes, and Table 3-2 for a sample of HCPCS level II injection codes.

MODIFIERS

modifier a two-character alphabetic, numeric, or alphanumeric descriptor used to signify that a procedure or service has been altered by an unusual or specific circumstance, although the code itself has not changed. Additional use includes referencing a specific body site.

There are occasions in medical billing when specific or additional information is needed when billing with a CPT or HCPCS national code. In these instances, the medical biller must attach a **modifier** to the appropriate code.
Modifiers are used when:

- A service or procedure has a technical component
- A service or procedure has a professional component
- A service or procedure was performed by more than one physician
- A service or procedure was increased or reduced
- Only part of a service was performed

TABLE 3-1   **Sample of HCPCS Level II DME Codes**

HCPCS Code	Description
AMBULATION DEVICES	
Canes and Crutches	
A4635	Underarm pad, crutch, replacement, each
A4636	Replacement handgrip, cane, crutch, or walker, each
A4637	Replacement tip, cane, crutch, or walker, each
E0100	Cane; includes canes of all materials, adjustable or fixed, with tip
E0105	Cane, quad or three-prong; includes canes of all materials, adjustable or fixed, with tips
E0111	Crutch, forearm; includes crutches of various materials, adjustable or fixed, each, with tip and handgrips
E0113	Crutch, underarm, wood, adjustable or fixed, each, with pad, tip, and handgrip
E0116	Crutch, underarm, other than wood, adjustable or fixed, each, with pad, tip, and handgrip
E0117	Crutch, underarm, articulating, spring-assisted, each
Walkers	
E0130	Rigid (pick-up), adjustable or fixed height
E0135	Folding (pick-up), adjustable or fixed height
E0144	Enclosed, framed folding walker, wheeled, with posterior seat
E0147	Heavy-duty, multiple-braking-system, variable-wheel-resistance walker
E0148	Walker, heavy-duty, without wheels, rigid or folding, any type, each
E0149	Walker, heavy-duty, wheeled, rigid or folding, any type, each
E0155	Wheel attachment, rigid pick-up walker, per pair
E0159	Brake attachment for wheeled walker, replacement, each
BATHROOM EQUIPMENT	
E0163	Commode chair, mobile or stationary, with fixed arms
E0165	Commode chair, mobile or stationary, with detachable arms
E0167	Pail or pan for use with commode chair, replacement only

TABLE 3-2   Sample of HCPCS Level II Injection Codes

J1460	Gamma globulin, intramuscular, 1 cc, injection
J1470	Gamma globulin, intramuscular, 2 cc, injection
J9999	Abarelix, 100 mg, injection (Plenaxis)
J0128	Abarelix, 10 mg, injection (Plenaxis)
J0130	Abciximab, 10 mg, injection (ReoPro)
J1120	Acetazolamide sodium, up to 500 mg, injection (Diamox)
J0133	Acyclovir, 5 mg, injection
J0150	Adenosine, 6 mg, injection (not to be used to report any adenosine phosphate compounds; instead use A9270) (Adenocard)
J0152	Adenosine, 30 mg, injection (not to be used to report any adenosine phosphate compounds; use A9270)
J0180	Agalsidase beta, 1 mg, injection (Fabrazyme)
J9015	Aldesleukin, per single-use vial (Proleukin, etc.)
J0215	Alefacept, 0.5 mg, injection (Amevive)
J9010	Alemtuzumab, 10 mg, injection (Campath)
J0205	Alglucerase, per 10 units, injection (Ceredase)
J2997	Alteplase recombinant, 1 mg, injection (Activase)
J0278	Amicacin sulfate, 100 mg, injection
J0207	Amifostine, 500 mg, injection (Ethyol)
J0280	Aminophylline, up to 250 mg, injection
J1320	Amitriptyline HCl, up to 20 mg, injection (Elavil, Enovil)
J0300	Amobarbital, up to 125 mg, injection (Amytal)
J0285	Amphotericin B, 50 mg, injection
J0288	Amphotericin B cholesteryl sulfate complex, 10 mg, injection (Amphotee)
J0287	Amphotericin B lipid complex, 10 mg, injection
J0289	Amphotericin B liposome, 10 mg, injection (Ambisome)
J0290	Ampicillin sodium, 500 mg, injection (Omnipen-N, Totacillin-N)
J0295	Ampicillin sodium/sulbactam sodium, per 1.5 g, injection (Unasyn)

Continued

TABLE 3-2   Sample of HCPCS Level II Injection Codes (Continued)

J0350	Anistreplase, per 30 units, injection (Eminase)
J7197	Antithrombin III (human), per IU (Throbate III, ATnativ)
J0395	Arbutamine HCl, 1 mg, injection
J9017	Arsenic trioxide, 1 mg, injection (Trisenox)
J9020	Asparaginase, 10,000 units (Elspar)
J9025	Azacitidine, 1 mg, injection (Vidaza)
J0456	Azithromycin, 500 mg, injection (Zithromax)

- An additional service was performed
- A bilateral procedure was performed more than once
- Referencing a specific body site
- Unusual events occurred

CPT Modifiers

CPT modifier
a two-character numeric descriptor used only with CPT codes.

It is extremely important that the medical biller use the most accurate **CPT modifier** in a given situation. Incorrect modifier usage can result in denial of the claim or, worse, an **audit** by the insurance company. Each physician's office should have a CPT manual on hand for the medical biller to refer to. See Table 3-3.

audit
a formal examination of an individual's or organization's accounts.

HCPCS Modifiers

HCPCS modifier
a two-character alphabetic or alphanumeric descriptor used with both CPT level I and level II national codes.

The **HCPCS modifier** can be used with both a CPT level I and a level II national code. It is in this list of modifiers that you will find reference to specific body sites. See Table 3-4.

ICD-9-CM CODES

ICD-9-CM
International Classification of Diseases, 9th Revision, Clinical Modification. The ICD-9 codes are used to report diagnoses, signs, and symptoms of a patient.

The **ICD-9-CM** code, referred to here as the *ICD-9 code*, is used to report a patient's **diagnosis**. ICD-9 codes can be found in an ICD-9-CM coding manual. The ICD-9-CM is arranged into three volumes:

diagnosis (plural: diagnoses)
the conclusion reached about a patient's ailment by thorough review of the patient's history, examination, and review of laboratory data.

- Volume 1 (Tabular List)
- Volume 2 (Index to Diseases)
- Volume 3 (Index to Procedures and Tabular List) — hospitals

Medical billing done in the physician's offices uses only the codes found in Volumes 1 and 2. Volume 3 is used by hospitals and therefore will not be covered in this text.

ICD-9 codes that are strictly numeric in nature are three to five digits long. A three-digit code is considered to be the heading of a category of codes. When an

TABLE 3-3   CPT Modifiers

22	Unusual procedural service—Surgeries for which services performed are significantly greater than usually required; may be billed with the 22 modifier added to the CPT code. Include a concise statement about how the service differs from the usual. Supportive documentation (e.g., operative reports, pathology reports, etc.) must be submitted with the claim.
23	Unusual anesthesia.
24	Unrelated evaluation and management (E&M) service by the same physician during a postoperative period.
25	Significant, separately identifiable E&M service by the same physician on the same day of the procedure or other therapeutic service that has a 0- to 10-day global period. A separate diagnosis is not needed. This modifier is used on the E&M service.
26	Professional component—Certain procedures that are combined with a physician's professional component may be identified by adding the modifier 26 to the usual procedure number. All diagnostic testing with a technical or professional component, whether done in an outpatient or inpatient setting, must reflect the 26 modifier. The fiscal intermediary (Part A Medicare) will reimburse the facility for the technical component.
50	Bilateral procedure—*Bilateral services* are procedures performed on both sides of the body during the same operative session or on the same day. Medicare will approve 150 percent of the fee-schedule amount for those services.
51	Multiple procedures—For internal use by carrier only.
52	Reduced services—Use modifier 52 (reduced service) to indicate a service or procedure that was partially reduced or eliminated at the physician's election. If claims are submitted electronically with modifier 52, the insurer or payor will request medical records from the provider before processing the claims.
53	Discontinued procedure—Under certain circumstances, the physician may elect to terminate a surgical or diagnostic procedure. Due to extenuating circumstances, or those that threaten the well-being of the patient, it may be necessary to indicate that a surgical or diagnostic procedure was started but discontinued. If claims are submitted electronically with modifier 53, the insurer or payor will request medical records from the provider before processing the claims. One of the most common examples of use of modifier 53 is when an incomplete colonoscopy is performed. Add modifier 53 to CPT code 45378. No documentation is required (this is an exception to the rule).
54	Surgical care only—When one physician performs a surgical procedure and another physician provides preoperative and/or postoperative management, the surgical service should be identified by adding modifier 54 to the usual procedure code.
55	Postoperative management only—Used for a physician's postoperative services when one physician performs the postoperative management and another physician has performed the surgical procedure.
57	Initial decision for surgery (90-day global period)—This modifier is used on E&M service, the day before or the day of surgery, to exempt it from the global surgery package.
58	Staged or related procedure or service by the same physician during the postoperative period—If a less extensive procedure fails and a more extensive procedure is required, the second procedure is payable separately. Modifier 58 must be reported with the second procedure.
59	Distinct procedural service—The physician may need to indicate that a procedure or service was distinct or separate from other services performed on the same day. This may represent a different session or patient encounter, different procedure or surgery, different site, separate lesion, or separate injury. However, when another already established modifier is appropriate, it should be used rather than modifier 59.

Continued

TABLE 3-3   CPT Modifiers (Continued)

62	Two surgeons (co-surgery)—Under certain circumstances, the skills of two surgeons (usually different skills) may be required in the management of a specific surgical procedure. Adding modifier 62 to the procedure code used by each surgeon should identify the separate service.
66	Surgical team—Under some circumstances, highly complex procedures requiring the accompanying services of several physicians, often of different specialties, plus other highly skilled or specially trained personnel, and various types of complex equipment, are carried out under the surgical team concept. Claims with modifier 66 cannot be processed without a copy of the operative report.
73	Discontinued outpatient hospital/ambulatory surgery center (ASC) procedure prior to the administration of anesthesia.
74	Discontinued outpatient hospital/ambulatory surgery center (ASC) procedure after administration of anesthesia.
76	Repeat procedure by same physician—Indicate the reason or the different times for the repeat procedure in item 19 of the CMS 1500 form or the electronic equivalent.
77	Repeat procedure by another physician—Indicate the reason or the different times for the repeat procedure in item 19 of the CMS 1500 form or the electronic equivalent.
78	Return to the operating room for a related procedure during the postoperative period—The physician may need to indicate that another procedure was performed during the postoperative period of the initial procedure. When this subsequent procedure is related to the first, and requires use of the operating room, it should be reported by adding modifier 78 to the related procedure.
79	Unrelated procedure or service by the same physician during the postoperative period—The physician may need to indicate that the performance of a procedure or service during the postoperative period was unrelated to the original procedure.
80	Assistant surgeon—Add modifier 80 to the usual procedure in a nonteaching setting to identify surgical assistant services.
82	Assistant surgeon when qualified resident surgeon not available in a teaching setting.
90	Reference (outside) laboratory—When laboratory procedures are performed by a party other than the treating or reporting physician, the procedure may be identified by adding the modifier 90 to the usual procedure number. For the Medicare program, this modifier is used by independent clinical laboratories when referring tests to a reference laboratory for analysis.
91	Repeat clinical diagnostic lab tests performed on same day to obtain subsequent reportable test value(s)—This modifier is used to report a separate specimen(s) taken at a separate encounter.
99	The Multi-Carrier System (MCS) now allows you to send up to four modifiers per line of service on your claims, for both electronically submitted and paper claims. Please indicate the pricing modifiers in the first two positions and processing or informational modifiers in the third and fourth positions. Use modifier 99 when more than four modifiers are needed on a line of service. In situations that require five or more modifiers, indicate modifier 99 in the first modifier field on the line of service and enter the remaining modifiers in the narrative field of an EMC claim or item 19 of a CMS 1500 claim form. For example: 79, RT, LT, QU, GA—99 in the first modifier field on the line of service, and 79, RT, LT, QU, GA in the narrative field of an EMC claim or item 19 of a CMS 1500 claim form.

TABLE 3-4   HCPCS Modifiers

AA	Anesthesia services personally furnished by an anesthesiologist.
AD	Medical supervision by physician: more than four concurrent anesthesia services.
AQ	Physician providing a service in a health professional shortage area (HPSA) (for dates of service on or after January 1, 2006).
AR	Physician provider services in a physician scarcity area.
AS	Physician assistant, nurse practitioner, or clinical nurse specialist service for assistant at surgery.
AT	Acute or chronic active/corrective treatment (effective October 1, 2004).
CB	Services ordered by a dialysis-facility physician as part of the ESRD [end-stage renal disease] beneficiary's dialysis benefit; this is not part of the composite rate and is separately reimbursable.
CC	Procedure code change (the carrier uses CC when the procedure code submitted was changed either for administrative reasons or because an incorrect code was filed).
CR	Catastrophe/disaster related.
EJ	Subsequent claim for EPO [epoetin alfa] course of therapy.
E1	Upper left, eyelid.
E2	Lower left, eyelid.
E3	Upper right, eyelid.
E4	Lower right, eyelid.
FA	Left hand, thumb.
F1	Left hand, second digit.
F2	Left hand, third digit.
F3	Left hand, fourth digit.
F4	Left hand, fifth digit.
F5	Right hand, thumb.
F6	Right hand, second digit.
F7	Right hand, third digit.
F8	Right hand, fourth digit.
F9	Right hand, fifth digit.
GA	Advance Beneficiary Notification on file.

Continued

TABLE 3-4   HCPCS Modifiers (Continued)

GC	This service has been performed in part by a resident under the direction of a teaching physician.
GE	This service has been performed by a resident without the presence of a teaching physician, under the primary care exception.
GG	Performance and payment of screening mammogram and diagnostic mammogram on the same patient, same day (effective for dates of service on or after January 1, 2002).
GJ	"OPT OUT" physician or practitioner emergency or urgent service.
GM	Multiple patients on one ambulance trip.
GN	Service delivered under an outpatient speech-language pathology plan of care.
GO	Service delivered under an outpatient occupational therapy plan of care.
GP	Service delivered under an outpatient physical therapy plan of care.
GQ	Via asynchronous telecommunications system.
GT	Via interactive audio and video telecommunication system.
GV	Attending physician not employed or paid under arrangement by the patient's hospice provider (effective for dates of service on or after January 1, 2002).
GW	Service not related to the hospice patient's terminal condition (effective for dates of service on or after January 1, 2002).
GY	Item or service statutorily excluded or does not meet the definition of any Medicare benefit.
GZ	Item or service expected to be denied as not reasonable and necessary and Advance Beneficiary Notification has not been signed.
J1	Competitive acquisition program (CAP) no-pay submission for a prescription number.
J2	CAP restocking of emergency drugs after emergency administration.
J3	CAP drug not available through CAP as written; reimbursed under average sales price methodology.
KD	Infusion drugs furnished through implanted durable medical equipment (effective January 1, 2004).
KX	Claims for therapy services that have exceeded therapy caps (either by automatic exception or by approved request), for which specific required documentation is on file.
KZ	New coverage not implemented by managed care.
LC	Left circumflex coronary artery.

Continued

TABLE 3-4   HCPCS Modifiers (Continued)

LD	Left anterior descending coronary artery.
LR	Laboratory round trip.
LT	Left side (use to identify procedures performed on the LEFT side of the body).
QA	FDA investigational device exemption.
QB	Physician providing service in a rural HPSA.
QC	Single-channel monitoring (recording device for Holter monitoring).
QD	Recording and storage in solid-state memory by a digital recorder (digital recording/storage for Holter monitoring).
QJ	Services/items provided to a prisoner or patient in state or local custody. However, the state or local government, as applicable, meets the requirements in 42 C.F.R. § 411.4.
QK	Medical direction of two, three, or four concurrent anesthesia procedures involving qualified individuals.
QL	Patient pronounced dead after ambulance called.
QP	Documentation is on file showing that the laboratory test(s) was ordered individually or ordered as a CPT-recognized panel other than automated profile codes.
QR	Services that are covered under a clinical study/trial.
QS	Monitored anesthesia care service.
QT	Recording and storage on tape by an analog tape recorder.
QU	Physician providing services in an urban HPSA (for dates of service prior to January 1, 2006).
QV	Item or service provided as routine care in a Medicare qualifying clinical trial.
QW	CLIA waived test.
QX	Certified registered nurse anesthetist (CRNA) service with medical direction by a physician.
QY	Medical direction of one CRNA by an anesthesiologist.
QZ	CRNA service without medical direction by a physician.
Q3	Live kidney donor surgery and related services.
Q5	Service furnished by a substitute physician under a reciprocal billing arrangement.
Q6	Service furnished by a locum tenens physician.

Continued

TABLE 3-4   **HCPCS Modifiers** (Continued)

Q7	One class "A" finding.
Q8	Two class "B" findings. Class "B" findings: Absent posterior tibial pulse; advanced tropic changes (hair growth, nail changes, pigmentary changes, or skin texture—three required); absent dorsalis pedis pulse.
Q9	One class "B" and two class "C" findings. Class "C" findings: Claudication; temperature changes, edema, paresthesias; burning.
RC	Right coronary artery.
RT	Right side (use to identify procedures performed on the RIGHT side of the body).
SG	Ambulatory surgical center (ASC) facility charges. This modifier is used only by the ASC for identifying the facility charge. It should not be reported by the physician when reporting the physician's professional service rendered in an ASC.
TA	Left foot, great toe.
T1	Left foot, second digit.
T2	Left foot, third digit.
T3	Left foot, fourth digit.
T4	Left foot, fifth digit.
T5	Right foot, great toe.
T6	Right foot, second digit.
T7	Right foot, third digit.
T8	Right foot, fourth digit.
T9	Right foot, fifth digit.
TC	Technical component. Under certain circumstances, a charge may be made for the technical component of a diagnostic test only. Under those circumstances, the technical component charge is identified by adding modifier TC to the usual procedure number.
TS	Pre-diabetic screening is paid twice within a rolling 12-month period. Second screening should be billed with TS modifier.
UN	Transportation of portable X-rays, two patients served (effective January 1, 2004).
UP	Transportation of portable X-rays, three patients served (effective January 1, 2004).
UQ	Transportation of portable X-rays, four patients served (effective January 1, 2004).
UR	Transportation of portable X-rays, five patients served (effective January 1, 2004).
US	Transportation of portable X-rays, six or more patients served (effective January 1, 2004).

ICD-9 code requires a fourth digit (subcategory) or fifth digit (subclassification), the additional digit(s) is preceded by a decimal point. A three-digit ICD-9 code should be used only if the code does not require further subdivision. When a code requires a fourth or fifth digit, as provided in the ICD-9 manual, these additional digits *must* be used. Use of these additional digits provides greater specificity.

Volume 1 (Tabular List)

Codes in Volume 1 of the ICD-9 manual are listed numerically according to diseases and disorders of the body systems. This volume also contains V codes and E codes. Because Volume 1 contains the fourth-digit subcategories and fifth-digit subclassification descriptions, the coder in the physician's office should always refer to this volume to be certain whether an ICD-9 code requires further subdivision.

V codes
ICD-9 codes assigned for preventive medicine services and for reasons other than disease or injuries.

E codes
codes used to describe external causes of injury, poisoning, or other adverse reactions affecting the patient's health.

V Codes

V codes are assigned when a patient is seen in the office for a reason other than injury or disease. Preventive medicine for both children and adults is always designated with a V code as a diagnosis. For example, the ICD-9 code for a well-baby checkup is V20.2, and the ICD-9 code for an annual physical examination is V70.0.

E Codes

E codes are assigned to describe external causes of injury, poisoning, or other adverse reactions affecting the patient's health. When a code from this section is applicable, it is intended to be used in *addition* to the main numeric ICD-9 code indicating the nature of the condition.

For example, a child falls while running around the bases at his baseball game. He is diagnosed with a closed fracture of the wrist (814.00). The additional E code E849.4 would follow to indicate the location where the injury occurred.

Volume 2 (Index to Diseases)

This volume of the ICD-9 manual is an alphabetical listing of diseases and injuries. The novice medical biller may at first experience some difficulty when looking for an ICD-9 code in this section, because diagnoses with more than one word are not always listed alphabetically by the first term.

For example, a patient is diagnosed with back pain. When searching Volume 2 in the ICD-9 manual under the letter B, once you locate the term "back," you will find that the following words are "*see condition*." This means that the ICD-9 code is listed by the condition first. In this example, the condition is "pain." Once you have found the listing for the condition "pain," you will find an alphabetical listing of anatomical sites (in this example, "back"). Here you will find that the ICD-9 code for back pain is 724.5.

This volume of the ICD-9 manual is usually referenced first, followed by Volume 1, to see if the code requires further subdivision. If it does, you must include an additional fourth or fifth digit.

Note
Because this text *is not* an instructional coding text, information given on the CPT and ICD-9 manuals is very basic. To see a complete list of codes and appendices in these manuals, visit your local library, if copies are not available from your instructor.

SUMMARY

The novice medical biller must practice the language of codes repeatedly to become familiar and comfortable with it and use it accurately. The three types of codes used by the physician-based medical biller include CPT, level II, and ICD-9 codes. CPT and national level II codes are used to determine what was done *to* and *for* the patient (office visits, medicine, supplies, etc.). ICD-9 codes are used to describe what is ailing the patient or for certain preventive diagnoses.

It is not the medical biller's job duty to assign these codes; the physician or coder will complete that task. However, it is important for the medical biller to become familiar with both CPT and HCPCS modifiers. It *is* the medical biller's job to attach these modifiers when needed in specific billing scenarios. Accurate use of codes and modifiers when billing reduces the chance of the physician's office being audited by an insurance company.

REVIEW QUESTIONS

1. Numbers, letters, or a combination of both describing procedures, services, and diagnoses are called _codes_.

2. The coding system used to report procedures, services, supplies, medicine, and durable medical equipment is called:
   a. ICD-9
   b. HCPCS
   c. level II
   d. none of the above

3. The coding manual that includes Evaluation and Management codes (99201–99499) is the _CPT_ manual.

4. A durable medical equipment code is called a _HCPCS_ or _National level II_ code.

5. Five-digit numeric codes are called _CPT_ codes.

6. A modifier is a _2_ character _alpha_, _numeric_, or _alphanumeric_ descriptor.

7. Give four examples of modifier usage.
   technical component
   professional component
   performed by one or more physician
   produce or service increased or reduced

8. Two types of modifiers are _CPT modifiers_ and _HCPCS modifiers_.

9. The _HCPCS_ modifier can be used with either a CPT or a national code.

10. A code used to report a diagnosis is called a(n) _ICD-9_ code.

11. Name the two volumes of ICD-9-CM used for physician billing.
    Vol 1 - Tabular list
    Vol 2 - Index to Diseases

12. Which volume of the ICD-9 manual is listed alphabetically?
    Vol 2 - Index

13. Codes used to report external causes of injury are called __E__ codes.

14. The ICD-9 code used to report an annual physical examination is called a(n)
    __V__ code.

15. Accurate coding reduces the risk of a(n) _audit_ by an insurance company.

Chapter 4

The Forms (Patient Registration, Superbill, and Hospital Sheet)

KEY TERMS

admit	documentation	hospital billing sheet
admit/discharge sheet	encounter form	medical chart
authorization	established patient	new patient
coder	follow-up visit	nursing home visit
consult	guarantor information	patient registration form
demographics	HIPAA	PHI
discharge	home visit	superbill

OBJECTIVES

Upon completion of this chapter, the student should be able to:

- Describe the use of various forms in the office.
- Decipher data from the superbill and hospital sheet.
- Explain the importance of a completed patient registration form.
- Define key terms.

PATIENT REGISTRATION FORM

some annually

new patient
a patient who has never been seen before, or who has not been seen in the past 36 months.

patient registration form
a form used to gather all patient information, including demographics and insurance information.

established patient
a patient who has been seen in the past 36 months.

demographics
statistical information on a patient.

guarantor information
information on the person financially responsible for the patient's account.

Each time a **new patient** comes to a physician's office, a **patient registration form** must be filled out (see Figure 4-1). The **established patient** does not have to do this. This form includes the patient's **demographics**, **guarantor information**, and health insurance information. A thorough patient registration form will include spaces for the patient's work telephone number, cellular telephone number, and next of kin. The more contacts available for reaching a patient, the better: these will assist the office in collecting money from that patient. The best advice a medical biller can give to the front-desk staff is to make sure the patient registration form is filled out in its entirety! Registration forms that are consistently found to be missing information will create unnecessary additional work for the medical biller.

Authorization to Release Protected Health Information

Depending on the office you are working for, there will be an **authorization** to release protected health information (PHI) at the bottom of the patient

Practice Name
PATIENT REGISTRATION

Welcome to our office. In order to serve you properly, we will need the following information. **(Please Print)**
All information will be strictly confidential.

| Patient's Name | Sex
M
F | Birth Date ____/____/____

Age_____ | Marital Status
Single [ ] Married [ ]
Widowed [ ] Divorced [ ] |

| Residence address | City | State | Zip | Home Phone: | Patient's Social Security # |

| Person financially responsible for this account | Self
Spouse
Parent | Responsible Party's Birthdate
____/____/____ | Responsible Party's Social Security # |

| Responsible Party Drivers License # State: Number | Occupation | How Long at current Employer? |

| Credit Card:
Number:
Type [ ] Mastercard [ ] Visa [ ] Discover | Expiration Date: | Name On Card |

| Name of employer Address | Business Phone | Occupation |

| Name of Spouse/Parent | Birth date | Social security # | Business phone |

| Reason for Visit: | Referred by: (include address and phone) |

| Person to contact in case of emergency: | Relationship to patient | Phone |

| **Medicare** Yes [ ] No [ ] | Medicare # | Medicaid Yes [ ] No [ ] | Medicaid # | Effective Date |

| Medicare Secondary insurance name Address | Policy # | Group # |

| Workers' Yes [ ] Motor Yes [ ]
Compensation? No [ ] Vehicle? No [ ]
If Yes-put W/C or MVA carrier below | Date of Accident | Treatment authorized by | Claim # | W/C or MVA Insurance Phone # |

| Primary insurance company Address | Is insurance through your employer? |

| Subscriber Name | Subscriber birth date | Policy # | Group # |

| Secondary insurance name Address | Policy # | Group # |

Medicare Lifetime Signature on File:
I request that payment of authorized Medicare benefits be made on my behalf to Practice Name for any services furnished me by the physician. I authorize any holder of medical information about me to release to the Health Care Financing Administration and its agents any information to determine these benefits payable for related services

_____   _____
Patient Signature   Date

Private Insurance Authorization for Assignment of Benefits/Information Release:
I, the undersigned authorize payment of medical benefits to Practice Name for any services furnished me by the physician. I understand that I am financially responsible for any amount not covered by my contract. I also authorize you to release to my insurance company or their agent information concerning health care, advice, treatment or supplies provided to me. This information will be used for the purpose of evaluating and administering claims of benefits.

_____   _____
Patient, Parent or Guardian Signature (if child is under 18 years old)   Date

Figure 4-1 Sample patient registration form.

authorization
a patient's signed approval.

PHI
protected health information.

medical chart
a confidential document that contains detailed and comprehensive information on the individual patient and the care given to that patient.

HIPAA
the Health Insurance Portability and Accountability Act of 1996, a law that stipulates patients' privacy rights regarding their PHI.

superbill
a form listing CPT, HCPCS, and ICD-9 codes used to record services performed for the patient and the patient's diagnosis(es) for a given visit.

registration form or on a separate sheet. This authorization will be signed by the patient or a parent, if the patient is a minor. By signing this, the patient gives the medical office permission to use the PHI for billing purposes when submitting a health insurance claim to the insurance company. This authorization need be signed only once, and will remain in the patient's **medical chart**.

HIPAA Release

Offices will also have the patient sign a variety of **HIPAA** forms. These will include a form regarding the office's privacy policies and a form asking the patient to whom medical information about the patient may be released, including names and telephone numbers. Some offices update these forms at the beginning of the calendar year, in case the patient wishes to change the previous information.

THE SUPERBILL

Chart slip

The **superbill** or **encounter form** is a form used to record the services performed for a patient and the patient's diagnoses for a given visit (see Figure 4-2). On the superbill are the CPT, HCPCS, and ICD-9 codes used specifically by that office.

Office Codes

New Pt	Established Pt	Consult
_____99201	_____99211	_____99241
_____99202	_____99212	_____99242
_____99203	_____99213	_____99243
_____99204	_____99214	_____99244
_____99205	_____99215	_____99245

_____93000 EKG	_____82270 Hemocult
_____36415 Venipuncture	_____J3420 Vitamin B-12 injection
_____90772 Therapeutic injection	_____J1030 Depo-Medrol
_____69210 Cerumen removal	_____87070 Throat culture
_____99000 Specimen handling	_____90471 Immunization admin
_____81002 Urinalysis	_____11200 Skin tag removal

ICD-9 Codes

_____789.00 Abdominal pain	_____V70.0 Routine visit
_____477.9 Allergies	_____784.0 Headache
_____285.9 Anemia	_____401.1 Hypertension
_____427.9 Arrhythmia	_____458.9 Hypotension
_____466.0 Bronchitis, acute	_____272.4 Hyperlipidemia
_____436 Cardiovascular accident	_____410.91 Myocardial infarction
_____414.00 Coronary artery disease	_____382.90 Otitis media
_____250.00 DM–controlled	_____462 Pharyngitis
_____782.3 Edema	_____482 Pneumonitis
_____780.79 Fatigue	_____461.9 Sinusitis
_____530.81 GERD	_____599.0 Urinary tract infection

Name _____ Date _____

Prim ins _____ Sec ins _____

Self-pay _____ Co-pay _____ Pd-ck _____ Chg _____ Cash _____

Figure 4-2 Sample superbill.

encounter form
another name for the superbill.

coder
the person whose job it is to assign CPT, HCPCS, and ICD-9 codes on the superbill, based on the physician's documentation.

documentation
the process of recording information in the medical chart, or the materials in a medical chart.

admit
term used when the patient is checked in to the hospital.

follow-up visit
subsequent visit made by the physician following an admission.

No two offices will have the exact same superbill, as the form will vary according to the specialty of the physician.

After a patient has been seen by the physician in the examination room, the physician is usually responsible for checking off on the superbill the level of office visit, procedures (if any), and diagnosis(es) for that patient on that given day. Some offices, particularly large group practices, may employ a **coder**, whose job it is to assign billing codes based on the physician's **documentation** in the medical chart.

HOSPITAL BILLING SHEET

As stated in Chapter 1, the medical biller is responsible for submitting health insurance claims, not only for patients seen in the office, but also for patients who are seen by the physician in the hospital. These visits include **admits, follow-up visits, consults,** and **discharges**. The CPT codes used for a physician's visit in the hospital setting are listed on a **hospital billing sheet** (see Figure 4-3) or an **admit/discharge sheet** (see Figure 4-4). The hospital sheet usually will not list ICD-9 codes on it; therefore, the physician will write in the ICD-9 code(s), or will write out the diagnosis, leaving the coder or medical biller to assign the correct code. The **admit/discharge** sheet is similar to the office version of the patient registration form. It lists demographics and insurance information pertaining to the patient. Some physicians will attach the hospital sheet directly to the admit/discharge sheet. Other physicians will write the CPT and ICD-9 codes directly on the admit/discharge sheet, and the medical biller will gather claims submission information directly from these sheets. Regardless of how your physician prepares hospital billing, the codes will be the same.

Name _____   Date Admitted _____   Date Discharged _____

Month _____   Year _____   Patient's Insurance _____

01	02	03	04	05	06	07	08	09	10	11	12	13	14	15	16	17	18	19	20	21	22	23	24	25	26	27	28	29	30	31	CPT Codes
																															99221
																															99222
																															99223
																															99231
																															99232
																															99233
																															99251
																															99252
																															99253
																															99254
																															99255
																															99238
																															99239

Diagnosis(es)

1 _____
2 _____
3 _____
4 _____

Figure 4-3 Sample hospital billing sheet.

MedRec#:22-000478

Admit Date_____Discharge Date_____
Physician Signature_____

Patient Name: Admit Date and Time:

Address: Discharge Date and Time:

City: State: Zip code: Phone#:

Soc sec#:   Date of Birth: Sex: M/S:

Emp. Status:

Emp. Address:

Guarantor Name: Rel: DOB:

Soc sec#:   Address:

Phone:

Insurance #1:   ID#:   Gr#:

Insured: Rel to patient:

Insurance #2:   ID#:   Gr#:

Insured: Rel to patient:

Admitting Physician: Attending Physician:

Admitting Diagnosis:
Comments:

Principal Diagnosis: Procedures:
Secondary Diagnosis:

ABC Hospital
125 Rt 70
Brick, NJ 08724

Figure 4-4 Sample admit/discharge sheet.

CPT & location diff

NURSING HOME VISITS

If the physician you are billing for visits patients in the nursing homes where they reside, you will submit claims for these visits and services also. The CPT codes for nursing home visits will differ from those listed on your superbill or hospital sheet. Your office may have a special sheet designed for these visits, or the physician may use an admit/discharge sheet from the nursing home and write the CPT codes directly on that sheet.

HOME VISITS

not cost effective

Home visits to a patient are rare these days, but you may nonetheless end up working for a physician who performs them. Again, the codes are different for these visits. A physician who performs home visits will most likely have these codes listed on the superbill used in the office.

FREQUENCY OF BILLING

The frequency with which an office submits health insurance claims can vary. Some medical billers submit claims on a daily basis, while others may submit once or twice per week. If working for a medical billing company, the biller will most likely receive the assigned work for the physician accounts for which the biller is responsible on a weekly basis. If a physician gives the biller hospital billing on a daily basis after making hospital rounds, the biller will not bill for the patient's entire stay at the hospital, but for each day the patient is seen.

consult
term used when a physician calls upon another physician to evaluate and make an assessment on a patient in the hospital setting.

discharge
term used for the patient's release from the hospital.

hospital billing sheet
form used by the physician to record hospital codes for inpatient visits.

admit/discharge sheet
a sheet generated by the hospital listing all patient information, including demographics and insurance information.

nursing home visit
a visit made by the physician to a patient who resides in a nursing home.

home visit
a visit made by the physician to the patient's home.

SUMMARY

Although the medical biller must become familiar with many forms, three very important ones are the patient registration form, the superbill, and the hospital sheet. It is appropriate to emphasize to the front-desk staff the importance of a completed registration form. The CPT codes listed on the superbill will vary from those on the hospital sheet or admit/discharge sheet. It is the medical biller's job to read these codes correctly when submitting a health insurance claim. The billing process for both medical offices and medical billing companies is the same; however, the frequency of claims submission may vary. Never make an assumption about missing form information. Call the patient if need be, or ask the physician if you are unsure of a code. It is the medical biller's responsibility to create and submit accurate claims.

REVIEW QUESTIONS

1. A new patient is one who has never been seen in the office, or who has not been seen in the past:
   a. 12 months
   b. 24 months
   c. 36 months
   d. none of the above

2. Another name for the superbill is:
   a. bill form
   b. payment form
   c. encounter form
   d. none of the above

3. Privacy enforcement in the office is regulated by:
   a. HIPPA
   b. HIPPO
   c. HIPAA
   d. none of the above

4. Two types of codes found on the superbill are:
   a. CPT and ICD-9
   b. ICD-9 and ICD-10
   c. CPT and CMA
   d. none of the above

5. The history, physical exam information, and diagnoses related to a patient are kept in the:
   a. file
   b. superbill
   c. medical chart
   d. HIPAA envelope

6. The person responsible for assigning an ICD-9 code on a superbill is the:
   a. biller
   b. coder
   c. physician
   d. a or c
   e. b or c

7. Codes used for hospital visits are found on the:
   a. superbill
   b. encounter form
   c. hospital sheet
   d. none of the above

8. Explain the importance of a thoroughly completed patient registration form.
   _____
   _____

9. How might a physician present his hospital billing to the medical biller if a hospital sheet is not used?
   _____
   _____
   _____

10. Explain how the frequency of billing may vary from office to office, or if working for a medical billing company.
    _____
    _____
    _____

See Figure 4-5 to answer the following questions.

Practice Name
PATIENT REGISTRATION

Welcome to our office. In order to serve you properly, we will need the following information. **(Please Print)**
All information will be strictly confidential.

Patient's Name	Sex	Birth Date	Marital Status
Sarah Jones	M __ F **X**	04 / 18 / 1940	Single [ ] Married **[X]** Widowed [ ] Divorced [ ]

Residence address	City	State	Zip	Home Phone:	Cell phone:	Patient's Social Security #
999 Apple Lane	Brick	NJ	08724	732-999-9999	848-999-9999	999-99-9999

Person financially responsible for this account		X Self __Spouse __Parent	Responsible Party's Birthdate 04/18/1940	Responsible Party's Social Security # 999-99-9999
Sarah Jones				

Responsible Party Drivers License #	State: NJ	Number 4478-9978-7788-7440	Relation to patient: self	Phone:

Patient Employer	Address	Occupation retired	How Long at current Employer?

Name of Spouse/Parent	Birth date	Home phone	Cell phone	Social security #
Michael Jones	01/28/1940	same	848-222-0000	888-77-9999

Name of Spouse employer	Address	Business Phone	Occupation

Reason for Visit:	Referred by: (include address and phone)

Person to contact in case of emergency:	Relationship to patient	Phone

Medicare Yes [X] No [ ]	Medicare # 999-99-9999A	Medicaid Yes [ ] No [X]	Medicaid #	Effective Date

Medicare Secondary insurance name	Address	Policy #	Group #

Workers' Yes [ ] Motor Yes [ ] Compensation? No [X] Vehicle? No [X] **If Yes-put W/C or MVA carrier below**	Date of Accident	Treatment authorized by	Claim #	W/C or MVA Insurance Phone #

Primary insurance company	Address	Is insurance through your employer?

Subscriber Name	Subscriber birth date	Policy #	Group #

Secondary insurance name	Address	Policy #	Group #
BCBS			

Subscriber Name	Subscriber birth date	Policy #	Group #

Medicare Lifetime Signature on File:
I request that payment of authorized Medicare benefits be made on my behalf to Practice Name for any services furnished me by the physician. I authorize any holder of medical information about me to release to the Health Care Financing Administration and its agents any information to determine these benefits payable for related services

Sarah Jones   05/01/XX
Patient Signature   Date

Private Insurance Authorization for Assignment of Benefits/Information Release:
I, the undersigned authorize payment of medical benefits to Practice Name for any services furnished me by the physician. I understand that I am financially responsible for any amount not covered by my contract. I also authorize you to release to my insurance company or their agent information concerning health care, advice, treatment or supplies provided to me. This information will be used for the purpose of evaluating and administering claims of benefits.

Patient, Parent or Guardian Signature (if child is under 18 years old)   Date

Figure 4-5 Sample completed patient registration form.

11. What is the patient's work telephone number?

_____

12. Which insurance is primary for this patient?

_____

13. Who is the policyholder for the secondary insurance plan?

_____

14. Is there a group number for the primary insurance plan?

_____

15. What important piece of information is missing from this patient registration form?

_____

See Figure 4-6 to answer the following questions.

Office Codes

New Pt	Established Pt	Consult
_____99201	_____99211	_____99241
_____99202	_____99212	_____99242
_____99203	__X__99213	_____99243
_____99204	_____99214	_____99244
_____99205	_____99215	_____99245

_____93000 EKG   _____82270 Hemocult
_____36415 Venipuncture   _____J3420 Vitamin B-12 injection
_____90772 Therapeutic injection   _____J1030 Depo-Medrol
_____69210 Cerumen removal   _____87070 Throat culture
__X__99000 Specimen handling   _____90471 Immunization admin
__X__81002 Urinalysis   _____11200 Skin tag removal

ICD-9 Codes

_____789.00 Abdominal pain   _____V70.0 Routine visit
_____477.9 Allergies   _____784.0 Headache
_____285.9 Anemia   _____401.1 Hypertension
_____427.9 Arrhythmia   _____458.9 Hypotension
_____466.0 Bronchitis, acute   _____272.4 Hyperlipidemia
_____436 Cardiovascular accident   _____410.91 Myocardial infarction
_____414.00 Coronary artery disease _____382.90 Otitis media
_____250.00 DM–controlled   _____462 Pharyngitis
_____782.3 Edema   _____482 Pneumonitis
_____780.79 Fatigue   _____461.9 Sinusitis
_____530.81 GERD   __X__599.0 Urinary tract infection

Name __Patty Patient_____   Date __April 19, 20XX____
Prim ins __Great West_____   Sec ins _____
Self-pay _____ Co-pay _$20____ Pd-ck _____ Chg _____ Cash _$20_____

Figure 4-6 Sample completed superbill.

16. Which CPT codes will be billed out for this visit?

_____

_____

17. What are the patient's diagnoses for this visit?

_____

_____

18. What is the level of office visit for this date of service?

_____

See Figure 4-7 to answer the following questions.

19. What date was the patient admitted?

_____

20. What is the level of the admit?

_____

21. How many follow-up visits are on this hospital sheet?

_____

22. According to this hospital sheet, has the patient been discharged?

_____

23. How many total visits will be billed from this hospital sheet?

_____

Name __Sarah Jones_____   Date Admitted __10/15/20XX____   Date Discharged __10/19/20XX___

Month __October_____   Year __20XX____   Patient's Insurance __Medicare-pri BCBS-sec_____

01	02	03	04	05	06	07	08	09	10	11	12	13	14	15	16	17	18	19	20	21	22	23	24	25	26	27	28	29	30	31	CPT Codes
																															99221
																															99222
														X																	99223
																	X														99231
															X	X															99232
																															99233
																															99251
																															99252
																															99253
																															99254
																															99255
																		X													99238
																															99239

Diagnosis(es)

1 __786.50__

2 __272.4___

3 _____

4 _____

Figure 4-7 Sample completed hospital billing sheet.

Chapter 5

The Heart of Medical Billing: The CMS-1500 Form

KEY TERMS

intelligence-free legacy number	National Provider Identifier (NPI)	payer

OBJECTIVES

Upon completion of this chapter, the student should be able to:

- Differentiate between patient data fields and physician data fields on the CMS-1500 form.
- Discuss requirements for specific blocks on the CMS-1500 form.
- Explain multiple uses for different blocks on the CMS-1500 form.
- Define key terms.

INTRODUCTION

Implementation of the newest CMS-1500 form (see Figure 5-1) was phased in over about a two-year period. Following approval of the claim filing instructions by the National Uniform Claim Committee (NUCC), a timeline was established for adoption of the form. The NUCC Web site states that:

- By October 1, 2006, health plans, clearinghouses, and other support vendors should be using the revised 1500 form.
- From October 1, 2006, to March 31, 2007, providers may use either the existing 12/90 version or the revised (08/05) version of the 1500 form.
- As of April 1, 2007, the 12/90 version of the 1500 form is discontinued; only the revised (08/05) form is to be used.

Because these timelines and mandatory-use dates may be revised, it is advisable for the medical biller to check the NUCC Web site frequently to stay abreast of current changes and new requirements.

Several changes were made in the new version of the form. Most importantly, shaded areas were added to several blocks to accommodate the new **National Provider Identifier (NPI)** number issued to all HIPAA-covered entities. Use of the NPI on all CMS-1500 forms became mandatory

National Provider Identifier (NPI) a 10-digit, intelligence-free, numeric identifier.

1500

HEALTH INSURANCE CLAIM FORM

APPROVED BY NATIONAL UNIFORM CLAIM COMMITTEE 08/05

NUCC Instruction Manual available at: www.nucc.org

APPROVED OMB-0938-0999 FORM CMS-1500 (08/05)

Figure 5-1 Blank CMS-1500 form (08/05 version).

effective May 23, 2007. The NPI, a 10-digit, **intelligence-free**, numeric identifier, was designed to replace all previous provider **legacy numbers**. A physician's NPI number identifies the physician universally to all payers.

CLAIM FILING INSTRUCTIONS

The following CMS-1500 claim form instructions are generic; that is, they are not specific to any one individual **payer**. For specific payer guidelines, contact the individual payer in question.

Carrier or Payer Block

Payer block: Enter the name and address of the payer in the upper right-hand side of the form.

1500

HEALTH INSURANCE CLAIM FORM

APPROVED BY NATIONAL UNIFORM CLAIM COMMITTEE 08/05

PICA

PICA

CARRIER

Blocks 1–13: Patient and Insured Information

Block 1: Check the payer type for the claim by marking an "X" in the appropriate box.

- Options are Medicare, Medicaid, Tricare Champus, Champva, Group Health Plan, FECA BLK Lung, and Other.
- The "OTHER" box can include HMO, commercial, motor vehicle, liability, or workers' compensation insurance.

1. MEDICARE	MEDICAID	TRICARE CHAMPUS	CHAMPVA	GROUP HEALTH PLAN	FECA BLK LUNG	OTHER
(Medicare #)	(Medicaid #)	(Sponsor's SSN)	(Member ID#)	(SSN or ID)	(SSN)	(ID)

Block 2: Enter the patient's full legal name, beginning with the last name, then first name and middle initial.

- Insert a comma between the last name and first name and before the middle initial.
- If patient's last name includes a suffix (e.g., Jr. or Sr.), enter the suffix after the last name.
- Do not enter professional credentials or designations (e.g., M.D., Esq.) in this box.
- A hyphen may be inserted for hyphenated last names.
- Do not enter a period in this block.

2. PATIENT'S NAME (Last Name, First Name, Middle Initial)

Block 3: Enter the patient's date of birth in an eight-digit format (MM/DD/CCYY). Enter an "X" in the appropriate box for the patient's gender.

3. PATIENT'S BIRTH DATE — MM DD YY — SEX — M — F

Block 4: Enter the insured's full legal name, beginning with last name, the first name, and the middle initial.

- Do not insert professional credentials, designations, or periods in this block.
- If the insured is the patient, may enter "Same" in this block.

> 4. INSURED'S NAME (Last Name, First Name, Middle Initial)

Block 5: Enter the patient's address and telephone number.

- If using a nine-digit Zip Code to include the rural route, use a hyphen.
- Although a hyphen is not required in manual completion of the form for the telephone number, most software programs are formatted to include a hyphen.
- Do not use commas, periods, or other punctuation marks in this block.

> 5. PATIENT'S ADDRESS (No., Street)

Block 6: Enter an "X" in the correct box indicating the patient's relationship to the insured.

> **Note**
> The reason for this is that, for workers' compensation claims, the insured is always the patient's employer.

- For workers' compensation claims, check the "Other" box.

> 6. PATIENT RELATIONSHIP TO INSURED
> Self ☐ Spouse ☐ Child ☐ Other ☐

Block 7: Enter the insured's address here.

- Do not use commas, periods, or other punctuation in this block.
- If the insured's address is the same as the patient's, may enter "Same."
- For workers' compensation claims, enter the patient's employer's address.

> 7. INSURED'S ADDRESS (No., Street)

Block 8: Enter the patient's marital and employment status here.

- If the patient is a part-time or full-time student in a postsecondary school or university, check the appropriate box.

> 8. PATIENT STATUS
> Single ☐ Married ☐ Other ☐
> Employed ☐ Full-Time Student ☐ Part-Time Student ☐

Block 9: If Box 11d is checked "YES," complete this block.

- Enter the name of the insured who holds the secondary/supplemental insurance.
- If the insured's name is the same as in Block 2, may leave this block blank.

Block 9a: Enter the policy and/or group number of the secondary/supplemental insurance.

- It is not necessary to include a hyphen or space between the policy and group number for handwritten claims; however, most software programs are formatted to indicate a space between the two numbers.

Block 9b: Enter the date of birth in an eight-digit (MM/DD/CCYY) format for the insured listed in Block 9. Enter an "X" to indicate the gender of the insured listed in Block 9.

Block 9c: Enter the employer's name or school attended by the insured listed in Block 9.

- For Medicare claims, if the insured listed in Block 9 is retired, enter "Retired" in this block.

Block 9d: Enter the name of the secondary/supplemental insurance plan or program.

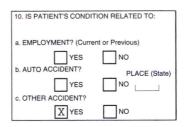

Blocks 10a–10c: Place an "X" in the "NO" box if the patient's condition is not related to employment injury, an automobile accident, or another accident.

- If the patient's condition is the result of an injury that occurred on the job, place an "X" in the "YES" box in 10a.
- If the patient's condition is the result of an automobile accident, place an "X" in the "YES" box in 10b and enter the two-character Postal Service abbreviation in the "(State)" line for the state in which the accident occurred.
- If the patient's condition is the result of another accident (e.g., a fall on the ice outside a condominium complex), place an "X" in the "YES" box in 10c.

Block 10d: This block is reserved for local use. It is not a data-required field for most claims. Contact individual payers for their guidelines.

- For workers' compensation claims, may enter the adjuster's name or case manager's name in this block.

Block 11: Enter the primary insurance policy's group number as listed on the health insurance identification card (if one is listed).

- For workers' compensation claims, enter the FECA number (a nine-digit alphanumeric identifier assigned to a patient claiming a work-related condition).
- For Medicare claims, enter the word "None" here.

Block 11a: Enter the insured's (person named in Block 4) date of birth in an eight-digit (MM/DD/CCYY) format. Enter an "X" in the correct box for the insured's gender.

Block 11b: Enter the insured's employer's name or school name here.

- For Medicare claims, if the insured is retired, enter "Retired" here.

Block 11c: Enter the primary insurance payer's plan or program name (this may be listed on the health insurance identification card).

- Some payers require an identification number here (contact the individual payer for specific guidelines).
- If no plan or program name is listed on the health insurance identification card and the payer in question does not require data in this block, leave this block blank.

Block 11d: Enter an "X" in the "YES" box if there is health insurance coverage other than the insurance checked in Block 1. (For primary claims, checking "YES" indicates that there is a secondary/supplemental plan.)

- If "YES" is checked, continue and complete Blocks 9 through 9d.
- If there is no other health insurance coverage, mark an "X" in the "NO" box.

```
11. INSURED'S POLICY GROUP OR FECA NUMBER


a. INSURED'S DATE OF BIRTH                SEX
      MM   DD   YY              M [ ]        F [ ]

b. EMPLOYER'S NAME OR SCHOOL NAME


c. INSURANCE PLAN NAME OR PROGRAM NAME


d. IS THERE ANOTHER HEALTH BENEFIT PLAN?
    [ ] YES    [ ] NO    If yes, return to and complete item 9 a-d.
```

Block 12: This block is for the patient's or authorized person's signature.

- If a legal signature is not available, enter "Signature on file" or "SOF" in this field, as long as the patient's or authorized person's signature is on file in the medical chart.
- If there is no signature on file, leave blank or enter "No signature on file."
- Enter the date the form was signed or the date of service, in either a six-digit (MM/DD/YY) or an eight-digit (MM/DD/CCYY) format.

```
                    READ BACK OF FORM BEFORE COMPLETING & SIGNING THIS FORM.
12. PATIENT'S OR AUTHORIZED PERSON'S SIGNATURE I authorize the release of any medical or other information necessary
    to process this claim. I also request payment of government benefits either to myself or to the party who accepts assignment
    below.

    SIGNED _____    DATE _____
```

Block 13: Enter the insured's or authorized person's signature here. When signed, the person is requesting that benefits be paid directly to the provider. This is known as *assignment of benefits*.

```
13. INSURED'S OR AUTHORIZED PERSON'S SIGNATURE I authorize
    payment of medical benefits to the undersigned physician or supplier for
    services described below.

    SIGNED _____
```

Blocks 14–33: Provider or Supplier Information

Block 14: This block is used to enter the six-digit (MM/DD/YY) or eight-digit (MM/DD/CCYY) format for the first date of the present illness, injury, or pregnancy.

- For workers' compensation, motor vehicle accidents, or other accidents, enter the date of the injury or accident here.
- For pregnancy claims, enter the date of the patient's last menstrual period (LMP) here.

```
14. DATE OF CURRENT:        ILLNESS (First symptom) OR
    MM   DD   YY            INJURY (Accident) OR
                           PREGNANCY(LMP)
```

Block 15: Enter a six-digit (MM/DD/YY) or an eight-digit (MM/DD/CCYY) date in this block for the first date the patient had the same or a similar illness.

- Previous pregnancies are not considered a similar illness.
- This block is *not* a required field.
- Leave block blank if original illness date is unknown.

```
15. IF PATIENT HAS HAD SAME OR SIMILAR ILLNESS.
    GIVE FIRST DATE   MM   DD   YY
```

Block 16: If known, enter a six-digit (MM/DD/YY) or an eight-digit (MM/DD/CCYY) date in both the "FROM" and "TO" sections of this block, indicating the dates the patient was unable to work in his or her current occupation.

- If the "TO" date is unknown, some software programs will allow "N/A" (not applicable) or no date at all in this field.
- Entry in this block is usually related to a workers' compensation claim.

```
16. DATES PATIENT UNABLE TO WORK IN CURRENT OCCUPATION
    MM   DD   YY              MM   DD   YY
FROM                     TO
```

Block 17: This block is used for a referring provider, ordering provider, or other source who referred or ordered the service, or procedures rendered on the claim.

- Enter the first name, middle initial, last name, and credentials of the referring provider, ordering provider, or other source of services, procedures, or supplies to be billed on the claim.
- Do not enter commas or periods in this block.
- May enter hyphen for hyphenated names.

```
17. NAME OF REFERRING PROVIDER OR OTHER SOURCE
```

Block 17a: In the small box to the left, enter the two-character qualifier designated for the ID (identification) number to be entered in the following section. The ID number is a non-NPI provider legacy number.

The provider legacy qualifiers are as follows:

0B   state license number
1B   Blue Shield provider number
1C   Medicare provider number
1D   Medicaid provider number
1G   provider UPIN number
1H   CHAMPUS ID number
E1   employer's ID number
G2   provider commercial number

LU   location number
N5   provider plan network ID number
SY   Social Security number (may not be used for Medicare)
X5   State Industrial Accident provider number
ZZ   provider taxonomy

- As of May 2007, Medicare provider legacy numbers may not be reported on *paper* claims sent to Medicare.

Block 17b: Enter the 10-digit NPI number of the referring provider, ordering provider, performing provider, or other source in this block. As of May 23, 2007, all claims must include the NPI number.

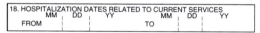

Block 18: Enter the six-digit (MM/DD/YY) or eight-digit (MM/DD/CCYY) hospitalization dates related to current services here.

- This block relates to inpatient stays only. If the patient has not yet been discharged, may enter "N/A" or leave the "TO" field blank.

Block 19: This block may be used when the CPT/HCPCS code billed in Block 24 requires more than four modifiers. Enter the modifiers in this field.

- For Medicare claims, enter the description of the HCPCS level II national code for J codes billed in Block 24 here.
- Contact individual payers for additional claim requirements for this block.

Block 20: Enter an "X" in the "YES" box when billing for purchased services.

- Checking "YES" indicates that the service was performed by an entity other than the billing provider. The other entity will be listed in Block 32.
- Enter the dollar amount under "CHARGES" for the purchased services. Enter "00" to the right of the vertical line if the dollar amount is a whole number.
- Do not enter dollar signs.
- Enter an "X" in the "NO" box when no purchased services are reported on the claim.

Block 21: Enter the patient's diagnosis/condition (ICD-9-CM) code(s) in this block.

- This block may contain up to four ICD-9 codes.
- For ICD-9 codes containing more than three digits, enter the first three digits before the period and the fourth and fifth (if required) digits after the period.

- For E codes beginning with more than three digits, enter the fourth digit above the period.
- The numbers 1, 2, 3, and 4 listed in this block are referred to as *diagnosis reference numbers* and must correlate to the correct CPT/HCPCS codes billed in Block 24D.

```
21. DIAGNOSIS OR NATURE OF ILLNESS OR INJURY (Relate Items 1, 2, 3 or 4 to Item 24E by Line)

1. |____ . _____                    3. |____ . _____

2. |____ . _____                    4. |____ . _____
```

Block 22: This block is used for Medicaid claims.

- Enter the Medicaid resubmission code and original reference number assigned by the Medicaid payer.
- Because Medicaid payers vary by state, contact each payer about its guidelines for this block.

```
22. MEDICAID RESUBMISSION
    CODE              ORIGINAL REF. NO.
```

Block 23: Enter any of the following in this block:

- Prior authorization number, if assigned by payer.
- Precertification number, if assigned by payer.
- Clinical Laboratory Improvement Amendments (CLIA) number, if billing for lab services.

```
23. PRIOR AUTHORIZATION NUMBER
```

Block 24A: Enter the "From" and "To" dates for service(s) rendered.

- Some payers may require a "To" date even when it is the same as the "From" date; it is advisable always to enter both sections to reduce the risk of claim rejection.
- If billing for multiple units for the same service (e.g., follow-up hospital visits for same level of service), may reflect this by listing the "From" date as the first day of the service and the "To" date as the last date this same service was rendered.

Block 24B: Enter the appropriate two-digit place-of-service code for each billable item. See Table 5-1.

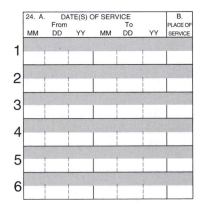

TABLE 5-1   Place-of-Service Codes

03*	School
04*	Homeless shelter
11	Office
12	Home
13**	Assisted living facility
14**	Group home
15*	Mobile unit (see note)
20*	Urgent care facility
21	Inpatient hospital
22	Outpatient hospital
23	Emergency room—hospital
24	Ambulatory surgical center (free-standing)
25	Birthing center
26	Military treatment facility
31	Skilled nursing facility (covered Part A stay patient)
32	Nursing facility
33	Custodial care facility
34	Hospice
41	Ambulance (land)
42	Ambulance (air or water)
49**	Independent clinic
50	Federally qualified health center
51	Inpatient psychiatric facility
52	Psychiatric facility partial hospitalization
53	Community mental health center
54	Intermediate care facility/mentally retarded
55	Residential substance abuse treatment facility

Continued

TABLE 5-1   **Place-of-Service Codes** (Continued)

56	Psychiatric residential treatment center
57**	Nonresidential substance abuse treatment facility
60	Mass immunization center
61	Comprehensive inpatient rehabilitation facility
62	Comprehensive outpatient rehabilitation facility
65	End-stage renal disease treatment facility
71	State or local public health clinic
72	Rural health clinic
81	Independent laboratory
99	Other unlisted facility

*Valid January 1, 2003, and thereafter.
**Place-of-service code valid October 1, 2003, and thereafter.

Block 24C: This block is used if the service rendered is deemed an "emergency service."

- Check the individual payer's requirements for completion of this block. If deemed an emergency, usually a "Y" will be required in this block; if not an emergency, leave blank.

Block 24D: Enter the CPT/HCPCS and modifier (if applicable) code(s) in the unshaded area of this block.

- CPT/HCPCS codes are listed to the left; up to four modifiers may be listed per line item.
- Up to six CPT/HCPCS line items may be billed on one claim form.
- If payers require additional anesthesia services information (e.g., begin and end times) or a narrative description of an unspecified code, enter this information in the shaded area of the block, directly above the CPT/HCPCS code.
- If payers require specific codes (e.g., NCD code for drugs) for durable medical equipment or supplies, enter these codes in the shaded area of the block.

```
D. PROCEDURES, SERVICES, OR SUPPLIES
       (Explain Unusual Circumstances)
  CPT/HCPCS  |        MODIFIER
```

Block 24E: Enter the diagnosis reference number from Block 21 that pertains to each billable line item.

- The primary reference number should always be listed first.
- This block can contain a "1," "2," "3," or "4" or any combination of the four diagnosis reference numbers.
- Do not list the actual ICD-9 code in this block.
- Do not use commas to separate the numbers.

```
     E.
 DIAGNOSIS
  POINTER
```

Block 24F: Enter the dollar amount for each billable service, procedure, or item.

- Do not enter dollar signs.
- Enter "00" in the cents field to the right of the perforated line if the amount is a whole number.

```
     F.
 $ CHARGES
```

Block 24G: Enter the number of days or units for the CPT/HCPCS code listed in Block 24D.

- The most common use of this block is for multiple visits, units of supplies, anesthesia units or minutes, or oxygen volume.
- If only one day or unit was needed, enter "1" in this block. If reporting a fraction of a unit, use a decimal point.
- Contact individual payers regarding guidelines for NDC units when using HCPCS billing codes for drugs.

Block 24H: This block is reserved for Medicaid claims.

- If the claim is related to early and periodic screening, diagnosis, treatment, or family planning, enter "Y" for yes.
- Check with each state's Medicaid payers to find out if an "N" is required for non-EPSDT/family planning services.

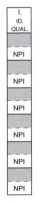

Block 24I: Enter the non-NPI qualifier as directed in Block 17a (refer to list of qualifiers).

Block 24J: Enter the non-NPI legacy number in the shaded area.

- Enter the 10-digit NPI number in the unshaded area.
- For Medicare claims, when the rendering physician is part of a group practice, the individual NPI number is reported in the unshaded area.
- Use of the NPI number is mandatory as of May 23, 2007.

J.
RENDERING
PROVIDER ID. #

Block 25: Enter the provider or supplier's tax identification number here with an ''X'' in the appropriate box.

- For rendering physicians who are part of a group practice, enter the *group's* tax identification number.

25. FEDERAL TAX I.D. NUMBER   SSN EIN

Block 26: Enter the patient's account number assigned by the provider or supplier's manual or computerized software system.

26. PATIENT'S ACCOUNT NO.

Block 27: Enter an ''X'' in the appropriate box.

- An ''X'' in the ''YES'' box indicates that the provider has agreed to accept assignment on the claim. An ''X'' in the ''NO'' box indicates that the provider does not accept assignment on the claim (a ''NO'' would indicate that the provider does not have a contract with or does not participate with the payer in question).

27. ACCEPT ASSIGNMENT?
(For govt. claims, see back)
☐ YES   ☐ NO

Block 28: Enter the total charges from lines 1 through 6 in Block 24F.

- Do not enter dollar signs.
- Enter ''00'' to the right of the perforated line if the total amount is a whole number.

28. TOTAL CHARGE
$

Block 29: Enter amount the patient or primary payer paid (for secondary claims).

- Some software programs are not formatted to reflect a patient payment (co-payment or co-insurance) in this block.
- If no payment is made, may leave blank or enter ''0'' to the left of the perforated line and ''00'' to the right of the perforated line.

> **29. AMOUNT PAID**
> $

Block 30: Enter the balance-due amount here.

- If the software program used does not reflect an amount in Block 29, this block will equal the dollar amount in Block 28.

> **30. BALANCE DUE**
> $

Block 31: Enter the signature of the provider or supplier.

- Include degrees or credentials after the name.
- For computerized claims, a printed signature is acceptable.
- "Signature on file" or "SOF" is acceptable in this block.
- Enter the six-digit (MM/DD/YY) or eight-digit (MM/DD/CCYY) date on which the claim was signed or billed (for computerized claims).

> **31. SIGNATURE OF PHYSICIAN OR SUPPLIER**
> **INCLUDING DEGREES OR CREDENTIALS**
> (I certify that the statements on the reverse
> apply to this bill and are made a part thereof.)
>
> SIGNED   DATE

Block 32: Enter the name and address of the location where billed items (Block 24D) were rendered.

- If the provider is billing for purchased diagnostic tests, enter the supplier's name and address here.
- If the provider is part of a group practice, enter the name of the group here.
- Do not use commas, periods, or other punctuation in the address.

Block 32a: Enter the NPI of the provider, supplier, or facility listed in Block 32.
Block 32b: Enter the two-digit qualifier (see instructions for Block 17a) followed by the non-NPI legacy number of the provider, supplier, or facility listed in Block 32.

> **32. SERVICE FACILITY LOCATION INFORMATION**
>
> a.   NPI   b.

Block 33: Enter the name, address, and telephone number of the billing entity (legal name of the practice) here. If the provider is part of a group practice, enter the group's name here.
Block 33a: Enter the NPI number of the billing entity listed in Block 33. If the billing entity is a group practice, enter the group's NPI number here.
Block 33b: Enter the two-digit qualifier (see instructions for Block 17a) followed by the non-NPI legacy number of the billing entity.

> **33. BILLING PROVIDER INFO & PH #** (   )
>
> a.   NPI   b.

Several sample bills and claims on the CMS-1500 form appear in Chapters 6 and 7, and in Appendix I at the back of this textbook.

SUMMARY

After the NUCC approved the claim filing instructions of the new CMS-1500 form, version 8/05, use of that form became mandatory according to a phase-in timeline.

Each payer may require completion of certain blocks, boxes, or items, or may require specific information to be listed in different blocks on this form. If the medical biller is in doubt about a payer's requirements regarding a block or box, the biller should contact the payer to get its claim filing instructions.

REVIEW QUESTIONS

1. Which fields of the CMS-1500 form require information about the patient and insured?

   Blocks 1-13

2. Which fields require information about the physician or supplier?

   Blocks 14-33

3. Where on the CMS-1500 form are the name and address of the payer placed?

4. True or False: Is the term "signature on file" or "SOF" is acceptable in all blocks requiring a signature?

   _T_

5. What is the purpose of the shaded fields in Block 24d on the CMS-1500 form?

6. Why was the NPI number developed?

Chapter 6
Billing for Office Services and Procedures

KEY TERMS

| office visit | referred | specialist |

OBJECTIVES

Upon completion of this chapter, the student should be able to:

- Distinguish between new patient and established patient office visit codes.
- Accurately complete a CMS-1500 form for a patient encounter in the physician's office.
- Determine codes used for an encounter at a specialist's office and the important CMS-1500 form box requirements for such.
- Define key terms.

GATHERING DATA

Q16 Medical billers working in physicians' offices extract data from the patient registration form and the superbill (introduced in Chapter 4).

The evaluation and management CPT codes for all physicians (except psychiatrists) for new, established, and consult visits will be found on most practices' superbills. See Figure 6-1.

Pediatricians will have additional preventive medicine evaluation and management codes on their superbills to reflect services for well-baby and well-child visits.

Billing for a New Patient

Before submitting a claim for a new patient, the data gathered from the patient registration form must be entered into the computer system's software program. The photocopies of the patient's insurance card(s) will have been placed in the patient's medical chart. The medical biller will need to reference these copies for correct claim submission addresses.

Once all patient data has been entered, the medical biller can then enter the claim information and prepare the claim for submission.

office visit
an encounter in the physician's office.

The CPT codes used for billing an **office visit** for a new patient vary in levels ranging from 1 to 5 (1 being the lowest, 5 being the highest). The level of office visit a patient is assigned is determined by the physician or coder, based on documentation in the medical chart. See Figure 6-2.

New		Established		Consult	
Level 1	99201	Level 1	99211	Level 1	99241
Level 2	99202	Level 2	99212	Level 2	99242
Level 3	99203	Level 3	99213	Level 3	99243
Level 4	99204	Level 4	99214	Level 4	99244
Level 5	99205	Level 5	99215	Level 5	99245

Figure 6-1 CPT codes for office visits.

Code	Description
99201	Level I New Patient
99202	Level II New Patient
99203	Level III New Patient
99204	Level IV New Patient
99205	Level V New Patient

Figure 6-2 Office visit codes for a new patient.

Code	Description
99211	Level I Est. Patient
99212	Level II Est. Patient
99213	Level III Est. Patient
99214	Level IV Est. Patient
99215	Level V Est. Patient

Figure 6-3 Office visit codes for an established patient.

Billing for an Established Patient

Billing for established patients is less time-consuming, as their patient and insurance information has already been entered into the computer's software program. Occasionally, the medical biller may need to add or edit the patient's information if the patient has moved or switched insurance carriers.

The CPT codes for established patients are similar to those for new patients, with the exception of the fourth digit in each level. The "0" in new patient codes is replaced by a "1" in established patient codes. See Figure 6-3.

Billing for a Consult

referred
patient is sent to a specialist for evaluation and testing.

specialist
physician who concentrates on a particular area of medicine (for example, cardiology or gastroenterology).

When a patient is **referred** by a physician (usually a primary care doctor) to another physician (usually a **specialist**), this visit is called a *consultation* or a *consult.*

All specialists should have consult evaluation and management visit codes on superbills used in their offices. Occasionally, primary care physicians will also have consult codes on their superbills. These are to be used when the patient is at the office for surgical clearance prior to surgery.

The fees for consult codes are higher than those for office visits. Specialists can expect to receive more for their services, because of their additional training and experience in a particular area of medicine.

Code	Description
99241	Level I Consult
99242	Level II Consult
99243	Level III Consult
99244	Level IV Consult
99245	Level V Consult

Figure 6-4 Consultation codes used for office encounters (same for both new and established patients).

Note that there is no distinction in consult codes between new and established patients. The codes used are the same for both. See Figure 6-4.

Billing for Procedures and HCPCS Level II Codes

Office visits and consults are not the only items to be billed from the superbill. Depending on the practice you are billing for, there will also be codes for:

- Immunizations
- Injections
- Minor procedures

It is important not to miss any of these other services when preparing the claim.

DETERMINING MODIFIER USAGE

Note

For the purpose of completing CMS-1500 forms for billing exercises, the patient registration form and superbill have been combined into one form called a case study form (see Figure 6-5). You can gather the information needed to prepare the claim for submission from each case study form. Sample case study forms requiring modifiers are listed in Appendix I at the back of this textbook.

Because most superbills in physicians' offices do *not* have the modifiers listed on the superbill next to the appropriate CPT or HCPCS level II code, the medical biller's knowledge of modifier usage is crucial to the process of submitting clean claims.

Billing for services and procedures performed in the physician's office becomes easier with practice and time. The same codes are used on a daily basis, which enables the medical biller to become familiar with these codes fairly quickly.

Case Study

PATIENT INFORMATION:

Name:

Social Security #:

Address:

City:

State:

Zip Code:

Home Telephone:

Date of Birth:

Gender:

Occupation:

Employer:

Employer Telephone:

Spouse:

Spouse's Social Security #:

Spouse's Employer:

Spouse's Date of Birth:

INSURANCE INFORMATION:

Patient Number:

Place of Service:

Primary Insurance Plan:

Primary Insurance Plan ID #:

Group #:

Primary Policyholder:

Policyholder Date of Birth:

Relationship to Patient:

Secondary Insurance Plan:

Secondary Insurance Plan ID #:

Secondary Policyholder:

Patient Status ☐ Married ☐ Divorced ☐ Single ☐ Student ☐ Other

DIAGNOSIS INFORMATION

	Diagnosis	Code		Diagnosis	Code
1.			5.		
2.			6.		
3.			7.		
4.			8.		

PROCEDURE INFORMATION

	Description of Procedure or Service	Date	Code	Charge
1.				
2.				
3.				
4.				
5.				
6.				

SPECIAL NOTES:

Figure 6-5 Sample blank case study form.

SUMMARY

The only challenge that should arise in office billing is the use of modifiers. Determining when a modifier is needed, and choosing the correct modifier, both require research and understanding of the modifiers if the medical biller is to correctly apply them.

REVIEW QUESTIONS

1. From which two forms is data extracted to prepare a claim?
   _____
   _____

2. What is the difference between an office visit code and a consult code for the office?
   _____
   _____

3. What is the only difference between new patient and established patient office visit codes?
   _____
   _____

4. Define:
   a. office visit
   _____

   b. referred
   _____

   c. specialist
   _____

5. What is normally not found on a superbill that may present a challenge for the biller?
   _____
   _____

Before completing the following exercises, see Figure 6-6 and Figure 6-7.

6. Using the case study form in Figure 6-8a, complete the CMS-1500 form in Figure 6-8b.

7. Using the case study form in Figure 6-9a, complete the CMS-1500 form in Figure 6-9b.

Michael Rowe, M.D.

123 Apple Lane • Brick, NJ 08723 • (732) 222-3333
Tax ID# 11-2345678
NPI# 9933993399

Case Study

PATIENT INFORMATION:

Name:	Anne Adams
Social Security #:	000-11-0000
Address:	111 Rail Road
City:	Brick
State:	New Jersey
Zip Code:	08724
Home Telephone:	(732) 000-1111
Date of Birth:	04-12-1972
Gender:	Female
Occupation:	Cashier
Employer:	Groceries 'R' Us
Employer Telephone:	(732) 111-2222
Spouse:	
Spouse's Social Security #:	
Spouse's Employer:	
Spouse's Date of Birth:	

INSURANCE INFORMATION:

Patient Number:	Adaan000
Place of Service:	Office
Primary Insurance Plan:	Aetna
Primary Insurance Plan ID #:	723Z92660
Group #:	9800-00
Primary Policyholder:	Anne Adams
Policyholder Date of Birth:	04-12-1972
Relationship to Patient:	Self
Secondary Insurance Plan:	
Secondary Insurance Plan ID #:	
Secondary Policyholder:	

Patient Status ☐ Married ☐ Divorced ☒ Single ☐ Student ☐ Other

---

DIAGNOSIS INFORMATION

Diagnosis	Code	Diagnosis	Code
1. Headache	784.0	5.	
2.		6.	
3.		7.	
4.		8.	

PROCEDURE INFORMATION

Description of Procedure or Service	Date	Code	Charge
1. Level 2 office visit - new patient	04-01-YYYY	99202	$75.00
2.			
3.			
4.			
5.			
6.			

SPECIAL NOTES:

Figure 6-6 Case study form for new patient Anne Adams.

1500

HEALTH INSURANCE CLAIM FORM

INSTRUCTIONAL FORM ONLY - NOT APPROVED FOR USE

PICA | | | PICA | |

1. MEDICARE	MEDICAID	TRICARE CHAMPUS	CHAMPVA	GROUP HEALTH PLAN	FECA BLK LUNG	OTHER	1a. INSURED'S I.D. NUMBER	(For Program in Item 1)
(Medicare #)	(Medicaid #)	(Sponsor's SSN)	(Member ID#) X	(SSN or ID)	(SSN)	(ID)	723Z92660	

2. PATIENT'S NAME (Last Name, First Name, Middle Initial)	3. PATIENT'S BIRTH DATE MM DD YY	SEX	4. INSURED'S NAME (Last Name, First Name, Middle Initial)
ADAMS, ANNE	04 12 1972	M F X	SAME

5. PATIENT'S ADDRESS (No., Street)	6. PATIENT'S RELATIONSHIP TO INSURED	7. INSURED'S ADDRESS (No., Street)
111 RAIL ROAD	Self Spouse Child Other	SAME

CITY	STATE	8. PATIENT STATUS	CITY	STATE
BRICK	NJ	Single X Married Other		

ZIP CODE	TELEPHONE (Include Area Code)		ZIP CODE	TELEPHONE (Include Area Code)
08724	(732) 000 1111	Employed X Full-Time Student Part-Time Student		( )

9. OTHER INSURED'S NAME (Last Name, First Name, Middle Initial)	10. IS PATIENT'S CONDITION RELATED TO:	11. INSURED'S POLICY GROUP OR FECA NUMBER

a. OTHER INSURED'S POLICY OR GROUP NUMBER	a. EMPLOYMENT? (Current or Previous) YES NO X	a. INSURED'S DATE OF BIRTH MM DD YY SEX M F

b. OTHER INSURED'S DATE OF BIRTH MM DD YY SEX M F	b. AUTO ACCIDENT? PLACE (State) YES NO X	b. EMPLOYER'S NAME OR SCHOOL NAME GROCERIES R US

c. EMPLOYER'S NAME OR SCHOOL NAME	c. OTHER ACCIDENT? YES NO X	c. INSURANCE PLAN NAME OR PROGRAM NAME

d. INSURANCE PLAN NAME OR PROGRAM NAME	10d. RESERVED FOR LOCAL USE	d. IS THERE ANOTHER HEALTH BENEFIT PLAN? YES NO X If yes, return to and complete item 9 a-d.

READ BACK OF FORM BEFORE COMPLETING & SIGNING THIS FORM.

12. PATIENT'S OR AUTHORIZED PERSON'S SIGNATURE I authorize the release of any medical or other information necessary to process this claim. I also request payment of government benefits either to myself or to the party who accepts assignment below.	13. INSURED'S OR AUTHORIZED PERSON'S SIGNATURE I authorize payment of medical benefits to the undersigned physician or supplier for services described below.
SIGNED SOF DATE 0401YYYY	SIGNED SOF

14. DATE OF CURRENT: MM DD YY ILLNESS (First symptom) OR INJURY (Accident) OR PREGNANCY (LMP)	15. IF PATIENT HAS HAD SAME OR SIMILAR ILLNESS, GIVE FIRST DATE MM DD YY	16. DATES PATIENT UNABLE TO WORK IN CURRENT OCCUPATION MM DD YY TO MM DD YY FROM

17. NAME OF REFERRING PROVIDER OR OTHER SOURCE	17a.	18. HOSPITALIZATION DATES RELATED TO CURRENT SERVICES MM DD YY TO MM DD YY
	17b. NPI	FROM

19. RESERVED FOR LOCAL USE	20. OUTSIDE LAB? $ CHARGES YES NO X

21. DIAGNOSIS OR NATURE OF ILLNESS OR INJURY (Relate Items 1, 2, 3 or 4 to Item 24E by Line)	22. MEDICAID RESUBMISSION CODE ORIGINAL REF. NO.
1. 784 . 0 3. ___ . ___	23. PRIOR AUTHORIZATION NUMBER
2. ___ . ___ 4. ___ . ___	

24. A. DATE(S) OF SERVICE From MM DD YY To MM DD YY	B. PLACE OF SERVICE	C. EMG	D. PROCEDURES, SERVICES, OR SUPPLIES (Explain Unusual Circumstances) CPT/HCPCS MODIFIER	E. DIAGNOSIS POINTER	F. $ CHARGES	G. DAYS OR UNITS	H. EPSDT Family Plan	I. ID. QUAL.	J. RENDERING PROVIDER ID. #
1	04 01 YY 04 01 YY	11		99202		1	75 00	1		NPI	
2										NPI	
3										NPI	
4										NPI	
5										NPI	
6										NPI	

25. FEDERAL TAX I.D. NUMBER SSN EIN	26. PATIENT'S ACCOUNT NO.	27. ACCEPT ASSIGNMENT? (For govt. claims, see back)	28. TOTAL CHARGE	29. AMOUNT PAID	30. BALANCE DUE
112345678 X	ADAAN000	X YES NO	$ 75 00	$ 0 00	$ 75 00

31. SIGNATURE OF PHYSICIAN OR SUPPLIER INCLUDING DEGREES OR CREDENTIALS (I certify that the statements on the reverse apply to this bill and are made a part thereof.)	32. SERVICE FACILITY LOCATION INFORMATION	33. BILLING PROVIDER INFO & PH # (732) 222-3333
MICHAEL ROWE MD	MICHAEL ROWE MD	MICHAEL ROWE MD
	123 APPLE LANE	123 APPLE LANE
SIGNED DATE 0402YY	BRICK NJ 08723	BRICK NJ 08723
	a. 9933993399 b.	a. 9933993399 b.

NUCC Instruction Manual available at: www.nucc.org   INSTRUCTIONAL USE ONLY - NOT APPROVED FOR USE

Figure 6-7 Completed CMS-1500 form for Anne Adams.

Case Study

Michael Rowe, M.D.

123 Apple Lane • Brick, NJ 08723 • (732) 222-3333
Tax ID# 11-2345678
NPI# 9933993399

PATIENT INFORMATION:

Name:	Bella Berry
Social Security #:	111-22-3333
Address:	001 Trail Terrace
City:	Brick
State:	New Jersey
Zip Code:	08723
Home Telephone:	(732) 111-0000
Date of Birth	01-28-1969
Gender:	Female
Occupation:	Teacher
Employer:	Burns Elementary School
Employer Telephone:	(732) 999-2222
Spouse:	Bernie Berry
Spouse's Social Security #:	222-33-4444
Spouse's Employer:	QTA Corporation
Spouse's Date of Birth:	11-07-1968

INSURANCE INFORMATION:

Patient Number:	Berbe000
Place of Service:	Office
Primary Insurance Plan:	Cigna
Primary Insurance Plan ID #:	33B427A16
Group #:	624700
Primary Policyholder:	Bernie Berry
Policyholder Date of Birth:	11-07-1968
Relationship to Patient:	Spouse
Secondary Insurance Plan:	
Secondary Insurance Plan ID #:	
Secondary Policyholder:	

Patient Status   [X] Married   ☐ Divorced   ☐ Single   ☐ Student   ☐ Other

---

DIAGNOSIS INFORMATION

	Diagnosis	Code		Diagnosis	Code
1.	UTI	599.0	5.		
2.			6.		
3.			7.		
4.			8.		

PROCEDURE INFORMATION

	Description of Procedure or Service	Date	Code	Charge
1.	Level 3 office visit - est. patient	03-15-YYYY	99213	$60.00
2.	Urinalysis	03-15-YYYY	81002	$15.00
3.				
4.				
5.				
6.				

SPECIAL NOTES:

Figure 6-8a Case study form for an established patient.

1500

HEALTH INSURANCE CLAIM FORM

INSTRUCTIONAL FORM ONLY - NOT APPROVED FOR USE

☐☐ PICA | PICA ☐☐

| 1. MEDICARE   MEDICAID   TRICARE CHAMPUS   CHAMPVA   GROUP HEALTH PLAN   FECA BLK LUNG   OTHER | 1a. INSURED'S I.D. NUMBER   (For Program in Item 1) |

☐ (Medicare #) ☐ (Medicaid #) ☐ (Sponsor's SSN) ☐ (Member ID#) ☐ (SSN or ID) ☐ (SSN) ☐ (ID)

| 2. PATIENT'S NAME (Last Name, First Name, Middle Initial) | 3. PATIENT'S BIRTH DATE   MM ¦ DD ¦ YY   SEX   M ☐ F ☐ | 4. INSURED'S NAME (Last Name, First Name, Middle Initial) |

| 5. PATIENT'S ADDRESS (No., Street) | 6. PATIENT'S RELATIONSHIP TO INSURED   Self ☐ Spouse ☐ Child ☐ Other ☐ | 7. INSURED'S ADDRESS (No., Street) |

| CITY | STATE | 8. PATIENT STATUS   Single ☐ Married ☐ Other ☐ | CITY | STATE |

| ZIP CODE | TELEPHONE (Include Area Code) ( ) | Employed ☐ Full-Time Student ☐ Part-Time Student ☐ | ZIP CODE | TELEPHONE (Include Area Code) ( ) |

| 9. OTHER INSURED'S NAME (Last Name, First Name, Middle Initial) | 10. IS PATIENT'S CONDITION RELATED TO: | 11. INSURED'S POLICY GROUP OR FECA NUMBER |

| a. OTHER INSURED'S POLICY OR GROUP NUMBER | a. EMPLOYMENT? (Current or Previous)   ☐ YES ☐ NO | a. INSURED'S DATE OF BIRTH   MM ¦ DD ¦ YY   SEX   M ☐ F ☐ |

| b. OTHER INSURED'S DATE OF BIRTH   MM ¦ DD ¦ YY   SEX   M ☐ F ☐ | b. AUTO ACCIDENT?   PLACE (State)   ☐ YES ☐ NO | b. EMPLOYER'S NAME OR SCHOOL NAME |

| c. EMPLOYER'S NAME OR SCHOOL NAME | c. OTHER ACCIDENT?   ☐ YES ☐ NO | c. INSURANCE PLAN NAME OR PROGRAM NAME |

| d. INSURANCE PLAN NAME OR PROGRAM NAME | 10d. RESERVED FOR LOCAL USE | d. IS THERE ANOTHER HEALTH BENEFIT PLAN?   ☐ YES ☐ NO   If yes, return to and complete item 9 a-d. |

READ BACK OF FORM BEFORE COMPLETING & SIGNING THIS FORM.
12. PATIENT'S OR AUTHORIZED PERSON'S SIGNATURE I authorize the release of any medical or other information necessary to process this claim. I also request payment of government benefits either to myself or to the party who accepts assignment below.

SIGNED _____ DATE _____

13. INSURED'S OR AUTHORIZED PERSON'S SIGNATURE I authorize payment of medical benefits to the undersigned physician or supplier for services described below.

SIGNED _____

| 14. DATE OF CURRENT: MM ¦ DD ¦ YY   ◄ ILLNESS (First symptom) OR INJURY (Accident) OR PREGNANCY (LMP) | 15. IF PATIENT HAS HAD SAME OR SIMILAR ILLNESS,   GIVE FIRST DATE MM ¦ DD ¦ YY | 16. DATES PATIENT UNABLE TO WORK IN CURRENT OCCUPATION   FROM MM ¦ DD ¦ YY   TO MM ¦ DD ¦ YY |

| 17. NAME OF REFERRING PROVIDER OR OTHER SOURCE | 17a. ¦   17b. NPI | 18. HOSPITALIZATION DATES RELATED TO CURRENT SERVICES   FROM MM ¦ DD ¦ YY   TO MM ¦ DD ¦ YY |

| 19. RESERVED FOR LOCAL USE | 20. OUTSIDE LAB?   ☐ YES ☐ NO $ CHARGES |

| 21. DIAGNOSIS OR NATURE OF ILLNESS OR INJURY (Relate Items 1, 2, 3 or 4 to Item 24E by Line)   1. └__.__   3. └__.__   2. └__.__   4. └__.__ | 22. MEDICAID RESUBMISSION CODE   ORIGINAL REF. NO.   23. PRIOR AUTHORIZATION NUMBER |

24. A. DATE(S) OF SERVICE From MM DD YY To MM DD YY	B. PLACE OF SERVICE	C. EMG	D. PROCEDURES, SERVICES, OR SUPPLIES (Explain Unusual Circumstances) CPT/HCPCS ¦ MODIFIER	E. DIAGNOSIS POINTER	F. $ CHARGES	G. DAYS OR UNITS	H. EPSDT Family Plan	I. ID. QUAL.	J. RENDERING PROVIDER ID. #
1									NPI
2									NPI
3									NPI
4									NPI
5									NPI
6									NPI

| 25. FEDERAL TAX I.D. NUMBER   SSN ☐ EIN ☐ | 26. PATIENT'S ACCOUNT NO. | 27. ACCEPT ASSIGNMENT? (For govt. claims, see back)   ☐ YES ☐ NO | 28. TOTAL CHARGE $ | 29. AMOUNT PAID $ | 30. BALANCE DUE $ |

| 31. SIGNATURE OF PHYSICIAN OR SUPPLIER INCLUDING DEGREES OR CREDENTIALS   (I certify that the statements on the reverse apply to this bill and are made a part thereof.)   SIGNED _____ DATE _____ | 32. SERVICE FACILITY LOCATION INFORMATION   a. NPI   b. | 33. BILLING PROVIDER INFO & PH # ( )   a. NPI   b. |

NUCC Instruction Manual available at: www.nucc.org | INSTRUCTIONAL USE ONLY - NOT APPROVED FOR USE

CARRIER ▲ / PATIENT AND INSURED INFORMATION / PHYSICIAN OR SUPPLIER INFORMATION

Figure 6-8b Blank CMS-1500 form for case study exercise.

Thomas Shue, M.D.

111 Peach Blvd • Brick, NJ 08723 • (732) 999-0000
Tax ID# 11-1122334
NPI# 1122223333

Case Study

PATIENT INFORMATION:

Name:	Cameron Carle
Social Security #:	222-33-4444
Address:	001 Queenie Road
City:	Brick
State:	New Jersey
Zip Code:	08724
Home Telephone:	(732) 002-0009
Date of Birth:	03-28-1975
Gender:	Male
Occupation:	IT Specialist
Employer:	BMB Industries
Employer Telephone:	(732) 003-2600
Spouse:	
Spouse's Social Security #:	
Spouse's Employer:	
Spouse's Date of Birth:	

INSURANCE INFORMATION:

Patient Number:	Carca000
Place of Service:	Office
Primary Insurance Plan:	Healthnet
Primary Insurance Plan ID #:	002003ZZQ
Group #:	H 12300
Primary Policyholder:	Cameron Carle
Policyholder Date of Birth:	03-28-1975
Relationship to Patient:	Self
Secondary Insurance Plan:	
Secondary Insurance Plan ID #:	
Secondary Policyholder:	

Patient Status ☐ Married ☐ Divorced ☒ Single ☐ Student ☐ Other

DIAGNOSIS INFORMATION

Diagnosis	Code	Diagnosis	Code
1. Stomach pain	536.8	5.	
2.		6.	
3.		7.	
4.		8.	

PROCEDURE INFORMATION

Description of Procedure or Service	Date	Code	Charge
1. Level 2 office consultation	05-12-YYYY	99242	$125.00
2.			
3.			
4.			
5.			
6.			

SPECIAL NOTES:

Patient was referred by Dr. Michael Rowe; NPI# 9933993399

Figure 6-9a Case study form for a consult visit.

1500

HEALTH INSURANCE CLAIM FORM

INSTRUCTIONAL FORM ONLY - NOT APPROVED FOR USE

CARRIER

PICA | | PICA

| 1. MEDICARE   MEDICAID   TRICARE   CHAMPVA   GROUP   FECA   OTHER | 1a. INSURED'S I.D. NUMBER   (For Program in Item 1) |

1. MEDICARE (Medicare #)   MEDICAID (Medicaid #)   TRICARE CHAMPUS (Sponsor's SSN)   CHAMPVA (Member ID#)   GROUP HEALTH PLAN (SSN or ID)   FECA BLK LUNG (SSN)   OTHER (ID)

1a. INSURED'S I.D. NUMBER   (For Program in Item 1)

2. PATIENT'S NAME (Last Name, First Name, Middle Initial)

3. PATIENT'S BIRTH DATE   MM   DD   YY   SEX   M ☐   F ☐

4. INSURED'S NAME (Last Name, First Name, Middle Initial)

5. PATIENT'S ADDRESS (No., Street)

6. PATIENT'S RELATIONSHIP TO INSURED   Self ☐   Spouse ☐   Child ☐   Other ☐

7. INSURED'S ADDRESS (No., Street)

CITY   STATE

8. PATIENT STATUS   Single ☐   Married ☐   Other ☐

CITY   STATE

ZIP CODE   TELEPHONE (Include Area Code) (   )

Employed ☐   Full-Time Student ☐   Part-Time Student ☐

ZIP CODE   TELEPHONE (Include Area Code) (   )

9. OTHER INSURED'S NAME (Last Name, First Name, Middle Initial)

10. IS PATIENT'S CONDITION RELATED TO:

11. INSURED'S POLICY GROUP OR FECA NUMBER

a. OTHER INSURED'S POLICY OR GROUP NUMBER

a. EMPLOYMENT? (Current or Previous)   YES ☐   NO ☐

a. INSURED'S DATE OF BIRTH   MM   DD   YY   SEX   M ☐   F ☐

b. OTHER INSURED'S DATE OF BIRTH   MM   DD   YY   SEX   M ☐   F ☐

b. AUTO ACCIDENT?   PLACE (State)   YES ☐   NO ☐

b. EMPLOYER'S NAME OR SCHOOL NAME

c. EMPLOYER'S NAME OR SCHOOL NAME

c. OTHER ACCIDENT?   YES ☐   NO ☐

c. INSURANCE PLAN NAME OR PROGRAM NAME

d. INSURANCE PLAN NAME OR PROGRAM NAME

10d. RESERVED FOR LOCAL USE

d. IS THERE ANOTHER HEALTH BENEFIT PLAN?   YES ☐   NO ☐   If yes, return to and complete item 9 a-d.

READ BACK OF FORM BEFORE COMPLETING & SIGNING THIS FORM.
12. PATIENT'S OR AUTHORIZED PERSON'S SIGNATURE I authorize the release of any medical or other information necessary to process this claim. I also request payment of government benefits either to myself or to the party who accepts assignment below.

SIGNED _____   DATE _____

13. INSURED'S OR AUTHORIZED PERSON'S SIGNATURE I authorize payment of medical benefits to the undersigned physician or supplier for services described below.

SIGNED _____

PATIENT AND INSURED INFORMATION

14. DATE OF CURRENT: MM   DD   YY   ILLNESS (First symptom) OR INJURY (Accident) OR PREGNANCY (LMP)

15. IF PATIENT HAS HAD SAME OR SIMILAR ILLNESS. GIVE FIRST DATE   MM   DD   YY

16. DATES PATIENT UNABLE TO WORK IN CURRENT OCCUPATION   FROM   MM   DD   YY   TO   MM   DD   YY

17. NAME OF REFERRING PROVIDER OR OTHER SOURCE

17a.
17b. NPI

18. HOSPITALIZATION DATES RELATED TO CURRENT SERVICES   FROM   MM   DD   YY   TO   MM   DD   YY

19. RESERVED FOR LOCAL USE

20. OUTSIDE LAB?   YES ☐   NO ☐ $ CHARGES

21. DIAGNOSIS OR NATURE OF ILLNESS OR INJURY (Relate Items 1, 2, 3 or 4 to Item 24E by Line)

1. ____.____   3. ____.____
2. ____.____   4. ____.____

22. MEDICAID RESUBMISSION CODE   ORIGINAL REF. NO.

23. PRIOR AUTHORIZATION NUMBER

24. A. DATE(S) OF SERVICE		B. PLACE OF SERVICE	C. EMG	D. PROCEDURES, SERVICES, OR SUPPLIES (Explain Unusual Circumstances) CPT/HCPCS MODIFIER	E. DIAGNOSIS POINTER	F. $ CHARGES	G. DAYS OR UNITS	H. EPSDT Family Plan	I. ID. QUAL.	J. RENDERING PROVIDER ID. #
From MM DD YY	To MM DD YY									
1									NPI	
2									NPI	
3									NPI	
4									NPI	
5									NPI	
6									NPI	

25. FEDERAL TAX I.D. NUMBER   SSN ☐ EIN ☐

26. PATIENT'S ACCOUNT NO.

27. ACCEPT ASSIGNMENT? (For govt. claims, see back)   YES ☐   NO ☐

28. TOTAL CHARGE $

29. AMOUNT PAID $

30. BALANCE DUE $

31. SIGNATURE OF PHYSICIAN OR SUPPLIER INCLUDING DEGREES OR CREDENTIALS (I certify that the statements on the reverse apply to this bill and are made a part thereof.)

SIGNED _____ DATE _____

32. SERVICE FACILITY LOCATION INFORMATION

a. NPI   b.

33. BILLING PROVIDER INFO & PH # (   )

a. NPI   b.

PHYSICIAN OR SUPPLIER INFORMATION

NUCC Instruction Manual available at: www.nucc.org   INSTRUCTIONAL USE ONLY - NOT APPROVED FOR USE

Figure 6-9b Blank CMS-1500 form for case study exercise.

Chapter 7
Billing for Inpatient and Nursing Facility Services

OBJECTIVES

Upon completion of this chapter, the student should be able to:

- Differentiate between initial and subsequent visit codes.
- Distinguish between admitting and consulting codes.
- Comprehend the use of critical care codes for inpatient services.
- Accurately complete the CMS-1500 form for inpatient and nursing facility services.
- Define key terms.

INPATIENT BILLING FOR PHYSICIAN SERVICES

inpatient
a patient who has been admitted to a hospital.

As used in this text, the term **inpatient** billing refers to the billing done for evaluation and management services performed by physicians for patients who have been admitted to a hospital. This type of billing is not the same as performed by medical billers working at the hospital and billing for the hospital's services (such as a private or semi-private room charge).

Billing for the Admitting Physician

initial hospital care
the first hospital inpatient encounter with a patient by the admitting physician.

Physicians will charge with an **initial hospital care** code for all evaluation and management services provided to a patient that are related to that patient's admission. This code can be used only once and *only* by the admitting physician.

There are three CPT evaluation and management codes to choose from when billing for initial hospital care:

- 99221 (level one)
- 99222 (level two)
- 99223 (level three)

Remember, it is *not* the medical biller's job to select the level of care provided by the physician. The physician will choose the appropriate level, and the code will be listed on the hospital billing sheet given to the medical biller to prepare the claim.

Billing for the Consulting Physician

Very often, an admitting physician will place a call to a specialist and request a consult on a patient who has been admitted to the hospital. The type of specialist called will depend on the nature of the patient's problems. For example, if the patient is experiencing persistent chest pains, a cardiologist will be called as a **consulting physician**.

> **consulting physician**
> the physician called upon to provide a consultation regarding a patient who is in the hospital.

A primary care physician can also be called upon to perform a consult on an in-hospital patient if the admitting physician seeks that doctor's advice or second opinion on a patient's care or diagnosis.

There are five CPT evaluation and management codes for the initial inpatient consultation:

- 99251 (level one)
- 99252 (level two)
- 99253 (level three)
- 99254 (level four)
- 99255 (level five)

Again, the level of care is chosen by the consulting physician.

Subsequent Hospital Care

> **subsequent hospital care**
> care provided to a patient (per day) following the initial hospital care.

The evaluation and management of a patient following the initial hospital care is considered **subsequent hospital care**. These visits made to the inpatient are frequently referred to as *follow-ups*.

Follow-ups do not necessarily occur on the day after admission, nor must they occur on a daily basis for the patient in the hospital. The frequency of these visits is determined by the physician, based on the patient's condition and need.

Although the initial hospital care codes for admitting and consulting physicians differ, the subsequent hospital care CPT evaluation and management codes for both doctors are the same. These CPT codes are:

- 99231 (level one)
- 99232 (level two)
- 99233 (level three)

Critical Care Services

> **critical care**
> direct delivery by a physician of medical care for a critically ill or critically injured patient.

The precedents for use of **critical care** service codes, when billing for a patient in the hospital setting, include:

- The injury or illness acutely impairs one or more vital organ systems with threat of possible failure to an organ system. Vital organ system problems include, but are not limited to:
  - Central nervous system failure
  - Circulatory failure

- Shock
- Renal failure
- Hepatic failure
- Metabolic failure
- Respiratory failure
- High-complexity decision making
- Assessment to treat single or multiple vital organ system failure
- Assessment to prevent further life-threatening deterioration of the patient's condition

These evaluation and management CPT codes are based on the total duration of time spent by a physician in providing the critical care services. The time spent on these services can be devoted to a single patient only. Therefore, for billing purposes, the physician cannot perform critical care services for multiple critically ill or injured patients in a given time period. The length of time spent with or on an individual patient must be documented in that patient's medical record. The total duration of time spent can include:

- Time spent engaged in work directly related to the individual patient's care (at immediate bedside or elsewhere on the hospital floor or unit)
- Time spent discussing the patient's care with other medical staff
- Time spent in discussions with family members or surrogate decision makers

The codes used to report these services are:

- 99291 (30–74 minutes)
- 99292 (additional block of time of up to 30 minutes each beyond the first 74 minutes)

Critical care codes can be used in conjunction with initial hospital and subsequent hospital care evaluation and management codes. However, critical care services totaling less than 30 minutes are not reported. Instead, the physician should only charge for the initial and/or subsequent evaluation and management, using the appropriate E&M codes.

Hospital Discharge Services

discharge
the patient's release from the hospital.

The management of a patient's **discharge** is reported with hospital-day discharge management codes. These, too, are based on the duration of time spent by the physician on a patient's discharge. Qualifiers for discharge services include:

- Final examination of the patient
- Discussion of the hospital stay
- Instructions on continuing care to relevant caregivers
- Preparation of discharge records, prescriptions, and referral forms

Evaluation and management codes for hospital discharge services are:

- 99238 (30 minutes or less)
- 99239 (more than 30 minutes)

Admitting Physician		Consulting Physician	
Initial Visit	Subsequent/Follow-up Visit	Initial Visit	Subsequent/Follow-up Visit
99221	99231	99251	99231
99222	99232	99252	99232
99223	99233	99253	99233
		99254	
		99255	
Critical Care Codes		Hospital Discharge	
99291 - 30 to 74 minutes		99238 - 30 minutes or under	
99292 - each additional 30 minutes		99239 - more than 30 minutes	

Figure 7-1 Inpatient hospital visit codes.

Unlike critical care codes, CPT code 99239 is *not* used in addition to CPT code 99238. Only one discharge-day management code can be billed for a patient.

A reference sheet used by the medical biller who is billing for inpatient hospital services might look like the sample in Figure 7-1.

BILLING FOR NURSING FACILITY SERVICES

Medical billers will bill out using nursing facility service evaluation and management codes when the physician visits a patient in:

nursing facility
a facility that provides continuous medical supervision via 24-hour-a-day nursing care and related services, in addition to food, shelter, and personal care.

- A **nursing facility** (formerly called a skilled nursing facility)
- An **intermediate care facility**
- A **long-term care facility**

Codes used for the initial care of a patient for admission (new patient) or readmission (established patient) to a facility are:

intermediate care facility
an institution that provides health-related care and services to individuals who do not require the degree of care and treatment that a hospital or nursing facility is designed to provide.

- 99304 (low severity)
- 99305 (moderate severity)
- 99306 (high severity)

Codes used for subsequent care in a facility are:

- 99307 (straightforward decision making)
- 99308 (low-complexity decision making)
- 99309 (moderate-complexity decision making)
- 99310 (high-complexity decision making)

long-term care facility
a facility that provides medical services and assistance to patients over an extended period of time, and is designed to meet the medical, personal, and social needs of the patient.

Evaluation and management codes used for discharge services from a nursing facility involve the same criteria as those used for discharging a patient from the hospital. Discharge service codes are:

- 99315 (30 minutes or less)
- 99316 (more than 30 minutes)

A reference sheet used by the medical biller who is billing for nursing facility services might look like the sample in Figure 7-2.

Initial (New/Est.)	Subsequent	Discharge
99304	99307	99315 30 minutes or less
99305	99308	99316 more than 30 minutes
99306	99309	
	99310	

Figure 7-2 Nursing facility services codes.

SUMMARY

It is important for the medical biller who is billing for inpatient, nursing facility, or critical care services to become familiar with these codes and their appropriate use. Physicians are human, so they might make errors such as reporting an initial visit two days in a row, instead of day one as the admission and day two as a follow-up. An astute medical biller will pick up this error and bring it to the physician's attention. Failure to notice such an error could result in rejection of the claim and therefore delay payment to the physician.

REVIEW QUESTIONS

1. Define the following key terms:
   a. inpatient

   _____

   _____

   _____

   b. initial hospital care

   _____

   _____

   _____

   c. subsequent hospital care

   _____

   _____

   _____

   d. critical care

   _____

   _____

   _____

   e. discharge

   _____

   _____

   _____

f. nursing facility

_____

_____

_____

g. intermediate care facility

_____

_____

_____

h. long-term care facility

_____

_____

_____

2. Which evaluation and management codes introduced in this chapter are based on time?

_____

_____

3. List three vital organ systems involved in billing for critical care services.

_____

_____

_____

4. Why is it important for the medical biller to become familiar with inpatient, critical care, and nursing facility services codes?

_____

_____

5. Using the case study form in Figure 7-3a, complete the CMS-1500 form in Figure 7-3b.

6. Using the case study form in Figure 7-4a, complete the CMS-1500 form in Figure 7-4b.

7. Using the case study form in Figure 7-5a, complete the CMS-1500 form in Figure 7-5b.

8. Using the case study form in Figure 7-6a, complete the CMS-1500 form in Figure 7-6b.

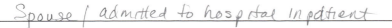

Spouse / admitted to hospital inpatient   *Hw dd 10/29*

Rindy Rain, M.D.

0072 Route 79 • Brick, NJ 08724 • (732) 999-9999
Tax ID# 11-9436799
NPI# 0001112223

Case Study

PATIENT INFORMATION:

Name:	Wendy Winters
Social Security #:	999-88-7777
Address:	009 Queen Court
City:	Neptune
State:	NJ
Zip Code:	00001
Home Telephone:	(732) 888-7777
Date of Birth:	12-01-1970
Gender:	Female
Occupation:	Clerk
Employer:	XYZ Gardens
Employer Telephone:	(732) 000-3333
Spouse:	Wayne Winters
Spouse's Social Security #:	333-44-5555
Spouse's Employer:	Marks Corporation
Spouse's Date of Birth:	07-30-1969

INSURANCE INFORMATION:

Patient Number:	Win We000
Place of Service:	(In-patient hospital)
Primary Insurance Plan:	Healthchoice
Primary Insurance Plan ID #:	A9723649
Group #:	0026
Primary Policyholder:	Wayne Winters
Policyholder Date of Birth:	07-30-1969
Relationship to Patient:	Spouse
Secondary Insurance Plan:	
Secondary Insurance Plan ID #:	
Secondary Policyholder:	

Patient Status   ☒ Married   ☐ Divorced   ☐ Single   ☐ Student   ☐ Other

DIAGNOSIS INFORMATION

Diagnosis	Code	Diagnosis	Code
1. Chest pain	786.50	5.	
2. Shortness of breath	786.05	6.	
3.		7.	
4.		8.	

PROCEDURE INFORMATION

Description of Procedure or Service	Date	Code	Charge
1. Initial hospital care - level 2 *admitted populate 18, 20*	04-07-YY	99222	$150.00
2.			
3.			
4.			
5.			
6.			

SPECIAL NOTES:

Ocean Grove Hospital
080 Route 99
Ocean Grove, NJ 00008
Facility NPI# 0006600001

Figure 7-3a Case study form for services provided by the admitting physician.

1500

HEALTH INSURANCE CLAIM FORM

INSTRUCTIONAL FORM ONLY - NOT APPROVED FOR USE

CARRIER

| | PICA | | | | | | | | | | PICA | | |

1. MEDICARE MEDICAID TRICARE CHAMPVA GROUP FECA OTHER   1a. INSURED'S I.D. NUMBER   (For Program in Item 1)
CHAMPUS   HEALTH PLAN BLK LUNG
(Medicare #) (Medicaid #) (Sponsor's SSN) (Member ID#) (SSN or ID) (SSN) (ID)

2. PATIENT'S NAME (Last Name, First Name, Middle Initial)

3. PATIENT'S BIRTH DATE   SEX
MM   DD   YY   M   F

4. INSURED'S NAME (Last Name, First Name, Middle Initial)

5. PATIENT'S ADDRESS (No., Street)

6. PATIENT'S RELATIONSHIP TO INSURED
Self   Spouse   Child   Other

7. INSURED'S ADDRESS (No., Street)

CITY   STATE

8. PATIENT STATUS
Single   Married   Other
Employed   Full-Time Student   Part-Time Student

CITY   STATE

ZIP CODE   TELEPHONE (Include Area Code)
(   )

ZIP CODE   TELEPHONE (Include Area Code)
(   )

9. OTHER INSURED'S NAME (Last Name, First Name, Middle Initial)

10. IS PATIENT'S CONDITION RELATED TO:

11. INSURED'S POLICY GROUP OR FECA NUMBER

a. OTHER INSURED'S POLICY OR GROUP NUMBER

a. EMPLOYMENT? (Current or Previous)
YES   NO

a. INSURED'S DATE OF BIRTH   SEX
MM   DD   YY   M   F

b. OTHER INSURED'S DATE OF BIRTH   SEX
MM   DD   YY   M   F

b. AUTO ACCIDENT?   PLACE (State)
YES   NO

b. EMPLOYER'S NAME OR SCHOOL NAME

c. EMPLOYER'S NAME OR SCHOOL NAME

c. OTHER ACCIDENT?
YES   NO

c. INSURANCE PLAN NAME OR PROGRAM NAME

d. INSURANCE PLAN NAME OR PROGRAM NAME

10d. RESERVED FOR LOCAL USE

d. IS THERE ANOTHER HEALTH BENEFIT PLAN?
YES   NO   If yes, return to and complete item 9 a-d.

READ BACK OF FORM BEFORE COMPLETING & SIGNING THIS FORM.

12. PATIENT'S OR AUTHORIZED PERSON'S SIGNATURE I authorize the release of any medical or other information necessary to process this claim. I also request payment of government benefits either to myself or to the party who accepts assignment below.

SIGNED_____   DATE_____

13. INSURED'S OR AUTHORIZED PERSON'S SIGNATURE I authorize payment of medical benefits to the undersigned physician or supplier for services described below.

SIGNED_____

14. DATE OF CURRENT: ILLNESS (First symptom) OR
MM   DD   YY   INJURY (Accident) OR
PREGNANCY (LMP)

15. IF PATIENT HAS HAD SAME OR SIMILAR ILLNESS,
GIVE FIRST DATE MM   DD   YY

16. DATES PATIENT UNABLE TO WORK IN CURRENT OCCUPATION
MM   DD   YY   MM   DD   YY
FROM   TO

17. NAME OF REFERRING PROVIDER OR OTHER SOURCE

17a.
17b. NPI

18. HOSPITALIZATION DATES RELATED TO CURRENT SERVICES
MM   DD   YY   MM   DD   YY
FROM   TO

19. RESERVED FOR LOCAL USE

20. OUTSIDE LAB? $ CHARGES
YES   NO

21. DIAGNOSIS OR NATURE OF ILLNESS OR INJURY (Relate Items 1, 2, 3 or 4 to Item 24E by Line)

1. ____.____   3. ____.____

2. ____.____   4. ____.____

22. MEDICAID RESUBMISSION
CODE   ORIGINAL REF. NO.

23. PRIOR AUTHORIZATION NUMBER

24. A. DATE(S) OF SERVICE						B. PLACE OF SERVICE	C. EMG	D. PROCEDURES, SERVICES, OR SUPPLIES (Explain Unusual Circumstances)		E. DIAGNOSIS POINTER	F. $ CHARGES	G. DAYS OR UNITS	H. EPSDT Family Plan	I. ID. QUAL.	J. RENDERING PROVIDER ID. #
From			To					CPT/HCPCS	MODIFIER						
MM	DD	YY	MM	DD	YY										
1														NPI	
2														NPI	
3														NPI	
4														NPI	
5														NPI	
6														NPI	

25. FEDERAL TAX I.D. NUMBER   SSN EIN

26. PATIENT'S ACCOUNT NO.

27. ACCEPT ASSIGNMENT?
(For govt. claims, see back)
YES   NO

28. TOTAL CHARGE
$

29. AMOUNT PAID
$

30. BALANCE DUE
$

31. SIGNATURE OF PHYSICIAN OR SUPPLIER INCLUDING DEGREES OR CREDENTIALS
(I certify that the statements on the reverse apply to this bill and are made a part thereof.)

SIGNED   DATE

32. SERVICE FACILITY LOCATION INFORMATION

a. NPI   b.

33. BILLING PROVIDER INFO & PH # (   )

a. NPI   b.

PHYSICIAN OR SUPPLIER INFORMATION

PATIENT AND INSURED INFORMATION

NUCC Instruction Manual available at: www.nucc.org   INSTRUCTIONAL USE ONLY - NOT APPROVED FOR USE

Figure 7-3b Blank CMS-1500 form for case study exercise.

Autumn Anderson, M.D.

0873 Route 10 • Lakewood, NJ 08701 • (732) 888-8888
Tax ID# 11-1122999
NPI# 5522998877

Case Study

PATIENT INFORMATION:

Name:	Frank Fields
Social Security #:	888-77-8888
Address:	002 Cherry Blvd
City:	Lakewood
State:	NJ
Zip Code:	08701
Home Telephone:	(732) 000-6652
Date of Birth:	06-27-1932
Gender:	Male
Occupation:	Retired
Employer:	
Employer Telephone:	
Spouse:	
Spouse's Social Security #:	
Spouse's Employer:	
Spouse's Date of Birth:	

INSURANCE INFORMATION:

Patient Number:	Fiefr000
Place of Service:	In-patient hospital
Primary Insurance Plan:	Medicare
Primary Insurance Plan ID #:	888-77-8888A
Group #:	
Primary Policyholder:	
Policyholder Date of Birth:	06-27-1932
Relationship to Patient:	Self
Secondary Insurance Plan:	AARP
Secondary Insurance Plan ID #:	BB 279639
Secondary Policyholder:	Frank Fields

Patient Status ☐ Married ☐ Divorced ☒ Single ☐ Student ☐ Other

DIAGNOSIS INFORMATION

Diagnosis	Code	Diagnosis	Code
1. GI bleeding	578.9	5.	
2.		6.	
3.		7.	
4.		8.	

PROCEDURE INFORMATION

Description of Procedure or Service	Date	Code	Charge
1. Initial In-patient consultation - level 4	11-22-YY	99254	$250.00
2. Subsequent hospital care - level 3	11-23-YY	99233	$175.00
3.			
4.			
5.			
6.			

SPECIAL NOTES: Referring physician: Rindy Rain M.D., NPI# 0001112223
Kendrall Hospital
0930 Route 10
Lakewood, NJ 08701
Facility NPI# 0202020211

Figure 7-4a Case study form for services provided by a consulting physician.

1500

HEALTH INSURANCE CLAIM FORM
INSTRUCTIONAL FORM ONLY - NOT APPROVED FOR USE

CARRIER

PICA						PICA

1. MEDICARE	MEDICAID	TRICARE CHAMPUS	CHAMPVA	GROUP HEALTH PLAN	FECA BLK LUNG	OTHER	1a. INSURED'S I.D. NUMBER (For Program in Item 1)
(Medicare #)	(Medicaid #)	(Sponsor's SSN)	(Member ID#)	(SSN or ID)	(SSN)	(ID)	

2. PATIENT'S NAME (Last Name, First Name, Middle Initial)

3. PATIENT'S BIRTH DATE MM DD YY SEX M F

4. INSURED'S NAME (Last Name, First Name, Middle Initial)

5. PATIENT'S ADDRESS (No., Street)

6. PATIENT'S RELATIONSHIP TO INSURED Self Spouse Child Other

7. INSURED'S ADDRESS (No., Street)

CITY STATE

8. PATIENT STATUS Single Married Other
Employed Full-Time Student Part-Time Student

CITY STATE

ZIP CODE TELEPHONE (Include Area Code) ( )

ZIP CODE TELEPHONE (Include Area Code) ( )

9. OTHER INSURED'S NAME (Last Name, First Name, Middle Initial)

10. IS PATIENT'S CONDITION RELATED TO:

11. INSURED'S POLICY GROUP OR FECA NUMBER

a. OTHER INSURED'S POLICY OR GROUP NUMBER

a. EMPLOYMENT? (Current or Previous) YES NO

a. INSURED'S DATE OF BIRTH MM DD YY SEX M F

b. OTHER INSURED'S DATE OF BIRTH MM DD YY SEX M F

b. AUTO ACCIDENT? PLACE (State) YES NO

b. EMPLOYER'S NAME OR SCHOOL NAME

c. EMPLOYER'S NAME OR SCHOOL NAME

c. OTHER ACCIDENT? YES NO

c. INSURANCE PLAN NAME OR PROGRAM NAME

d. INSURANCE PLAN NAME OR PROGRAM NAME

10d. RESERVED FOR LOCAL USE

d. IS THERE ANOTHER HEALTH BENEFIT PLAN? YES NO If yes, return to and complete item 9 a-d.

READ BACK OF FORM BEFORE COMPLETING & SIGNING THIS FORM.
12. PATIENT'S OR AUTHORIZED PERSON'S SIGNATURE I authorize the release of any medical or other information necessary to process this claim. I also request payment of government benefits either to myself or to the party who accepts assignment below.

SIGNED _____ DATE _____

13. INSURED'S OR AUTHORIZED PERSON'S SIGNATURE I authorize payment of medical benefits to the undersigned physician or supplier for services described below.

SIGNED _____

PATIENT AND INSURED INFORMATION

14. DATE OF CURRENT: MM DD YY ILLNESS (First symptom) OR INJURY (Accident) OR PREGNANCY (LMP)

15. IF PATIENT HAS HAD SAME OR SIMILAR ILLNESS, GIVE FIRST DATE MM DD YY

16. DATES PATIENT UNABLE TO WORK IN CURRENT OCCUPATION FROM MM DD YY TO MM DD YY

17. NAME OF REFERRING PROVIDER OR OTHER SOURCE
17a.
17b. NPI

18. HOSPITALIZATION DATES RELATED TO CURRENT SERVICES FROM MM DD YY TO MM DD YY

19. RESERVED FOR LOCAL USE

20. OUTSIDE LAB? YES NO $ CHARGES

21. DIAGNOSIS OR NATURE OF ILLNESS OR INJURY (Relate Items 1, 2, 3 or 4 to Item 24E by Line)
1. ____.____
2. ____.____
3. ____.____
4. ____.____

22. MEDICAID RESUBMISSION CODE ORIGINAL REF. NO.

23. PRIOR AUTHORIZATION NUMBER

24. A. DATE(S) OF SERVICE From MM DD YY To MM DD YY	B. PLACE OF SERVICE	C. EMG	D. PROCEDURES, SERVICES, OR SUPPLIES (Explain Unusual Circumstances) CPT/HCPCS MODIFIER	E. DIAGNOSIS POINTER	F. $ CHARGES	G. DAYS OR UNITS	H. EPSDT Family Plan	I. ID. QUAL.	J. RENDERING PROVIDER ID. #
1								NPI	
2								NPI	
3								NPI	
4								NPI	
5								NPI	
6								NPI	

25. FEDERAL TAX I.D. NUMBER SSN EIN

26. PATIENT'S ACCOUNT NO.

27. ACCEPT ASSIGNMENT? (For govt. claims, see back) YES NO

28. TOTAL CHARGE $

29. AMOUNT PAID $

30. BALANCE DUE $

31. SIGNATURE OF PHYSICIAN OR SUPPLIER INCLUDING DEGREES OR CREDENTIALS (I certify that the statements on the reverse apply to this bill and are made a part thereof.)

SIGNED _____ DATE _____

32. SERVICE FACILITY LOCATION INFORMATION
a. NPI b.

33. BILLING PROVIDER INFO & PH # ( )
a. NPI b.

PHYSICIAN OR SUPPLIER INFORMATION

NUCC Instruction Manual available at: www.nucc.org

INSTRUCTIONAL USE ONLY - NOT APPROVED FOR USE

Figure 7-4b Blank CMS-1500 form for case study exercise.

Rindy Rain, M.D.

0072 Route 79 • Brick, NJ 08724 • (732) 999-9999
Tax ID# 11-9436799
NPI# 0001112223

Case Study

PATIENT INFORMATION:

Name:	Jack Frost
Social Security #:	222-00-0002
Address:	0070 Birch Blvd
City:	Toms River
State:	NJ
Zip Code:	08755
Home Telephone:	(732) 555-5555
Date of Birth:	12-25-1925
Gender:	Male
Occupation:	Retired
Employer:	
Employer Telephone:	
Spouse:	
Spouse's Social Security #:	
Spouse's Employer:	
Spouse's Date of Birth:	

INSURANCE INFORMATION:

Patient Number:	Froja000
Place of Service:	In-patient hospital
Primary Insurance Plan:	Medicare
Primary Insurance Plan ID #:	222-00-0002A
Group #:	
Primary Policyholder:	Jack Frost
Policyholder Date of Birth:	12-25-1925
Relationship to Patient:	Self
Secondary Insurance Plan:	Blue Cross/Blue Shield
Secondary Insurance Plan ID #:	BB 1238976
Secondary Policyholder:	Jack Frost

Patient Status   ☐ Married   ☐ Divorced   ☒ Single   ☐ Student   ☐ Other

DIAGNOSIS INFORMATION

Diagnosis	Code		Diagnosis	Code
1. Respiratory failure	518.81	5.		
2.		6.		
3.		7.		
4.		8.		

PROCEDURE INFORMATION

Description of Procedure or Service	Date	Code	Charge
1. Initial In-patient hospital care - level 3	12-31-YY	99223	$175.00
2. Critical Care Services (30-74 minutes)	12-31-YY	99291	$275.00
3. Critical Care Services (ea add'l 30 minutes)	12-31-YY	99292	$250.00
4.			
5.			
6.			

SPECIAL NOTES: Physician Rindy Rain, M.D. spent a total of one and one half hours devoted to
KENDRALL HOSPITAL   the Critical Care Service of patient on 12-31-YY
0930 ROUTE 10
LAKEWOOD, NJ 08701
FACILITY NPI# 0202020211

Figure 7-5a Case study form for critical care services provided by the admitting physician.

Figure 7-5b Blank CMS-1500 form for case study exercise.

Autumn Anderson, M.D.

Case Study

0873 Route 10 • Lakewood, NJ 08701 • (732) 888-8888
Tax ID# 11-1122999
NPI# 5522998877

PATIENT INFORMATION:		INSURANCE INFORMATION:	
Name:	Serena Summers	Patient Number:	Sumse000
Social Security #:	772-77-2222	Place of Service:	Nursing facility
Address:	0099 Peach Lane	Primary Insurance Plan:	Medicare
City:	Wall	Primary Insurance Plan ID #:	772-77-2222A
State:	NJ		
Zip Code:	07719	Group #:	
Home Telephone:	(732) 666-6666	Primary Policyholder:	Serena Summers
Date of Birth:	08-08-1908		
Gender:	Female	Policyholder Date of Birth:	08-08-1908
Occupation:	Retired	Relationship to Patient:	Self
Employer:			
Employer Telephone:		Secondary Insurance Plan:	
Spouse:		Secondary Insurance Plan ID #:	
Spouse's Social Security #:			
Spouse's Employer:		Secondary Policyholder:	
Spouse's Date of Birth:			

Patient Status   ☐ Married   ☐ Divorced   ☒ Single   ☐ Student   ☐ Other

DIAGNOSIS INFORMATION

Diagnosis	Code	Diagnosis	Code
1. Dementia	294.8	5.	
2.		6.	
3.		7.	
4.		8.	

PROCEDURE INFORMATION

Description of Procedure or Service	Date	Code	Charge
1. Initial nursing facility care - level 1	03-27-YY	99304	$125.00
2. Subsequent + nursing facility care - level 1	03-28-YY	99307	$115.00
3.			
4.			
5.			
6.			

SPECIAL NOTES:
Sunnyvale Senior Home
0090 County Creek Road
Lakewood, NJ 08701
Facility NPI# 9988776655

Figure 7-6a Case study form for services provided in a nursing facility.

1500

HEALTH INSURANCE CLAIM FORM

INSTRUCTIONAL FORM ONLY - NOT APPROVED FOR USE

| | PICA | | PICA | |

1. MEDICARE MEDICAID TRICARE CHAMPUS CHAMPVA GROUP HEALTH PLAN FECA BLK LUNG OTHER

(Medicare #) (Medicaid #) (Sponsor's SSN) (Member ID#) (SSN or ID) (SSN) (ID)

1a. INSURED'S I.D. NUMBER   (For Program in Item 1)

2. PATIENT'S NAME (Last Name, First Name, Middle Initial)

3. PATIENT'S BIRTH DATE   SEX
MM DD YY   M   F

4. INSURED'S NAME (Last Name, First Name, Middle Initial)

5. PATIENT'S ADDRESS (No., Street)

6. PATIENT'S RELATIONSHIP TO INSURED
Self   Spouse   Child   Other

7. INSURED'S ADDRESS (No., Street)

CITY   STATE

8. PATIENT STATUS
Single   Married   Other

CITY   STATE

ZIP CODE   TELEPHONE (Include Area Code)
( )

Employed   Full-Time Student   Part-Time Student

ZIP CODE   TELEPHONE (Include Area Code)
( )

9. OTHER INSURED'S NAME (Last Name, First Name, Middle Initial)

10. IS PATIENT'S CONDITION RELATED TO:

11. INSURED'S POLICY GROUP OR FECA NUMBER

a. OTHER INSURED'S POLICY OR GROUP NUMBER

a. EMPLOYMENT? (Current or Previous)
YES   NO

a. INSURED'S DATE OF BIRTH   SEX
MM DD YY   M   F

b. OTHER INSURED'S DATE OF BIRTH   SEX
MM DD YY   M   F

b. AUTO ACCIDENT?   PLACE (State)
YES   NO

b. EMPLOYER'S NAME OR SCHOOL NAME

c. EMPLOYER'S NAME OR SCHOOL NAME

c. OTHER ACCIDENT?
YES   NO

c. INSURANCE PLAN NAME OR PROGRAM NAME

d. INSURANCE PLAN NAME OR PROGRAM NAME

10d. RESERVED FOR LOCAL USE

d. IS THERE ANOTHER HEALTH BENEFIT PLAN?
YES   NO   If yes, return to and complete item 9 a-d.

READ BACK OF FORM BEFORE COMPLETING & SIGNING THIS FORM.

12. PATIENT'S OR AUTHORIZED PERSON'S SIGNATURE I authorize the release of any medical or other information necessary to process this claim. I also request payment of government benefits either to myself or to the party who accepts assignment below.

SIGNED _____   DATE _____

13. INSURED'S OR AUTHORIZED PERSON'S SIGNATURE I authorize payment of medical benefits to the undersigned physician or supplier for services described below.

SIGNED _____

14. DATE OF CURRENT: ILLNESS (First symptom) OR
MM DD YY   INJURY (Accident) OR
PREGNANCY (LMP)

15. IF PATIENT HAS HAD SAME OR SIMILAR ILLNESS, GIVE FIRST DATE MM DD YY

16. DATES PATIENT UNABLE TO WORK IN CURRENT OCCUPATION
FROM MM DD YY   TO MM DD YY

17. NAME OF REFERRING PROVIDER OR OTHER SOURCE

17a.
17b. NPI

18. HOSPITALIZATION DATES RELATED TO CURRENT SERVICES
FROM MM DD YY   TO MM DD YY

19. RESERVED FOR LOCAL USE

20. OUTSIDE LAB? $ CHARGES
YES   NO

21. DIAGNOSIS OR NATURE OF ILLNESS OR INJURY (Relate Items 1, 2, 3 or 4 to Item 24E by Line)

1. ____.____   3. ____.____

2. ____.____   4. ____.____

22. MEDICAID RESUBMISSION
CODE   ORIGINAL REF. NO.

23. PRIOR AUTHORIZATION NUMBER

24. A. DATE(S) OF SERVICE						B. PLACE OF SERVICE	C. EMG	D. PROCEDURES, SERVICES, OR SUPPLIES (Explain Unusual Circumstances)		E. DIAGNOSIS POINTER	F. $ CHARGES	G. DAYS OR UNITS	H. EPSDT Family Plan	I. ID. QUAL.	J. RENDERING PROVIDER ID. #
From			To					CPT/HCPCS	MODIFIER						
MM	DD	YY	MM	DD	YY										
1														NPI	
2														NPI	
3														NPI	
4														NPI	
5														NPI	
6														NPI	

25. FEDERAL TAX I.D. NUMBER   SSN EIN

26. PATIENT'S ACCOUNT NO.

27. ACCEPT ASSIGNMENT?
(For govt. claims, see back)
YES   NO

28. TOTAL CHARGE
$

29. AMOUNT PAID
$

30. BALANCE DUE
$

31. SIGNATURE OF PHYSICIAN OR SUPPLIER INCLUDING DEGREES OR CREDENTIALS
(I certify that the statements on the reverse apply to this bill and are made a part thereof.)

SIGNED _____ DATE _____

32. SERVICE FACILITY LOCATION INFORMATION

a. NPI   b.

33. BILLING PROVIDER INFO & PH # ( )

a. NPI   b.

CARRIER → / PATIENT AND INSURED INFORMATION / PHYSICIAN OR SUPPLIER INFORMATION

NUCC Instruction Manual available at: www.nucc.org

INSTRUCTIONAL USE ONLY - NOT APPROVED FOR USE

Figure 7-6b Blank CMS-1500 form for case study exercise.

Chapter 8
Electronic Claims Submissions and Clearinghouses

KEY TERMS

batch
claim attachment
clean
clearinghouse

electronic claims submission
electronic data interchange (EDI)
electronically
encrypted

file
Internet-based medical billing
manual claims submission

OBJECTIVES

Upon completion of this chapter, the student should be able to:

- Describe the difference between manual claims billing and electronic claims billing.
- Describe the role of a clearinghouse.
- Explain the advantages of electronic claims submission.
- Define key terms.

BILLING VIA "SNAIL MAIL"

manual claims submission
the process of submitting health insurance claims via mail. The claim may be either handwritten or printed from the computer.

In today's advanced technological age, the probability of **manual claims submission** by medical establishments is low. Nevertheless, there are a few instances in which you might need to submit a claim manually. These include:

- Billing a secondary insurance company with the primary's explanation of benefits (EOB) attached.
- Billing critical care codes with the physician's progress notes from the patient's hospital medical record. *support w/ documentation*
- Billing an initial motor vehicle or workers' compensation claim with a personal injury protection (PIP) or a first report of injury form, respectively, attached. *we every claim nds documentation for workermans comp + auto ins claims*

claim attachment
additional information submitted with the health insurance claim (e.g., progress notes).

In these instances, each claim submitted must have a **claim attachment** in order for the claim to be considered for payment.

6-8wk

once yearly to remain active

ELECTRONIC CLAIMS SUBMISSION

Because of advances in computer and communications technology in the twenty-first century, it has become possible to submit health insurance

87

claims **electronically**. After the medical biller has completed a billing session, all the claims in that **batch** are then sent to a **file**.

Two common formats for **electronic claims submission** are NSF and ANSI.

electronically
via a computer modem.

batch
a set of claims.

file
an element of data storage.

electronic claims submission
the process of submitting health insurance claims via computer modem.

National Standard Format

When seen on a computer screen, the National Standard Format (NSF) claim format looks exactly like an actual completed CMS-1500 form, but without any lines.

American National Standards Institute

The American National Standards Institute (ANSI) is an organization that is responsible for approving U.S. standards involving computers and communications. The ANSI claim format contains all the patient and provider information that a completed CMS-1500 form has; however, the information is **encrypted** (see Figure 8-1). Most claims are now being sent this way to ensure security and confidentiality of patient information.

encrypted
information that is converted into code for security purposes.

THE ROLE OF A CLEARINGHOUSE

A **clearinghouse** acts as a middleman between the biller and the insurance company. Before electronic claims reach their final destination, which is the insurance company, the batch is first sent to a clearinghouse. The clearinghouse edits the claims for errors or missing information. If the claim is **clean**, the clearinghouse will forward it to the appropriate insurance company (see Figure 8-2). If the claim is not clean, it will be sent back to the biller for corrections (see Figure 8-3).

clearinghouse
an entity that forwards claims to insurance payers electronically.

clean
describes a claim with no errors.

ELECTRONIC DATA INTERCHANGE

The process of the biller sending claims electronically to the clearinghouse and the clearinghouse reporting back with the status of the claims is called **electronic data interchange (EDI)**. The reports you receive from the clearinghouse will also inform you of the following:

electronic data interchange (EDI)
a mutual exchange of data via computer modem.

- Report of all payers included in the batch
- Total amount of claims and dollar amount forwarded to each payer
- Claims that were forwarded manually to a specific payer (not all payers accept claims electronically)

BENEFITS OF ELECTRONIC CLAIMS SUBMISSION

There are several reasons why offices that are still submitting claims manually to insurance companies should strongly consider switching to electronic claims submission:

- Faster reimbursement
- Reduced error rate
- No excuses or delays from insurance carriers stating "claim never received"

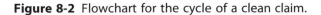

Figure 8-1 Sample of encrypted data.

Figure 8-2 Flowchart for the cycle of a clean claim.

Figure 8-3 Flowchart for the cycle of a claim with errors.

MEDICAL BILLING VIA THE WORLD WIDE WEB

Internet-based medical billing
the process of submitting health claims through a Web site on the Internet.

A new and growing trend in the submission of health insurance claims is **Internet-based medical billing**. This type of billing is not done on software in the physician's office. Instead, the biller (in the medical office or a medical billing company) uses a log-in identification (ID) and password to the Web site of a company that offers this service. Once the biller has logged onto the Web site, the page used to perform the medical billing function is similar to that produced by software used in physicians' offices.

When a physician or medical billing company signs a contract with a company offering this service, there is no software to purchase or install. There is typically a start-up fee and a subsequent monthly fee (for the subscription or maintenance) to pay.

This service may seem enticing to the new physician who is just starting a practice, or to the newly opened medical billing company, but there are several things to consider before choosing this option. Consider the following:

- How long has the company been in business?
- Can the company provide references from existing clients?
- How secure is the patient's private health information?
- What would happen to the data if the company were to shut down tomorrow?

SUMMARY

Most medical offices and medical billing companies today submit claims electronically rather than manually. The numerous advantages of electronic claims processing include quicker payment turnaround, reduced error rate, and avoidance of claim-receipt problems and excuses from insurance companies.

Clearinghouses act as liaisons between the medical biller and the insurance company. A clearinghouse will review and edit a claim for you but will not fix it. Within hours of electronic submission of claims, the medical biller can retrieve reports sent by the clearinghouse. These reports will detail the total batch submitted and note if there were any claims in need of correction. If there are any rejections, the biller can quickly fix and resubmit the claim. This mutual exchange of information is known as electronic data interchange.

Although Internet-based medical billing may seem intriguing, it is important to carefully investigate the company with which the medical practice is considering entering into a contract.

REVIEW QUESTIONS

1. The process of submitting claims through the mail is called _____ _____ _____.

2. Progress notes are an example of a _____ _____.

3. When claims are submitted via a computer modem, this is called _____ _____ _____.

4. A set of claims is referred to as a:
   a. file
   b. batch
   c. folder
   d. subdirectory

5. An element of data storage is a:
   a. folder
   b. bin
   c. file
   d. directory

6. Two types of electronic claim formats are _____ and _____.

7. The term used to describe information that has been converted into a code for security precautions is _____.

8. Which format looks like a CMS-1500 form without lines?
   a. ANSI
   b. EDI
   c. NSF
   d. MRA

9. Explain why the ANSI format is considered more desirable from a patient's point of view.

   _____

   _____

   _____

10. What is the role of a clearinghouse?

    _____

    _____

    _____

11. A claim with no errors is a _____ claim.

12. Within _____, the medical biller can retrieve a report on the computer from the clearinghouse.
    a. seconds
    b. minutes
    c. hours
    d. weeks

13. The mutual exchange of data between the medical biller and the clearinghouse is called _____ _____ _____.

14. List three benefits of submitting claims electronically.

    _____

    _____

    _____

15. Medical billing done through a company's Web site is called _____ _____ _____.

16. List three things to consider before choosing to submit claims through an Internet-based company.

    _____

    _____

    _____

Chapter 9
EOBs and Payments

KEY TERMS

decipher	explanation of benefits (EOB)	posting
electronic funds transfer (EFT)	insurance adjustment	

OBJECTIVES

Upon completion of this chapter, the student should be able to:

- Decipher the EOB.
- Describe the concept of insurance adjustments.
- Explain the importance of accurate posting of payments and insurance adjustments.
- Discuss the benefits of EFT.
- Define key terms.

DECIPHERING THE EXPLANATION OF BENEFITS

Once a claim has been processed, the insurance company sends an **explanation of benefits (EOB)** to the physician. The EOB lists such things as:

remittance advice (Ch 2 + 4)

explanation of benefits (EOB)
the form sent to a physician or patient detailing benefits paid or denied by the insurance company.

- Patient's name
- Policyholder's name
- Patient's account number *claim #*
- Health insurance identification number
- Health insurance group/plan name or number
- Date of service
- Procedures and services billed
- Allowed and disallowed amounts for procedures/services billed
- Amount applied to patient's deductible
- Patient's co-insurance or co-payment amount due
- Remark codes with explanation as to why claim was denied
- Payment amount to physician

decipher
to interpret the meaning of.

The medical biller must have the ability to **decipher** the EOB so that payments and insurance adjustments can be properly posted to patients' accounts. This is a critical skill for any medical biller! See Figure 9-1 for a sample EOB with explanations.

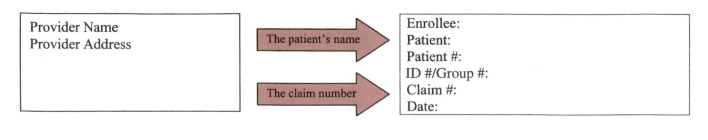

| Provider Name
Provider Address | The patient's name ➤ | Enrollee:
Patient: |
| The claim number ➤ | | Patient #:
ID #/Group #:
Claim #:
Date: |

| Employee Name & Address | Customer Service Information |

Date of Service	Procedure	Total Amount	Not Covered	Reason Code	Allowed Amount	Deductible Amount	Co-pay/ Co-ins Amount	Paid At	Payment Amount
Totals									

Other Insurance Credits or Adjustments

Total Net Payment

Total Patient Responsibility

Charges not eligible, which could be a discount written off by the provider, or a charge the patient is responsible to pay

Amount applied to the deductible on this claim

This could include an amount applied to the deductible, a co-pay, co-insurance, a charge excluded by the plan, or a charge previously considered

Accumulators   Payment to: Check No.   Amount

Your _____ deductible has been satisfied.

The total amount applied to the deductible year to date for the claimant and family

Service Code   Reason Code Description

Messages:

An explanation by line number of the reasons certain charges were excluded.

Figure 9-1 Example of how to read an explanation of benefits (EOB).

Depending on the insurance company, other names may be used for the EOB. These include:

- Remittance advice
- Standard paper remittance
- Medicare remittance notice (used by Medicare; see Figure 9-2)
- Explanation of payment report
- Provider voucher
- Provider claim summary

PAYMENT OF THE CLAIM

electronic funds transfer (EFT)
payment method in which funds are deposited directly into the physician's bank account.

The submission of clean claims results in payment to the physician. Payment is made in the form of a check sent by mail or in the form of an **electronic funds transfer (EFT).** Not all insurance companies offer EFT, but it is a wise choice for the physician to opt for this service if it is available. Choosing the EFT option reduces the risk of a check getting lost in the mail and allows the physician quicker reimbursement for services provided. See Figure 9-3 for a sample authorization form.

INSURANCE ADJUSTMENTS

By law, when a physician participates with an insurance company, the physician cannot bill the patient the difference between the dollar amount for the procedures and services billed and the allowed amount for these procedures and services as determined by the insurance company.

insurance adjustment
the dollar amount adjusted off the patient's account reflecting the difference between the fee for services billed and the allowed amount determined by the insurance company.

This dollar-amount difference, which is reflected by a change in the patient's account, is called an **insurance adjustment**. For example:

Physician fee for procedure 99203 is:	$100.00
Insurance company allowed amount for procedure 99203 is:	$ 80.00
Amount of the insurance adjustment is:	$ 20.00

The patient's account would be adjusted by subtracting the $20 difference between the billed fee and the allowed amount.

posting
the act of making an entry in the patient's account.

Insurance adjustments are done at the same time the biller is **posting** the insurance company's payment to that patient's account. It is imperative for the biller to accurately post insurance adjustments when necessary, as failure to do so directly affects the physician's accounts receivable balance. Errors can also result in incorrect patient balances on patient-due statements, prompting a telephone call from an irate patient.

SUMMARY

The medical biller must know how to read the EOB so that payments and insurance adjustments can be accurately posted to patients' accounts.

Although each insurance company may use a different name for the EOB, the purpose of the document is the same. Accurate posting of payments and insurance adjustments from the EOB is crucial so that patient-due statements will reflect the correct balance and the physician's accounts receivable balance will be correct.

Medicare Services
1 Insurance Avenue
Anycity, NY 12345
888-123-4567

Medicare Remittance Notice

Barbara Brown, MD
234 Physicians Way
Anytown, NY 13579

If patient has a supplemental insurance on file, Medicare will forward claim

ASG-Y or N for accepts assignment

NPI # 7722228888

Page 1 of 1

Date: 07/01/20YY

Check/ EFT # 103471897

Patient's Medicare health insurance claim number

Perf Prov	Serv Date	POS	NOS	Proc	Mods	Billed	Allowed	Deduct	Co-Ins	Grp/RC Amt	Prov Paid
Alden, Lisa		HIC 1124589XXA		ACNT Aldili00		ICN 020012459874		ASG-Y			
7722228888	6/01/YY	11	1	99214		125.00	84.01	0.00	16.80 CO-42	40.99	67.21
PT RESP 16.80				Claim totals		125.00	84.01	0.00	16.80	40.99	67.21 NET
Claim info forwarded to AARP											
Bart, Frank		HIC 1549856XXA		ACNT Barfr000		ICN 054125896525		ASG-Y			
7722228888	6/04/YY	21	1	99202		175.00	0.00	0.00	0.00	175.00 –ZZ01	0.00
PT RESP 0.00				Claim totals		175.00	0.00	0.00	0.00	175.00	0.00 NET
Class, Mary		HIC 1276325XXB		ACNT Clama000		ICN 041257896523		ASG-Y			
7722228888	6/05/YY	11	1	99213		75.00	63.20	63.20	0.00	11.80	0.00
PT RESP 63.20				Claim totals		75.00	63.20	63.20	0.00	11.80	0.00 NET
Davis, Louise		HIC 1748249XXHA		ACNT Davio000		ICN 092265489653		ASG-Y			
7722228888	6/02/YY	11	1	99245		225.00	0.00	0.00	0.00	225.00-MA130	0.00
PT RESP 0.00				Claim totals		225.00	0.00	0.00	0.00	225.00	0.00 NET
Engle, Diane		HIC 2234476XX		ACNT Eagdi000		ICN 021458974562		ASG-Y			
7722228888	6/03/YY	11	1	99214		110.00	0.00	0.00	0.00	110.00-MA104	0.00
PT RESP 0.00				Claim totals		110.00	0.00	0.00	0.00	110.00	0.00 NET

Totals						Billed	Allowed	Deduct	Co-Ins	Grp/RC Amt	Prov Paid
						710.00	147.21	63.20	16.80	562.79	67.21

The internal control number of claim — assigned by Medicare

Remark Codes:

MA104	HIC number does not match our files
CO-42	Contractual obligation
OA01	Other primary insurance
ZZ01	POS does not match CPT code
MA130	Refer phys NPI missing

Explanation of Column Headings:
Perf Prov — NPI # of performing provider
Serv Date — Date service was performed
POS — Place of service
NOS — Number or units of services
Proc — Procedure code of service
Mods — Modifier
Billed — The billed dollar amount
Allowed — The allowed amount of procedure
Deduct — Deductible
Co-Ins — Co-insurance due
Grp/RC Amt — The amount to be written off
Prov Paid — The amount provider paid for

Figure 9-2 Sample Medicare remittance notice.

DEPARTMENT OF HEALTH AND HUMAN SERVICES
CENTERS FOR MEDICARE & MEDICAID SERVICES

Form Approved
OMB No. 0938-0626

ELECTRONIC FUNDS TRANSFER (EFT) AUTHORIZATION AGREEMENT

PART I – REASON FOR SUBMISSION

Reason for Submission:　❑ New EFT Authorization

❑ Revision to Current Authorization (e.g. account or bank changes)

Chain Home Office:　❑ Check here if EFT payment is being made to the Home Office of Chain
Organization　(Attach letter authorizing EFT payment to Chain Home Office)

PART II – PROVIDER OR SUPPLIER INFORMATION

Name _____

Provider/Supplier Legal Business Name _____

Chain Organization Name_____

Home Office Legal Business Name (if different from Chain Organization Name) _____

Tax Identification Number: (Designate SSN ❑ or EIN ❑)___ ___ ___ ___ ___ ___ ___ ___ ___

Medicare Identification Number (if issued) _____

National Provider Identifier (NPI) _____

PART III – DEPOSITORY INFORMATION (Financial Institution)

Depository Name_____

Street Address_____

City _____State _____Zip Code _____

Depository Telephone Number _____

Depository Contact Person _____

Depository Routing Transit Number (nine digit) ___ ___ ___ ___ ___ ___ ___ ___ ___

Depositor Account Number _____

Type of Account (check one) ❑ Checking Account　❑ Savings Account

Please include a voided check or deposit slip or confirmation of account information on bank letterhead. When submitting the documentation, it should contain the name on the account, electronic routing transit number, account number and type, and the bank officer's name signature. This information will be used to verify your account number.

PART IV – CONTACT PERSON

First Name	Middle Initial	Last Name
Telephone Number		Fax Number (if applicable)

Address Line 1 (Street Name and Number)

Address Line 2 (Suite, Room, etc.)

City/Town	State	ZIP Code + 4

E-mail Address

FORM CMS-588 (08/06)　EF 09/2006

Figure 9-3 Example of an EFT authorization form from CMS.

PART V – AUTHORIZATION

I hereby authorize the Centers for Medicare & Medicaid Services fee-for-service contractor, _____ _____, hereinafter called the CONTRACTOR, to initiate credit entries, and in accordance with 31 CFR part 210.6(f) initiate adjustments for any credit entries made in error to the account indicated above. I hereby authorize the financial institution/bank named above, hereinafter called the DEPOSITORY, to credit and/or debit the same to such account.

If payment is being made to an account controlled by a Chain Home Office, the Provider of Services hereby acknowledges that payment to the Chain Office under these circumstances is still considered payment to the Provider, and the Provider authorizes the forwarding of Medicare payments to the Chain Home Office.

If the account is drawn in the Physician's or Individual Practitioner's Name, or the Legal Business Name of the Provider/ Supplier, the said Provider or Supplier certifies that he/she has sole control of the account referenced above, and certifies that all arrangements between the DEPOSITORY and the said Provider or Supplier are in accordance with all applicable Medicare regulations and instructions.

This authorization agreement is effective as of the signature date below and is to remain in full force and effect until the CONTRACTOR has received written notification from me of its termination in such time and such manner as to afford the CONTRACTOR and the DEPOSITORY a reasonable opportunity to act on it. The CONTRACTOR will continue to send the direct deposit to the DEPOSITORY indicated above until notified by me that I wish to change the DEPOSITORY receiving the direct deposit. If my DEPOSITORY information changes, I agree to submit to the CONTRACTOR an updated EFT Authorization Agreement.

Signature Line

Authorized/Delegated Official Name (Print) _____

Authorized/Delegated Official Title _____

Authorized/Delegated Official Signature _____Date _____

PRIVACY ACT ADVISORY STATEMENT

Sections 1842, 1862(b) and 1874 of title XVIII of the Social Security Act authorize the collection of this information. The purpose of collecting this information is to authorize electronic funds transfers.

Under 31 U.S.C. 3332(f)(1), all Federal payments, including Medicare payments to providers and suppliers, shall be made by electronic funds transfer.

The information collected will be entered into system No. 09-70-0501, titled "Carrier Medicare Claims Records," and No. 09-70-0503, titled "Intermediary Medicare Claims Records" published in the Federal Register Privacy Act Issuances, 1991 Comp. Vol. 1, pages 419 and 424, or as updated and republished. Disclosures of information from this system can be found in this notice.

You should be aware that P.L. 100-503, the Computer Matching and Privacy Protection Act of 1988, permits the government, under certain circumstances, to verify the information you provide by way of computer matches.

According to the Paperwork Reduction Act of 1995, no persons are required to respond to a collection of information unless it displays a valid OMB control number. The valid OMB control number for this information collection is 0938-0626. The time required to complete this information collection is estimated to average 60 minutes per response, including the time to review instructions, search existing data resources, gather the data needed, and complete and review the information collection. If you have any comments concerning the accuracy of the time estimate(s) or suggestions for improving this form, please write to: CMS, Attn: PRA Reports Clearance Officer, 7500 Security Boulevard, Baltimore, Maryland 21244-1850.

DO NOT MAIL THIS FORM TO THIS ADDRESS.
MAILING YOUR APPLICATION TO THIS ADDRESS WILL SIGNIFICANTLY DELAY PROCESSING.

FORM CMS-588 (08/06) EF 09/2006

Figure 9-3 (Continued).

REVIEW QUESTIONS

1. Define key terms:
   a. EOB
      by insurance co. to dr
      explanation of benefits - form detailing benefits pd/denied
   b. EFT
      electronic funds transfer - pmt deposited directly to dr bk acct.
   c. insurance adjustment   *amt determined by ins. co.*
      $ amt adj off pt acct of diff btwn fee for srv billed + allowed
   d. posting
      an entry in patient's acct.
   e. decipher
      interpret the meaning of.

2. Explain the importance of accurate posting of payments and insurance adjustments.
   So that patient-due statements will reflect the correct balance & the physician's acct receivable balance will be correct

Refer to Figure 9-4 to answer the following.

3. Who is the policyholder of the insurance?
   Mary Doe

4. What is the description of the procedure billed?
   99214

5. What is the reason for the not-covered amount?
   03 - exceeds fee schedule

6. The payment of $47.60 is ___80___ percent of ___$59.50___. *allowed amt*

7. What dollar amount will the biller adjust on this claim, presuming that the physician is a participating provider?
   $20.50

Refer to Figure 9-5 to answer the following.

8. Where were services performed for this patient?
   hospital

9. Why was no payment made for procedure code 99223?
   the allowed amt was applied to deductible amt

10. What is the patient's health insurance group number?
    197Q42A1(2799) → group #

Provider Name
Provider Address

Michael Moe, M.D.
0009 Brick Blvd
Brick, NJ 08724
NPI# 9922375892

Policyholder: Mary Doe

Patient: John Doe

Patient #: Doejo 111

ID #/Group #: 00327569/9937

Claim #: 72-4937JD

Date: 05-01-YYYY

Employee Name & Address

Mary Doe
002 Apple La
Brick, NJ 08724

Customer Service Information

(800) 999-8888

Date of Service	Procedure	Total Amount	Not Covered	Reason Code	Allowed Amount	Deductible Amount	Co-pay/ Co-ins Amount	Paid At	Payment Amount
04-01-YY	99214	$80.00	$20.50	03	$59.50		$11.90	80%	$47.60
Totals		$80.00	$20.50		$59.50		$11.90		$47.60
				Other Insurance Credits or Adjustments					
				Total Net Payment					$47.60
				Total Patient Responsibility					$11.90

Accumulators
Your YYYY deductible has been satisfied.

Payment to: Check No.   Amount

Michael Moe, M.D.   201197 $47.60

Service Code

Medical

Reason Code Description

03- Exceeds fee schedule

Messages:

Figure 9-4 Sample explanation of benefits for John Doe.

Provider Name
Provider Address

Charlie Chintz, DO
0020 Hooper Ave
Toms River, NJ 08755

Policyholder: Sally Sunrise
Patient: Sally Sunrise
Patient #: Salsu 000
ID #/Group #: 197Q42A/2799
Claim #: 622-590ss
Date: 03-07-YYYY

Employee Name & Address

Sally Sunrise
999 Sunny Lane
Brick, NJ 08723

Customer Service Information

(800) 999-1111

Date of Service	Procedure	Total Amount	Not Covered	Reason Code	Allowed Amount	Deductible Amount	Co-pay/ Co-ins Amount	Paid At	Payment Amount
02-01-YY	99223	$175.00	$25.00	03	$150.00	$150.00			$0.00
02-02-YY	99232	$150.00	$15.00	03	$135.00		$27.00	80%	$108.00
02-03-YY	99238	$125.00	$10.00	03	$115.00		$23.00	80%	$92.00
Totals		$450.00	$50.00		$400.00	$150.00	$50.00		$200.00
Other Insurance Credits or Adjustments									
Total Net Payment									$200.00
Total Patient Responsibility									$200.00

Accumulators
Your YYYY deductible has been satisfied.

Payment to: Check No.

Charlie Chintz, DO   79963

Amount

$200.00

Service Code

Hospital

Reason Code Description

03- Exceeds fee schedule

Messages:

Figure 9-5 Sample explanation of benefits for Sally Sunrise.

11. Is the $50.00 in the "Not Covered" column part of the "Total Patient Responsibility" amount that the patient must pay?

no

Refer to Figure 9-6 to answer the following.

12. Do any patients have supplemental insurance? If so, who?

yes

Lisa Alden – aarp

13. Were any of the patients' claims applied to their deductible? If so, whose?

yes

Mary Class

14. Which two claims were clean claims? no remark codes

Lisa Alden

Mary Class

15. Why was Frank Bart's claim denied? What does the biller need to do before resubmitting this claim?

2201 – POS does not match CPT code.

Vfy & correct location code
           place

16. Why was Louise Davis's claim denied? What does the biller need to do before resubmitting this claim?

MA130 – Ref phys NPI # missing

Obtain refering phys NPI # & resubmit

17. Why was Diane Engle's claim denied? What does the biller need to do before resubmitting this claim?

MA104 – HIC # as not match files

Vfy location of service V pfs card

18. What is the total dollar amount the biller will adjust on this remittance notice?

67.21   562.79

Medicare Services
1 Insurance Avenue
Anycity, NY 12345
888-123-4567

Medicare Remittance Notice

Barbara Brown, MD
234 Physicians Way
Anytown, NY 13579

NPI # 7722228888
Page 1 of 1
Date: 07/01/20YY
Check/ EFT # 103471897

Perf Prov	Serv Date	POS	NOS	Proc	Mods	Billed	Allowed	Deduct	Co-Ins	Grp/RC Amt	Prov Paid
Alden, Lisa		HIC 1124589XXA		ACNT Aldili00		ICN 020012459874		ASG-Y			
7722228888	061520YY	11	1	99214		125.00	84.01	0.00	16.80 CO-42	40.99	67.21
PT RESP 16.80				Claim totals		125.00	84.01	0.00	16.80	40.99	67.21 NET
Claim info forwarded to AARP											
Bart, Frank		HIC 1549856XXA		ACNT Barfr000		ICN 054125896525		ASG-Y			
7722228888	022220YY	21	1	99202		175.00	0.00	0.00	0.00	175.00 –ZZ01	0.00
PT RESP 0.00				Claim totals		175.00	0.00	0.00	0.00	175.00	0.00 NET
Class, Mary		HIC 1276325XXB		ACNT Clama000		ICN 041257896523		ASG-Y			
7722228888	013020YY	11	1	99213		75.00	63.20	63.20	0.00	11.80	0.00
PT RESP 63.20				Claim totals		75.00	63.20	63.20	0.00	11.80	0.00 NET
Davis, Louise		HIC 1748249XXHA		ACNT Davio000		ICN 092265489653		ASG-Y			
7722228888	061220YY	11	1	99245		225.00	0.00	0.00	0.00	225.00-MA130	0.00
PT RESP 0.00				Claim totals		225.00	0.00	0.00	0.00	225.00	0.00 NET
Engle, Diane		HIC 2234476XX		ACNT Eagdi000		ICN 021458974562		ASG-Y			
7722228888	061320YY	11	1	99214		110.00	0.00	0.00	0.00	110.00-MA104	0.00
PT RESP 0.00				Claim totals		110.00	0.00	0.00	0.00	110.00	0.00 NET
Totals						**Billed**	**Allowed**	**Deduct**	**Co-Ins**	**Grp/RC Amt**	**Prov Paid**
						710.00	**147.21**	**63.20**	**16.80**	**562.79**	**67.21**

Remark Codes:

MA104   HIC number does not match our files
CO-42   Contractual obligation
OA01   Other primary insurance
ZZ01   POS does not match CPT code
MA130   Refer phys NPI missing

Figure 9-6 Sample Medicare remittance notice for Barbara Brown, MD.

Chapter 10
Denials and Appeals

KEY TERMS

appeal	noncovered	unauthorized
denied	rejected	

OBJECTIVES

Upon completion of this chapter, the student should be able to:

- Explain the difference between a rejected claim and a denied claim.
- Comprehend the reasons for claim denial.
- Discuss the necessary actions to be taken following denial of a claim.
- List important things to remember when filing an appeal.
- Define key terms.

THE REJECTED CLAIM

rejected
refused to accept.

Errors made on claims submitted electronically are caught before they reach the insurance company, as they are first submitted through a clearinghouse. Claims that have been **rejected** by the clearinghouse will not be forwarded to the intended payer. Instead, they will be returned to the submitter for correction.

Reasons for claim rejection include, but are not limited to:

- Missing patient information
- Missing physician (provider) information
- Diagnosis code not specified to required digit   3,4,5 digits
- Place-of-service code does not match procedure code
- Required box items not checked
- Blocks or boxes requiring a signature or "SOF" notation are left blank
- Typographic errors (for example, date of service listed on claim is in the future)

See Figure 10-1 for a sample CMS-1500 form that contains errors.

Once the errors that caused rejection of the claim have been corrected, the claim can be resubmitted to the clearinghouse for processing.

THE DENIED CLAIM

denied
refused to grant (as in payment for the claim).

Acceptance of a claim by the clearinghouse does not guarantee the physician payment for that claim. Too often, claims are **denied**, resulting in delay of payment to the physician and additional work for the medical biller.

1500									ABC INS COMPANY

HEALTH INSURANCE CLAIM FORM

INSTRUCTIONAL FORM ONLY - NOT APPROVED FOR USE

100 RAIL ROAD
VEIL NJ 00003

CARRIER

| | PICA | | | | | | | | | | PICA | | |

1. MEDICARE (Medicare #)	MEDICAID (Medicaid #)	TRICARE CHAMPUS (Sponsor's SSN)	CHAMPVA (Member ID#) [X]	GROUP HEALTH PLAN (SSN or ID)	FECA BLK LUNG (SSN)	OTHER (ID)	1a. INSURED'S I.D. NUMBER (For Program in Item 1) QR7239603

2. PATIENT'S NAME (Last Name, First Name, Middle Initial) FIELDS, FRAN	3. PATIENT'S BIRTH DATE MM DD YY SEX M □ F [X]	4. INSURED'S NAME (Last Name, First Name, Middle Initial) Same

5. PATIENT'S ADDRESS (No., Street) 0039 FRAN ROAD	6. PATIENT'S RELATIONSHIP TO INSURED Self [X] Spouse □ Child □ Other □	7. INSURED'S ADDRESS (No., Street)
CITY FRANKLIN STATE NJ	8. PATIENT STATUS Single [X] Married □ Other □	CITY STATE
ZIP CODE 00007 TELEPHONE (Include Area Code) (908)	Employed [X] Full-Time Student □ Part-Time Student □	ZIP CODE TELEPHONE (Include Area Code) ( )

9. OTHER INSURED'S NAME (Last Name, First Name, Middle Initial)	10. IS PATIENT'S CONDITION RELATED TO:	11. INSURED'S POLICY GROUP OR FECA NUMBER
a. OTHER INSURED'S POLICY OR GROUP NUMBER	a. EMPLOYMENT? (Current or Previous) □ YES [X] NO	a. INSURED'S DATE OF BIRTH MM DD YY SEX M □ F □
b. OTHER INSURED'S DATE OF BIRTH MM DD YY SEX M □ F □	b. AUTO ACCIDENT? PLACE (State) □ YES □ NO	b. EMPLOYER'S NAME OR SCHOOL NAME
c. EMPLOYER'S NAME OR SCHOOL NAME	c. OTHER ACCIDENT? □ YES [X] NO	c. INSURANCE PLAN NAME OR PROGRAM NAME
d. INSURANCE PLAN NAME OR PROGRAM NAME	10d. RESERVED FOR LOCAL USE	d. IS THERE ANOTHER HEALTH BENEFIT PLAN? □ YES [X] NO If yes, return to and complete item 9 a-d.

READ BACK OF FORM BEFORE COMPLETING & SIGNING THIS FORM.

12. PATIENT'S OR AUTHORIZED PERSON'S SIGNATURE I authorize the release of any medical or other information necessary to process this claim. I also request payment of government benefits either to myself or to the party who accepts assignment below. SIGNED SOF ✓ DATE 0504YY	13. INSURED'S OR AUTHORIZED PERSON'S SIGNATURE I authorize payment of medical benefits to the undersigned physician or supplier for services described below. SIGNED SOF ✓

14. DATE OF CURRENT: MM DD YY ILLNESS (First symptom) OR INJURY (Accident) OR PREGNANCY (LMP)	15. IF PATIENT HAS HAD SAME OR SIMILAR ILLNESS, GIVE FIRST DATE MM DD YY	16. DATES PATIENT UNABLE TO WORK IN CURRENT OCCUPATION FROM MM DD YY TO MM DD YY
17. NAME OF REFERRING PROVIDER OR OTHER SOURCE LUKE LUCAS MD	17a. 17b. NPI	18. HOSPITALIZATION DATES RELATED TO CURRENT SERVICES FROM MM DD YY TO MM DD YY
19. RESERVED FOR LOCAL USE		20. OUTSIDE LAB? $ CHARGES □ YES [X] NO

21. DIAGNOSIS OR NATURE OF ILLNESS OR INJURY (Relate Items 1, 2, 3 or 4 to Item 24E by Line) 1. 784 0 3. 2. 4.	22. MEDICAID RESUBMISSION CODE ORIGINAL REF. NO.
	23. PRIOR AUTHORIZATION NUMBER

24. A. DATE(S) OF SERVICE From To MM DD YY MM DD YY	B. PLACE OF SERVICE	C. EMG	D. PROCEDURES, SERVICES, OR SUPPLIES (Explain Unusual Circumstances) CPT/HCPCS MODIFIER	E. DIAGNOSIS POINTER	F. $ CHARGES	G. DAYS OR UNITS	H. EPSDT Family Plan	I. ID. QUAL.	J. RENDERING PROVIDER ID. #
1 05 04 YY 05 04 YY	21		99244		175			NPI	
2								NPI	
3								NPI	
4								NPI	
5								NPI	
6								NPI	

25. FEDERAL TAX I.D. NUMBER SSN EIN [X]	26. PATIENT'S ACCOUNT NO. FIEFA000	27. ACCEPT ASSIGNMENT? (For govt. claims, see back) [X] YES □ NO	28. TOTAL CHARGE $ 175 00	29. AMOUNT PAID $ 0 00	30. BALANCE DUE $ 175 00
31. SIGNATURE OF PHYSICIAN OR SUPPLIER INCLUDING DEGREES OR CREDENTIALS (I certify that the statements on the reverse apply to this bill and are made a part thereof.) DINA DIAMOND MD SIGNED DATE 0510YY	32. SERVICE FACILITY LOCATION INFORMATION DINA DIAMOND MD 050 ROUTE 27 EDISON NJ 00099		33. BILLING PROVIDER INFO & PH # (732) DINA DIAMOND MD 050 ROUTE 27 EDISON NJ 00099		

(handwritten note in left margin: SOF does not work here ✓)

NUCC Instruction Manual available at: www.nucc.org

INSTRUCTIONAL USE ONLY - NOT APPROVED FOR USE

Figure 10-1 Sample CMS-1500 form with errors.

Denied

Reasons for denials can include, but are not limited to:

- Insurance coverage not yet effective
- Insurance coverage terminated prior to the date of service
- Insured's name does not match insurance company's database
- Incorrect health insurance identification number
- Other primary insurance on file
- Diagnosis code does not meet requirements for procedure or service
- Procedure or service is considered a **noncovered** benefit
- Procedure or service is **unauthorized**
- Maximum benefits reached for this procedure or service
- Submission of claim exceeds payer's claim filing deadline

noncovered
service or procedure not listed as a covered benefit in the payer's master benefit list.

unauthorized
authorization or approval not obtained prior to treatment.

The EOB for a denied claim will contain a reason or reasons for the denial. See Figure 10-2.

Responding to the Denied Claim

appeal
a procedure used when the payer denies a service the patient thinks is needed or refuses to pay for care that the patient has already received.

Once a reason for the claim denial has been determined, the claim balance must be transferred to the patient's account as the patient's responsibility. The patient can then choose to call her insurance company if she feels the denial was made in error, or call the physician's office with corrected information.

The following table lists reasons for denials and suggested actions to reverse or **appeal** the denial.

Denial Reason	Suggested Action
Insurance coverage not yet effective	Patient should contact the physician's office with correct insurance information.
Insurance coverage terminated	Patient should contact the physician's office with correct insurance information.
Other primary insurance on file	Patient should contact the physician's office with correct insurance information.
Insured's name does not match payer's database	Biller should check copy of ID card to see if name mismatch was a result of a typographical error.
Incorrect health insurance identification number	Biller should check copy of ID card to see if incorrect number was a result of a typographical error.
Diagnosis code does not meet requirements for procedure or service	If not a billing error, file an appeal with the insurance company.
Procedure or service is considered a noncovered benefit	An appeal may be attempted. If appeal is denied, the balance is the patient's responsibility.
Procedure or service is unauthorized	If the physician's office had the responsibility to obtain authorization, the physician decides whether to write off the claim balance.
	If the responsibility to obtain authorization was the patient's, the patient is responsible for paying the claim balance.

Continued

[handwritten at top: good denial – adheres – non covered services = showed w/ modifier 1st back up *bad denial – no recourse]*

Denial Reason	Suggested Action
Maximum benefits reached for this service	Attempt an appeal. If denied, responsibility for paying the claim balance is the patient's.
Submission of claim exceeds payer's filing deadline	Biller may attempt an appeal with explanation for late filing. If denied, the physician must approve a write-off of the claim balance.

Provider Name
Provider Address

Winston Wagner, DO
00330 Spring Lake Rd
Spring Lake, NJ 00004
NPI# 0000260000

Employee Name & Address
Vera Vonable
0030 Oakhurst Rd
Oakhurst, NJ 00007

Policyholder: Vera Vonable
Patient: Victor Vonable
Patient #: Vonvi 000
ID #/Group #: 339ZQ4372/996644
Claim #: 26-QRZ549
Date: 02-27-YY

Customer Service Information

(800) 555-5555

Date of Service	Procedure	Total Amount	Not Covered	Reason Code	Allowed Amount	Deductible Amount	Co-pay/ Co-ins Amount	Paid At	Payment Amount
02-01-YY	99203	$100.00	$100.00	02					$0.00
Totals		$100.00	$100.00						$0.00
				Other Insurance Credits or Adjustments					
				Total Net Payment					$0.00
				Total Patient Responsibility					$100.00

Accumulators
Your   deductible has been satisfied.

Payment to: Check No.   Amount
                                    $0.00

Service Code
Office visit

Reason Code Description
02- Coverage terminated prior to date of service

Messages:

Figure 10-2 Sample EOB for a denied claim.

Appealing the Denied Claim

Once a decision has been made to appeal the denial of a claim, it is important to remember the following:

document!

- Write down the date, the name of the person contacted, and details of all telephone conversations and/or correspondence relating to the denied claim in question.
- Keep original documents in the physician's office and send photocopies to the insurance company, with a letter outlining why the claim should be covered.
- Include copies of the patient's records (progress notes, lab results, diagnostic testing results) to assist when appealing for reasons of medical necessity.
- Adhere to the payer's appeal filing deadlines.
- Request a written reply.   *deadlines*

See Figures 10-3 through 10-6 for sample inquiry and appeal forms and letters.

If all efforts to appeal fail, the physician may decide to hire an attorney skilled in health insurance company matters to sue the insurance company.

SUMMARY

A rejected claim and a denied claim are not the same. A rejected claim is sent back to the physician's office via a clearinghouse report; errors may be corrected and the claim resubmitted. A denied claim was processed by the clearinghouse and presented to a payer that then denied the claim.

Appeals may be initiated by either the physician or the patient/insured. An appeal should include a list of reasons why the physician or patient feels the claim should be reconsidered for payment.

An excess number of rejected or denied claims results in delay of payment to the physician and additional work for the medical biller.

REVIEW QUESTIONS

1. See Figure 10-7 and circle errors that would cause the claim to be rejected.

2. See Figure 10-8; give an explanation for claim denial and suggest a course of action.

3. Define key terms:
   a. rejected

   _____

   b. denied

   _____

   c. noncovered

   _____

   d. unauthorized

   _____

   e. appeal

   _____

MEDICARE PART B CLAIM INQUIRY/APPEAL REQUEST FORM
Fields marked with an * are REQUIRED for an Appeal Request

This form may be used for one or more claims concerning the same issue. If your request involves multiple claims, you may attach a copy of your Standard Paper Remittance (SPR) to this form and highlight the services you want reviewed.

Please mail this form and pertinent documentation (Certificate of Medical Necessity, operative notes, test results, etc.) to:

New Jersey Providers Mail to:	New York Providers Mail to:	Date of Request:
Empire Medicare Services	Empire Medicare Services	
P.O. Box 69202	P.O. Box 2280	/ /
Harrisburg, PA 17106-9202	Peekskill, NY 10566-2280	

CLAIM INFORMATION

PROVIDER NUMBER:	*PATIENT HEALTH INSURANCE CLAIM NUMBER (HIC):
*PROVIDER NAME & ADDRESS:	*PATIENT NAME & ADDRESS:
*INTERNAL CONTROL NUMBER(S):	*PROCEDURE CODE(S):
*DATES OF SERVICE:	BILLED AMOUNT:

*REQUEST FOR: APPEAL: ☐ **INQUIRY:** ☐

*SPR DATE: / /

The date of the Standard Paper Remittance (SPR) for the claim in question:

If the appeal concerns Medicare Secondary Payment, please indicate if you participate with the

Primary insurance company _____ participate _____ do not participate

*REASON FOR APPEAL/INQUIRY (AND LATE FILING EXPLANATION IF APPLICABLE):
_____
_____
_____
_____
_____

* If your request has <u>exceeded the time limit</u> for an appeal, please include the <u>reason</u> for late filing with your request.

* If requesting an appeal of an unassigned claim, as the patient's representative, complete the Appointment of Representative Form (CMS 1696-U4). Otherwise, requests on behalf of the patient can be made through this form or any written statement; however, the outcome of the appeal will only be disclosed to the patient.

*REQUESTER'S NAME & TITLE:	TELEPHONE NUMBER:
*REQUESTER'S SIGNATURE:	DATE SIGNED:

A PHOTOCOPY OF THIS FORM IS ACCEPTABLE

SMC3123 Rev. 01/11/2005

Figure 10-3 Sample Medicare Part B claim inquiry/appeal request form.

Insurance Company
Address

Date

Dear Mr. _____:

We have received the explanation of benefits for the patient, Mr. Robert Crawford. However, we believe the charges, totaling **$480.00** for February 25, 20XX through March 14, 20XX, have been considered incorrectly.

The EOB states that the March 15th charge of **$80.00** is not a medical necessity. When I spoke to you at the claims center earlier this week, your explanation of the denial was because the patient is not homebound; the insurance company believes the visit was for patient convenience and not medically necessary.

In reviewing the nurse's notes for each skilled nursing visit, medical necessity appears to have been established. The March 15th visit should not have been denied. A new infusion therapy was started on that date and the patient required instruction on drug administration.

Skilled nursing visits are a medical necessity to follow up on how well the patient is learning; in this instance, errors in the patient's technique were in fact discovered. Throughout the therapy the patient was fatigued, weak, and felt sick. The patient also felt overwhelmed with the therapies, requiring further instruction and reinforcement. The results of not having skilled nursing visits could lead to further complications, such as the patient not following the drug schedule or performing inaccurate drug administration.

It appears that a review of the nurse's notes would support the medical necessity of the nursing charges. Please reconsider the denied portion of the charges and issue a payment to Valu Home Care in the amount of **$80.00**.

Sincerely,

_____ _____
Collections Manager, Valu Home Care

Figure 10-4 Sample appeal letter for "not medically necessary" denial of charges.

Insurance Company
Address

Date

Dear Ms. _____:

I am writing to you in regards to a claim submitted by White Oaks Hospital for my daughter, [name]. The charges were rendered on August 30, 20XX, and totaled $23,716.91. ABC Insurance Company has considered the charges and made a payment of $18,269.86, but this was after a penalty of $1,500.00 was deducted from the payment.

My daughter was involved in a serious car accident. We were unaware of a required preauthorization procedure and, under the circumstances, didn't think to investigate the policy booklet about preauthorizing inpatient hospital stays. The policy booklet does state that the preauthorization hotline must be called within three days of the patient's admittance to the hospital for emergency situations. However, both the hospital and attending physician were preferred providers. I called the PPO agency and they advised me that it is the medical provider's responsibility, if they are preferred providers, to initiate the preauthorization. [Name] from [name] PPO network, at (800) 555-1234, extension 567, was my contact for this information. Because of this, I believe the benefit penalty was applied in error.

Please reconsider the charges and issue the additional payment to the hospital. Thank you.

Sincerely,

[insured's name]

Figure 10-5 Sample appeal letter concerning reduction of payment for failure to preauthorize treatment.

Insurance Company
Address

Date

Dear Claims Review Department:

I am writing to you in regards to a claim submitted by Home Health Agency [medical provider] for [patient]. The charges were rendered on [date] and totaled [claim dollar total]. [Health plan] has denied payment for this procedure, stating that the home health agency was not licensed.

The State of Kentucky does not require a home health agency to be a licensed provider. The current condition requires that the services of a home health agency be obtained. Home health agency visits are a covered expense under my plan. I am requesting that you reconsider your denial of the claim for this service and immediately authorize payment. I am including, with this appeal letter, documentation that supports this statement.

As a member of [health plan], I am requesting your reconsideration of this denial and that you extend the coverage for me. If there is any additional information I could provide to you that would expedite this matter, please feel free to contact me. Thank you for your time and assistance in this matter.

Sincerely,

[insured's name]

Enclosures:
_____
_____

Figure 10-6 Sample appeal letter for "place of service" denial.

4. Explain the difference between a rejected claim and a denied claim:
   _____
   _____

5. List three reasons why a claim may be rejected:
   _____
   _____
   _____

6. List five reasons for denial of a claim and suggested actions to take thereafter:
   _____
   _____
   _____
   _____
   _____

7. What can a physician do if appeal requests have failed?
   _____
   _____

```
┌─────────┐
│  1500   │
└─────────┘
```

HEALTH INSURANCE CLAIM FORM

INSTRUCTIONAL FORM ONLY - NOT APPROVED FOR USE

LOCAL 00970
0055 ROUTE 22
GREENFIELD NJ 00399

[ ][ ] PICA | PICA [ ][ ]

1. MEDICARE MEDICAID TRICARE CHAMPUS CHAMPVA GROUP HEALTH PLAN FECA BLK LUNG OTHER	1a. INSURED'S I.D. NUMBER (For Program in Item 1)
(Medicare #) (Medicaid #) (Sponsor's SSN) (Member ID#) (SSN or ID) (SSN) (ID)	729P46R292

2. PATIENT'S NAME (Last Name, First Name, Middle Initial)	3. PATIENT'S BIRTH DATE / SEX	4. INSURED'S NAME (Last Name, First Name, Middle Initial)
KITE, KYLE	MM 02 DD 28 YY 92 M [ ] F [ ]	KITE KAREN

5. PATIENT'S ADDRESS (No., Street)	6. PATIENT'S RELATIONSHIP TO INSURED	7. INSURED'S ADDRESS (No., Street)
055 NECTAR LANE	Self [ ] Spouse [ ] Child [X] Other [ ]	055 NECTOR LANE

CITY	STATE	8. PATIENT STATUS	CITY	STATE
TOMS RIVER	NJ	Single [X] Married [ ] Other [ ]	TOMS RIVER	NJ

ZIP CODE	TELEPHONE (Include Area Code)		ZIP CODE	TELEPHONE (Include Area Code)
08753	(732)0552995	Employed [ ] Full-Time Student [ ] Part-Time Student [ ]	08753	(732)0552995

9. OTHER INSURED'S NAME (Last Name, First Name, Middle Initial)	10. IS PATIENT'S CONDITION RELATED TO:	11. INSURED'S POLICY GROUP OR FECA NUMBER
		639976
a. OTHER INSURED'S POLICY OR GROUP NUMBER	a. EMPLOYMENT? (Current or Previous) YES [ ] NO [X]	a. INSURED'S DATE OF BIRTH MM DD YY SEX M [ ] F [X]
b. OTHER INSURED'S DATE OF BIRTH MM DD YY SEX M [ ] F [ ]	b. AUTO ACCIDENT? PLACE (State) YES [ ] NO [X]	b. EMPLOYER'S NAME OR SCHOOL NAME IW CANE INC
c. EMPLOYER'S NAME OR SCHOOL NAME	c. OTHER ACCIDENT? YES [ ] NO [X]	c. INSURANCE PLAN NAME OR PROGRAM NAME IRON WORKERS UNION
d. INSURANCE PLAN NAME OR PROGRAM NAME	10d. RESERVED FOR LOCAL USE	d. IS THERE ANOTHER HEALTH BENEFIT PLAN? YES [ ] NO [X] If yes, return to and complete item 9 a-d.

READ BACK OF FORM BEFORE COMPLETING & SIGNING THIS FORM.

12. PATIENT'S OR AUTHORIZED PERSON'S SIGNATURE I authorize the release of any medical or other information necessary to process this claim. I also request payment of government benefits either to myself or to the party who accepts assignment below.

SIGNED __SOF__   DATE _____

13. INSURED'S OR AUTHORIZED PERSON'S SIGNATURE I authorize payment of medical benefits to the undersigned physician or supplier for services described below.

SIGNED __SOF__

14. DATE OF CURRENT: MM DD YY ◄ ILLNESS (First symptom) OR INJURY (Accident) OR PREGNANCY (LMP)	15. IF PATIENT HAS HAD SAME OR SIMILAR ILLNESS, GIVE FIRST DATE MM DD YY	16. DATES PATIENT UNABLE TO WORK IN CURRENT OCCUPATION FROM MM DD YY TO MM DD YY
17. NAME OF REFERRING PROVIDER OR OTHER SOURCE	17a. ___ 17b. NPI	18. HOSPITALIZATION DATES RELATED TO CURRENT SERVICES FROM MM DD YY TO MM DD YY
19. RESERVED FOR LOCAL USE		20. OUTSIDE LAB? YES [ ] NO [X] $ CHARGES

21. DIAGNOSIS OR NATURE OF ILLNESS OR INJURY (Relate Items 1, 2, 3 or 4 to Item 24E by Line)	22. MEDICAID RESUBMISSION CODE ORIGINAL REF. NO.
1. 477.9 _____ 3. _____	
2. _____ 4. _____	23. PRIOR AUTHORIZATION NUMBER

24. A. DATE(S) OF SERVICE			B. PLACE OF SERVICE	C. EMG	D. PROCEDURES, SERVICES, OR SUPPLIES (Explain Unusual Circumstances) CPT/HCPCS MODIFIER	E. DIAGNOSIS POINTER	F. $ CHARGES	G. DAYS OR UNITS	H. EPSDT Family Plan	I. ID. QUAL.	J. RENDERING PROVIDER ID. #
From MM DD YY	To MM DD YY										
1	04 29 YY	04 29 YY			99213		65 00			NPI	
2										NPI	
3										NPI	
4										NPI	
5										NPI	
6										NPI	

25. FEDERAL TAX I.D. NUMBER SSN EIN	26. PATIENT'S ACCOUNT NO.	27. ACCEPT ASSIGNMENT? (For govt. claims, see back) YES [ ] NO [ ]	28. TOTAL CHARGE	29. AMOUNT PAID	30. BALANCE DUE
119956788 [ ][ ]	KITKY000		$ 65 00	$ 0 00	$ 65 00

31. SIGNATURE OF PHYSICIAN OR SUPPLIER INCLUDING DEGREES OR CREDENTIALS (I certify that the statements on the reverse apply to this bill and are made a part thereof.)	32. SERVICE FACILITY LOCATION INFORMATION	33. BILLING PROVIDER INFO & PH # (732)010 1110
	HARRY HINES MD 011 HOOPER AVENUE BRICK NJ 08724	HARRY HINES MD 011 HOOPER AVENUE BRICK NJ 08724
SIGNED _____ DATE 0507YY	a. NPI b.	a. 1111000099 b.

NUCC Instruction Manual available at: www.nucc.org   INSTRUCTIONAL USE ONLY - NOT APPROVED FOR USE

Figure 10-7 Sample CMS-1500 form with errors for patient Kyle Kite.

Provider Name
Provider Address

Ben Foe, M.D.
002 Rainy Road
Neptune, NJ 00022
NPI# 0000777799

Employee Name & Address

John Doe
111 Fawn Road
Brick, NJ 08724

Policyholder: John Doe
Patient: Jane Doe
Patient #: Dojan 000
ID #/Group #: QRS2794Y33/694331
Claim #: 99-2278
Date: 04-15-YY

Customer Service Information

(800) 000-2222

Date of Service	Procedure	Total Amount	Not Covered	Reason Code	Allowed Amount	Deductible Amount	Co-pay/ Co-ins Amount	Paid At	Payment Amount
03-01-YY	58301	$500.00	$500.00	07					$0.00
Totals		$500.00	$500.00						$0.00
				Other Insurance Credits or Adjustments					
				Total Net Payment					$0.00
				Total Patient Responsibility					$500.00

Accumulators
Your YYYY deductible has been satisfied.

Payment to: Check No.   Amount

$0.00

Service Code

| Surgery |

Reason Code Description

| 07- POS not required for this procedure |

Messages:

Procedure code 58301 (removal of intrauterine device)
Does not meet guidelines for care in an out-patient hospital setting. Procedure could
have been performed in physician's office.

Figure 10-8 Sample EOB denial for patient Jane Doe.

Chapter 11
Maintaining Accounts Receivable, Aging Reports, and Rebilling

OBJECTIVES

Upon completion of this chapter, the student should be able to:

- Describe the function of rebilling.
- Explain the importance of claim follow-up.
- Decipher patient aging and insurance aging reports.
- Comprehend the significance of maintaining the office's accounts receivable.
- Define key terms.

THE AGING PROCESS

age
grow old.

follow-up
the process of checking the status of a claim.

rebill
to resubmit a claim.

insurance aging report
report showing monies owed to the physician from insurance companies.

patient aging report
report showing monies owed to the physician from patients (patient balances due).

outstanding
not yet paid.

Once a claim has been submitted, either via mail or electronically, it begins to **age**. The dollar amount submitted on this claim becomes part of the physician's accounts receivable. The older a claim gets, the more direct effect it has on the physician's monthly accounts receivable.

Offices vary on the protocol of claim **follow-up**. Some offices will **rebill** a claim after 30 days if no payment or denial has been received, before following up on that claim. Other offices will require the medical biller to call the insurance company first to find out the reason for the delay in payment. Each month, the medical biller should print an **insurance aging report** and a **patient aging report** as part of working the physician's accounts receivable.

Insurance Aging Report

The insurance aging report is a list of **outstanding** claims for each insurance company that owes the physician money. Depending on the software used in the office, an insurance aging report can be printed for one specific insurance company only, or for a summary of all companies (usually listed alphabetically). The report is broken into increments of

Tufts has 60 day aging

30 days per column. These columns indicate how many days old a claim is (see Figure 11-1). Other information on this report includes:

- Patient's name and account number
- Date of service
- Procedure or service rendered
- Total balance for each amount
- Telephone number of the insurance company

One goal of the medical biller is to reduce the dollar amount listed in the 120+ column of this report. The older a claim becomes, the harder it is to collect the money due on that claim.

> **Note**
> The insurance aging report shown in this text is only an example. Because software programs and capabilities vary among offices, the format of the insurance aging report will vary. Some reports have as few as three columns, reflecting claims that are 90 days old; other reports may extend beyond the 120+ column.

Date of Service	Procedure	0–30	31–60	61–90	91–120	120+	Total Balance
Aetna						Aetna Total	$175.00
Aplsu 000 Apples, Susan							
06-01-20XX	99214	$75.00					$75.00
Attal 000 Atty, Alice							
05-01-20XX	99203		$100.00				$100.00
Blue Cross Blue Shield						BC/BS Total	$205.00
Barbe 000 Barnes, Belinda							
04-07-20XX	99204			$125.00			$125.00
Beeba 000 Beeker, Barney							
01-17-20XX	69210					$80.00	$80.00
Cigna						Cigna Total	$155.00
Janja 000	81002				$20.00		
Jones, Janet	87070				$30.00		
02-27-20XX	99211				$40.00		$90.00
Scosa 000 Scott, Sarah							
04-01-20XX	99213			$65.00			$65.00
Healthnet						Healthnet Total	$225.00
Mapmi 000 Maples, Michelle							
01-22-20XX	99223				$175.00		$175.00
Truta 000 Trucker, Tammy							
06-07-20XX	93000	$50.00					$50.00
Medicare						Medicare Total	$220.00
Vasre 000 Vasquez, Vern							
05-02-20XX	99205		$150.00				$150.00
Zipze 000 Zippo, Zenny							
02-28-20XX	99212				$70.00		$70.00

Figure 11-1 Sample insurance aging report.

Account #	Name	0–30	31–60	61–90	91+	Total Balance
adamad01	Adam Adams	$10.60				$10.60
cohebe01	Betty Cohen			$150.00		$150.00
doejan01	Jane Doe	$7.80		$22.20		$30.00
flocfr03	Freda Flock		$14.60			$14.60
martma01	Martin Martinson	$11.20	$6.80		$16.50	$34.50
smitja10	John Jacob J. Smith		$12.30			$12.30
thomto02	Tom Thomas			$16.40		$16.40
westwa01	Wayne West	$4.80				$4.80

Figure 11-2 Sample patient aging report.

CIP – claim in process

Patient Aging Report

The patient aging report is an alphabetical list of all the patients of the practice who owe the physician money. Monies due on this list may include balances after the primary insurance has paid, balances after both the primary and supplemental insurances have paid, and balances for patients who have no insurance. Like the insurance aging report, it is sectioned into three columns (see Figure 11-2). The monies shown in each column represent how old the due-from-patient portion of the claim is for those patients with insurance. The age of monies listed for patients without insurance reflects back to the date of service. Methods of collecting balances due from patients are explored in Chapter 12.

> **Note**
> Like the insurance aging report, the patient aging report shown in this textbook is an example only. Report formats will vary from office to office.

3 statements & warning, then collections.

REBILLING

One job duty of the medical biller is rebilling. This means either reprinting and mailing a claim to the insurance company or electronically resubmitting the claim to the clearinghouse. A claim is rebilled when there has been no response *cell* from the insurance company regarding the claim. In other words, the claim has neither been paid nor denied. The time guidelines for rebilling of claims will vary according to office policy. One office may perform a rebilling of all claims if, after 30 days, the insurance company has not responded; other offices may wait 60 days before rebilling.

FOLLOW-UP

Another job duty of the medical biller is to follow up on claims. This is done by printing an insurance aging report, calling each insurance company listed on the report, and checking the status of each claim submitted to that insurance company. Responses from insurance companies as to why the claim has not yet been responded to may include:

- Claim never received (this response decreases when billing is done electronically).
- Claim received and is in process (this means the claim should be processed soon, with payment or denial following shortly thereafter).

- Claim has been processed and was denied on [date]. (Let the claims processor know that the denial was never received, and request the company to please send a replacement EOB.)
- Claim has been processed and check was sent to the patient. (If benefits were assigned to the physician, request a replacement check, or call the patient to verify that the check was received and ask that the patient please forward it to the office.)

Once follow-up is done, if an insurance company insists that the claim has not been received, the medical biller will then have to rebill the claim.

MAINTAINING THE ACCOUNTS RECEIVABLE

maintaining
keeping current.

cash flow
a stream of cash (income) used for disbursements.

overhead
a business expense.

Maintaining the physician's accounts receivable is of great significance in increasing **cash flow** for the office. If accounts are allowed to age beyond 90 days, cash flow will be restricted. The physician's practice cannot function at full capacity if all monies are spent on **overhead** costs (such as rent, utilities, malpractice insurance, and salaries) and not enough money is coming into the office.

An increasing balance of accounts receivable is high on any physician's list of complaints.

SUMMARY

The task of maintaining the practice's accounts receivable is of great importance. This task, which should be done on a monthly basis, includes:

- Printing insurance and patient aging reports
- Rebilling
- Following up on claims

If the physician sees a decrease, month after month, in the practice's accounts receivable (with no decrease in patient encounters), this signifies that the medical biller is working diligently to get claims paid in a timely fashion. A medical biller who can accomplish that will not only be a highly valued employee, but will be one of the office's greatest assets!

REVIEW QUESTIONS

1. Monies due the physician for services rendered are called _____ _____.

2. Two reports that total the physician's accounts receivable are the _____ and _____ _____ reports.

3. To resubmit a claim via by mail or electronically is called _____.

4. Calling an insurance company to check the status of a claim is known as _____.

5. Claims not yet paid are called _____.

6. Explain the importance of maintaining the physician's accounts receivable.

_____

_____

_____

Refer to Figure 11-3 to answer the following questions.

7. Which insurance company shows the highest accounts receivable?

_____

Date of Service	Procedure	0–30	31–60	61–90	91–120	120+	Total Balance
Aetna						Aetna Total	$175.00
Ablal 000 Ables, Allison 06-01-20XX	99214	$75.00					$75.00
Andag 000 Anders, Agnes 03-05-20XX	99203			$100.00			$100.00
Blue Cross Blue Shield						BC/BS Total	$280.00
Bonbe 000 Bones, Betty 01-03-20XX	99213 81002					$50.00 $25.00	$75.00
Bulbo 000 Bully, Bonnie 05-10-20XX	99204 69210		$125.00 $80.00				$205.00
Cigna						Cigna Total	$175.00
Culco 000 Cullen, Colleen 06-05-20XX	99215	$100.00					$100.00
Czeca 000 Czey, Cathy 05-11-20XX	99202		$75.00				$75.00
Healthnet						Healthnet Total	$210.00
Harhe 000 Harvey, Henry 12-15-20XX	99205					$150.00	$150.00
Hulho 000 Hulk, Howard 04-27-20XX	36415 81002		$35.00 $25.00				$60.00
Medicare						Medicare Total	$245.00
Meama 000 Mears, Marvin 03-07-20XX	99212				$45.00		$45.00
Mulma 000 Muller, Mary 04-01-20XX	20610			$200.00			$200.00

Figure 11-3 Sample insurance aging report for exercise.

8. Which patients' claims are current and do not yet need to be followed up?

   _____

   _____

9. Which patients' claims should be considered for rebilling?

   _____

   _____

10. Which patients' claims are approaching the status of hard to collect?

    _____

    _____

11. Which patients' claims are more than four months old?

    _____

    _____

12. Which patient has the oldest claim on this report?

    _____

Refer to Figure 11-4 to answer the following questions.

13. Which patients have balances reflecting that an insurance payment has been made in the last 15 days?

    _____

    _____

14. Which patient either has no insurance or has had the insurance company deny the claim?

    _____

15. Assuming that patient due statements are sent monthly, which patients have not been paying on the account?

    _____

16. Which patients will be hard to collect money from?

    _____

    _____

17. Which column from this report shows the highest balance due?

    _____

Account #	Name	0–30	31–60	61–90	91+	Total Balance
adamad01	Adam Adams	$20.70				$20.70
cohebe01	Betty Cohen				$175.00	$175.00
doejan01	Jane Doe	$7.40		$11.20		$18.60
flocfr03	Freda Flock		$21.60			$21.60
martma01	Martin Martinson		$7.20	$11.20	$6.80	$25.20
smitja10	John Jacob J. Smith	$11.20				$11.20
thomto02	Tom Thomas		$12.30			$12.30
westwa01	Wayne West	$5.60				$5.60

Figure 11-4 Sample patient aging report for exercise.

Chapter 12
Collections and the State Insurance Commissioner

KEY TERMS

collection agency	post-dated check	state insurance commissioner
Department of Insurance	soft collections	write off

OBJECTIVES

Upon completion of this chapter, the student should be able to:

- Describe the different approaches to collections.
- Comprehend the importance of collecting monies due up front.
- Explain the role of the state insurance commissioner in getting claims paid.
- Define key terms.

THE NEED TO COLLECT

Because accounts receivable will always exist in a physician's practice, the collections process will always be a part of the medical biller's job. To make the job of collection easier, efforts need to be increased at the front desk of the office.

Get the Money Up Front

Because some patients visit the office frequently (once per month or more), it is common for the front-desk personnel to have a friendly rapport with these patients. Asking patients to pay their past-due balances or their share of the cost responsibility for the current visit can be a difficult task for some front-desk personnel, who may feel awkward about "dunning" patients. Some patients are very adept at making the staff feel sorry for them. Some explanations or excuses for not paying include:

There should be a script.

- "I don't have any cash on me."
- "I left my checkbook at home."
- "Can I just pay next time?"
- "I'll send it in."

Accepting these excuses is detrimental to the physician's cash flow. Services have been rendered, and the physician deserves to be paid.

121

> "Okay, Mrs. Jones, the fee for *today's* services is $200. You can handle that *today* by cash, check, or credit card *today*, whichever works best for you *today*."

Figure 12-1 Sample time-of-treatment collection script.

Each office should have a "time-of-treatment collection" script posted at the front desk. This can be a constant reminder to *not* let patients leave without paying. Notice the emphasis on the word *today* in the sample script in Figure 12-1.

Co-Insurance Amount Due List

To assist the front-desk staff in their collection efforts, it is imperative that each office post a list of patients' co-insurance amounts due for insurance companies with which the practice participates. This can be done for indemnity plans and Medicare, as the patients' cost-share responsibility is 20 percent of the insurance company's allowed amount, according to the company's fee schedule. This 20-percent amount will remain constant throughout the year and will not increase unless and until the insurance company increases the dollar amounts on its fee schedule. See Figure 12-2.

The list of co-insurance amounts due is created by taking a blank superbill in the office and entering the 20 percent dollar amount (of the allowed amount) next to each CPT and HCPCS national level II code listed on the superbill. See Figure 12-3.

Collecting the 20 percent co-insurance amounts due from Medicare patients who have no supplemental insurance *before* these patients leave the office is a surefire way of maintaining cash flow and reducing the practice's accounts receivable.

Post-Dated Checks

Note

Although it is legal in all states to post-date checks, be sure to have patients contact their banks for policies and procedures regarding post-dated checks.

no

If the patient cannot pay a current balance in full, accept a partial payment at the time of service and request that the patient post-date a check or checks (depending on the balance) for the remainder due. Remember to keep **post-dated checks** in a secure location, and be sure *not* to deposit them until the date written on the check.

post-dated check
a check dated for the future.

Soft Collections

soft collections
mailing patient-due statements or calling patients to remind them of their past-due balances.

The **soft collections** process is done by a member of the physician's staff. Calls placed to the patient are intentionally kept nonthreatening and nonharassing in nature. The "patient-due" statements (invoices for the amounts due from the patient) are usually printed and sent out on a monthly basis. See Figure 12-4.

Remember these helpful hints when sending out patient-due statements:

- If writing anything on the statement, use red ink.
- If affixing collection labels to the statement, include insignia of credit cards the office accepts and a place for the credit-card account number, card expiration date, and the cardholder's signature.

 no longer

- Enclose a self-addressed, stamped envelope (so the patient will not have to pay postage).
- Print "Do Not Fold" across the front of the envelope (this indicates to patients that it is an important document so they will not throw it away).
- Include the practice's return address *only*. Omit the doctor's name.

NOTE	PROCEDURE CODE	MOD	PAR AMOUNT	NON-PAR AMOUNT	LIMITING CHARGE
	G0008		20.23	20.23	N/A
	G0009		20.23	20.23	N/A
	G0010		20.23	20.23	N/A
#	10021		76.79	72.95	83.89
	10021		145.49	138.22	158.95
#	10022		70.96	67.41	77.52
	10022		161.29	153.23	176.21
#	10040		81.99	77.89	89.57
	10040		91.32	86.75	99.76
#	10060		90.11	85.60	98.44
	10060		101.98	96.88	111.41
#	10061		168.06	159.66	183.61
	10061		182.06	172.96	198.90
#	10080		97.37	92.50	106.38
	10080		182.19	173.08	199.04
#	10081		169.30	160.84	184.97
	10081		278.71	264.77	304.49
#	10120		93.78	89.09	102.45
	10120		145.10	137.85	158.53
#	10121		194.41	184.69	212.39
	10121		267.77	254.38	292.54
#	10140		122.19	116.08	133.49
	10140		142.97	135.82	156.19
#	10160		98.39	93.47	107.49
	10160		120.45	114.43	131.59
#	10180		186.23	176.92	203.46
	10180		228.64	217.21	249.79
#	11000		35.63	33.85	38.93
	11000		50.89	48.35	55.60
#	11001		18.00	17.10	19.67
	11001		23.09	21.94	25.23
	11004		598.04	568.14	653.36
	11005		815.53	774.75	890.96
	11006		751.74	714.15	821.27
	11008		306.22	290.91	334.55
#	11010		301.49	286.42	329.38
	11010		482.14	458.03	526.73
#	11011		322.21	306.10	352.02
	11011		569.44	540.97	622.12
#	11012		477.59	453.71	521.77
	11012		829.15	787.69	905.84
#	11040		30.88	29.34	33.74
	11040		44.03	41.83	48.10
#	11041		50.09	47.59	54.73
	11041		64.09	60.89	70.02
#	11042		67.72	64.33	73.98
	11042		90.20	85.69	98.54
#	11043		216.13	205.32	236.12

- These amounts apply when service is performed in a facility setting. Limiting charge applies to unassigned claims by nonparticipating providers.

All Current Procedural Terminology (CPT) codes and descriptors copyrighted by the American Medical Association.

Figure 12-2 Sample Medicare fee schedule.

Office Codes

New Pt	Established Pt	Consult
7^{93} 99201	4^{73} 99211	10^{86}99241
14^{03}99202	8^{36} 99212	19^{76}99242
20^{84}99203	11^{37}99213	26^{35}99243
29^{42}99204	17^{80}99214	37^{10}99244
37^{30}99205	25^{78}99215	47^{92}99245

5^{89} 93000 EKG

$0 36415 Venípuncture

4^{05} 90772 Therapeutic injection

10^{53}69210 Cerumen removal

$0 99000 Specimen handling

.71 81002 Urinalysis

.91 82270 Hemocult

.17 J3420 Vitamin B-12 injection

1^{05} J1030 Depo-Medrol

2^{41} 87070 Throat culture

4^{05} 90471 Immunization admin

15^{20}11200 Skin tag removal

ICD-9 Codes

_____789.00 Abdominal pain	_____V70.0 Routine visit
_____477.9 Allergies	_____784.0 Headache
_____285.9 Anemia	_____401.1 Hypertension
_____427.9 Arrhythmia	_____458.9 Hypotension
_____466.0 Bronchitis, acute	_____272.4 Hyperlipidemia
_____436 Cardiovascular accident	_____410.91 Myocardial infarction
_____414.00 Coronary artery disease	_____382.90 Otitis media
_____250.00 DM-controlled	_____462 Pharyngitis
_____782.3 Edema	_____482 Pneumonitis
_____780.79 Fatigue	_____461.9 Sinusitis
_____530.81 GERD	_____599.0 Urinary tract infection

Name _____ Date _____

Prim ins _____ Sec ins _____

Self-pay _____ Co-pay _____ Pd-ck _____ CHG _____ Cash _____

Figure 12-3 Sample "Co-insurance Amounts Due" list for Medicare.

Write It Off

write off
to adjust the dollar amount due from the patient or insurance company to reflect a zero balance due on the claim in question, or sometimes the patient's entire balance. The amount adjusted is called a *write-off*.

There are instances in every medical office when the physician may instruct the biller to **write off** the balance due on an account. These situations may include when:

- The patient is deceased   [handwritten: Estate of]
- The patient has skipped town (or the state)   [handwritten: @ collection agency]
- The biller did not submit the claim in a timely fashion
- The patient is financially indigent   [handwritten: — financial info]

When write-offs are performed, the physician has essentially lost money on the services or procedures performed.

Time for Help

collection agency
an agency retained by the practice for the purpose of collecting debts.

When soft collection efforts have failed, some physicians will turn to an outside **collection agency** in an attempt to collect balances due from patients.

David Operatomy, MD
123 Shady Lane
Anycity, USA 12345

ADDRESS SERVICE REQUESTED

ANY QUESTIONS PLEASE CALL 999- 999-9999
TAX ID: 123456789
PATIENT: PATIENT, JOHN Q

JOHN Q. PATIENT
202 MAIN STREET
ANYTOWN, USA 12345-0000

HEALTHCARE, USA
1234 MAIN STREET
ANYTOWN, USA 12345-0000

11048574500000100000000000000000090123119950000089003   235352*OW5QA0000000000

☐ Please check box if your address is incorrect or insurance
☐ information has changed, please indicate change(s) on reverse side.   **STATEMENT**   PLEASE DETACH AND RETUN TOP PORTION WITH YOUR PAYMENT

DATE	PATIENT	CPT	DESCRIPTION OF SERVICE	CHARGE	RECEIPT	ADJUSTMENT	LINE ITEM BALANCE
00/00/00	STEVE	99212	EST. PATIENT LEVEL 2	50.00	0.00	0.00	50.00
00/00/00	STEVE	99213	EST. PATIENT LEVEL 3	75.00	0.00	0.00	75.00
00/00/00	STEVE	99211	EST. PATIENT LEVEL 1	40.00	0.00	0.00	40.00

ACCOUNT NO.	CURRENT	30 DAYS	60 DAYS	90 DAYS	120 DAYS	TOTAL ACCOUNT BALANCE
031284 82	165.00	0.00	0.00	0.00	0.00	$165.00

PLEASE PAY THIS AMOUNT ▶▶▶▶	$165.00

Figure 12-4 Sample patient-due statement.

Most collection agencies do not charge an up-front fee to the physician. The usual arrangement is for the agency to get paid only if it is successful in collecting on an account. These agencies usually charge the physician a percentage on money collected for each account (for example, 10 percent. If the agency collected $100 on a patient-due statement, the agency would be paid $10 on that account.).

Some collection agencies will have the patients send their money directly to the physician's office. At the end of the month, the physician will tally the total dollar amount collected specifically through the agency's efforts and send the agency a check for the agreed-upon percentage amount. Other agencies require that patients pay the agency directly. In this latter scenario, the agency tallies the total amount collected on the physician's account and deducts its percentage fee amount before forwarding a check for the remainder to the physician. See Figures 12-5, 12-6, and 12-7.

INSURANCE COMPANIES BEWARE

Chapter 11 explained the need for claim follow-up with insurance companies and the excuses these companies may give to the medical biller who calls to check on the status of claims. Unfortunately, many physician's offices are not aware of state laws and regulations regarding the timely payment of claims. See Table 12-1 for a state-by-state listing of these laws. For the exact text of your state's statute (and the legal citation of the statute section or number), and to be sure that you have the most up-to-date information, check the Web site of your state government or state insurance commissioner.

It is imperative that the medical biller inform the insurance companies of their legal obligation to obey these prompt-payment statutes, and stress that their failure to do so may result in financial penalties and the need for the practice to contact a higher authority.

The State Insurance Commissioner

Department of Insurance
the governmental agency in charge of controlling and regulating insurance companies.

state insurance commissioner
the appointed official in charge of each state's Department of Insurance.

Each insurance company offering insurance in any given state must be licensed with that state's **Department of Insurance**.

When these companies ignore inquiries and delay payment of claims, a complaint should be filed with the **state insurance commissioner**. A complaint of this nature could result in a financial penalty, or worse, for the insurance company. If enough complaints are filed against an individual company, that company could lose its license to practice insurance in that state. See Figure 12-8.

Doctor-Initiated Complaint

When a complaint is filed with the state insurance commissioner, the complaint should include the following:

- Letter to the insurance commissioner
- Copy of claim in question
- Printout from patient's account of all documented inquiries to and correspondence with the insurance company in question

A copy of the complaint should be sent to the insurance company in question. See Figure 12-9.

ABC Credit Services LLC
P.O. Box 12345
City, ST 67890

Date: April 21, 20YY

To: FirstName LastName   RE: Your account with:
       DebtorCompany   Creditor
       Address   Address
       City, State, ZIP   City, State, ZIP

                                              For the amount of $Amount
                                              Phone: xxx-xxx-xxxx
                                              Account ID: 1234567890

                    * * * * COURTESY NOTICE * * * *

The above client has requested that we contact you regarding the above referenced account. We realize that this amount due could be an oversight on your part and not a willful disregard of an apparent obligation.

Unless you notify this office within 30 days after receiving this notice that you dispute the validity of this debt or any portion thereof, this office will assume this debt is valid. If you notify this office in writing within 30 days from receiving this notice that you dispute the validity of this debt or any portion thereof, this office will obtain verification of the debt or obtain a copy of a judgment and mail you a copy of such judgment or verification. If you request this office in writing within 30 days after receiving this notice this office will provide you with the name and address of the original creditor, if different from the current creditor.

This communication is from a debt collector. **ABC Credit Services, LLC** is a collection agency attempting to collect a debt and any information obtained will be used for that purpose. Send correspondence, other than PAYMENTS, to this collection agency at P.O. Box 767095, City, ST 67890.

                    SEE REVERSE SIDE FOR IMPORTANT INFORMATION

*************************************Detach and return with payment to*************************************

Date: April 21, 20YY

Make check payable to: Creditor   Account ID: 1234567890

                                             Amount Paid: _____

Mail payment to:
                                             Home Phone: _____

       Creditor
       CreditorAddress
       CreditorCity, State, ZIP

                    Please make any address corrections: Debtor Firstname Debtor Lastname
                                                          Debtor Address
                                                          Debtor City, State, ZIP

Figure 12-5 Sample courtesy notice letter from collection agency.

ABC Credit Services LLC
P.O. Box 767095
City, ST 67890

Date: April 21, 20YY

To: FirstName LastName   RE: Your account with:
       DebtorCompany   Creditor
       Address   Address
       City, State, ZIP   City, State, ZIP

                                                    For the amount of $Amount
                                                    Phone: xxx-xxx-xxxx
                                                    Account ID: 1234567890

* * * * 2nd PAST DUE NOTICE * * * *

Our client, **CREDITOR NAME,**
continues to show a past due balance on your account.

We are attempting to resolve this matter amicably; however, unless you forward payment to our client listed above, we will have no choice but to continue collection attempts.

This communication is from a debt collector. **ABC Credit Services, LLC** is a collection agency attempting to collect a debt and any information obtained will be used for that purpose. Send correspondence, other than PAYMENTS, to this collection agency at P.O. Box 767095, City, ST 67890.

SEE REVERSE SIDE FOR IMPORTANT INFORMATION

**************************************Detach and return with payment to**************************************

Make check payable to: Creditor   Account ID: 1234567890

                                               Amount Paid: _____

Mail payment to: Home Phone: _____

       Creditor   Please make any address corrections:
       Address   Debtor Firstname Debtor Lastname
       City, State, ZIP   Debtor Address
                                               Debtor City, State, ZIP

Figure 12-6 Sample second past-due notice letter from collection agency.

ABC Credit Services LLC
P.O. Box 12345
City, ST

Date: April 21, 20YY

To: FirstName LastName
      DebtorCompany
      Address
      City, State, ZIP

RE: Your account with:
      Creditor
      Address
      City, State, ZIP

For the amount of $Amount
Phone: xxx-xxx-xxxx
Account ID: 1234567890

* * * * FINAL NOTICE * * * *

The statutory dispute period has expired. We are now permitted under Federal law to assume that this debt to **CREDITOR NAME** is valid.

Please make further collection efforts unnecessary by resolving this matter immediately.

This communication is from a debt collector. **ABC Credit Services, LLC** is a collection agency attempting to collect a debt and any information obtained will be used for that purpose. Send correspondence, other than PAYMENTS, to this collection agency at P.O. Box 767095, City, ST 67890.

SEE REVERSE SIDE FOR IMPORTANT INFORMATION

*************************************** Detach and return with payment to ***************************************

Make check payable to: Creditor

Account ID: 1234567890

Amount Paid: _____

Mail payment to:

Home Phone: _____

Creditor
Address
City, State, ZIP

Please make any address corrections:
Debtor Firstname Lastname
Debtor Address
Debtor City, State, ZIP

Figure 12-7 Sample final-notice letter from collection agency.

TABLE 12-1   **State Laws on Insurance Claim Payment Timing**

State	Status/Terms of Law
Alabama	Clean claims must be paid within 45 working days; applies to HMOs only.
Alaska	Clean claims must be paid within 30 working days.
Arizona	Clean claims must be paid within 30 days or interest payments are required (usually about 10%).
Arkansas	Clean, electronic claims must be paid or denied within 30 calendar days, paper claims within 45 days; 12% per annum interest after 60 days.
California	Claims must be paid within 45 working days for an HMO, 30 days for other health service plans. Interest accrues at 15% per annum or $15 penalty, whichever is greater.
Colorado	Claims must be paid within 30 calendar days if submitted electronically, or 45 days if submitted on paper. 10% annual interest penalty.
Connecticut	Claims must be paid within 45 days. Interest accrues at 15% per annum.
Delaware	Clean claims must be paid within 30 days.
District of Columbia	Clean claims will be paid within 30 days. Interest payable at 1.5% for days 31–60, 2% for days 61–120, and 2.5% after 120 days. Applies to claims received on or after October 16, 2002.
Florida	Clean HMO claims (paper or electronic) must be paid within 35 days; non-HMO claims within 45 days. Claims for which information was requested must be paid within 120 days. Interest penalty is 10% per year.
Georgia	Claims must be paid within 15 working days. Interest accrues at 18% per annum.
Hawaii	Clean, paper claims must be paid within 30 days; electronic claims within 15 days. Interest accrues at 15% per annum. Commissioner may impose fines.
Idaho	Paper claims settled within 45 days; electronic claims within 30 days.
Illinois	Clean claims must be paid within 30 days. Interest accrues at 9% per annum.
Indiana	Paper claims must be paid within 45 days; electronic claims must be paid within 30 days.
Iowa	Payment to be made within 30 days. Penalty is 10% per annum.
Kansas	Claims will be paid within 30 days. Interest accrues at a rate of 1% per month.
Kentucky	Claims must be paid or denied within 30 calendar days. Interest accrues at 12% per annum when 31–60 days late, at 18% when 61–90 days late, and at 21% when 91 or more days late.
Louisiana	Claims submitted electronically must be paid within 25 days. If not paid within 25 days, the health insurance issuer shall pay to the claimant an additional late payment adjustment equal to 1% of the unpaid balance due for each month.
Maine	Clean claims must be paid within 30 days. Interest accrues at 1.5% per month.
Maryland	Clean claims must be paid within 30 days. Interest accrues at monthly rates of 1.5% (31–60 days late), 2% (61–120 days late), or 2.5% (121 or more days late) respectively.
Massachusetts	Claims must be paid within 45 days.

Continued

TABLE 12-1   State Laws on Insurance Claim Payment Timing (Continued)

State	Status/Terms of Law
Michigan	A clean claim submitted to an insurance company with all the correct information shall be paid within 45 days. Penalty is 12% interest. The legislation also holds Medicaid and HMOs to this 45-day schedule.
Minnesota	Clean claims must be paid within 30 days. Interest accrues at 1.5% per month if not paid or denied.
Mississippi	Clean claims must be paid within 25 days if electronic, 35 days if paper. Interest accrues at 1.5% per month.
Missouri	Claims must be acknowledged within 10 days and paid or denied within 15 days of receipt of requested additional information. Interest penalty of 1% per month applies to claims not paid within 45 days. After 40 processing days, provider is entitled to a per-day penalty of 50% of the claim (up to $20) if the provider notifies the carrier. This penalty will accrue for 30 days only, unless the provider serves notice again. Rules also stipulate that recontracted providers may file claims up to one year from date of service; contracted providers may file for up to 6 months unless contract states otherwise. Refunds cannot be requested after 12 months.
Montana	Clean claims must be paid within 30 days. Interest accrues at 18% per annum.
Nebraska	Claims must be paid or denied within 15 days of affirmation of liability.
Nevada	Claims must be paid within 30 days. Penalty interest accrues at rate set forth in state code.
New Hampshire	Effective January 1, 2001, clean paper claims must be paid within 45 days, electronic claims within 15 days; 1.5% monthly interest penalty.
New Jersey	Clean electronic claims must be paid within 30 days, paper claims within 40 days.
New Mexico	Clean claims must be paid within 30 days if electronic, 45 days if paper. Interest accrues at 1.5% per month.
New York	Claims must be paid within 45 days. Interest accrues at greater of 12% per year or corporate tax rate determined by commissioner. Fines up to $500 per day are possible.
North Carolina	Claims must be paid or denied within 30 days. Annual interest penalty of 18%.
North Dakota	Claims must be paid within 15 days.
Ohio	Payer must notify provider within 15 days of receipt if claim is materially deficient; payer must process claims within 30 days if no supporting documentation is needed. If payer needs additional information, request must be made within 30 days of receipt of claim. Claim must be processed within 45 days of receipt of requested information.
Oklahoma	Clean claims must be paid within 45 days. Penalty of 10% of claim as interest for late claims payment.
Oregon	Effective January 1, 2002, clean claims must be paid within 30 days; 12% interest penalty applies.
Pennsylvania	Clean claims must be paid within 45 days. Provider must be licensed in Pennsylvania to benefit from this provision.
Rhode Island	Written claims to be paid within 40 calendar days, electronic claims within 30 days.
South Carolina	Group health insurers must pay claims within 60 days.
South Dakota	Electronic claims must be paid within 30 days, paper claims within 45 days.

Continued

TABLE 12-1   State Laws on Insurance Claim Payment Timing (Continued)

State	Status/Terms of Law
Tennessee	Clean, commercial claims sent electronically must be paid within 21 days, paper claims within 30 days. Interest accrues at 1% per month.
Texas	Effective September 1, 2003, paper claims must be paid within 45 days, electronic claims within 30 days. Interest accrues at 18%.
Utah	Effective September 1, 2001, claims must be paid or denied within 30 days. Penalty interest may be applied according to a statutory formula.
Vermont	Claims must be paid or denied within 45 days. Interest penalty is 12% per annum.
Virginia	Clean claims must be paid within 40 days.
Washington	95% of the monthly volume of clean claims shall be paid within 30 days. 95% of the monthly volume of all claims shall be paid or denied within 60 days.
West Virginia	Claims must be paid within 30 days if electronic, 40 days if paper. Interest and fines may apply. Interest penalty of 10% per annum.
Wisconsin	If clean claims are not paid within 30 days, the insurance company is subject to a penalty interest rate of 12% per year.
Wyoming	Claims must be paid within 45 days. Penalties and fines may accrue.

Federal Ruling

A quote from Judge Rafeedie in the federal court case of: Kanne v. Connecticut General Ins. Co., 607 F. Supp. 899 (1985) on upholding $750,000 in additional damages for unreasonable delay in payment of medical claims:

"Repeated requests for payment of the bills were made to the claims representative, and copies of the bills were in the Insurance Company's possession. Under these circumstances, it is not proper for the insurer to sit back and delay payment claims, under the pretextual theory that the Doctors have not dotted all the i's and crossed all the t's. On the contrary, the insurer has the duty to see to it that the promised protection is delivered when needed. It must act to facilitate the claims instead of searching for reasons not to do so."

Figure 12-8 Example of a federal ruling against insurance company.

Patient-Initiated Complaint

A patient-initiated complaint is similar to that from a physician. A patient complaint can be used to:

- Support the physician's decision to file a complaint
- Express the patient's anger to the insurance company (some practices may turn over the claim balance to the patient if the insurance company does not respond to a claim in a timely fashion). See Figure 12-10.

The complaint letters shown in Figures 12-9 and 12-10 are particularly helpful in claims for treatment of injuries suffered in motor vehicle accidents or covered by workers' compensation.

Practice Name _____   Date _____

Address _____

City, State, Zip _____

Phone _____

We filed the attached claim form with the __(insert name of company)__ Insurance Company
on ___(insert date)_____ . It has not been paid or denied.

Please accept this letter as a formal written complaint against the ___(insert name of company)___
Insurance Company.

Figure 12-9 Sample doctor-initiated complaint to a state insurance commissioner.

Practice Name _____

Address _____

City, State, Zip _____

Phone _____   Date _____

__(practice name)__ filed the attached claim form with the __(insert name of company)__ Insurance
Company on _____(insert date)_____ . It has not been paid or denied.

Benefits were assigned to ____(insert practice name)____ and, as of today's date, payment has not been
received. I am now responsible for payment of this bill.

Please accept this letter as a formal written complaint against the __(insert name of company)__
Insurance Company.

Patient's Signature _____

Figure 12-10 Sample patient-initiated complaint to a state insurance commissioner.

SUMMARY

The task of collecting monies is an ongoing process for the medical biller in any given practice. To ease this process, it is strongly advised that the front-desk staff keep available a list of co-insurance amounts due from insurance companies with which the physician participates, especially Medicare.

The strength of collections efforts done from the practice's offices varies among practices, according to the physician's or office manager's desire to proceed. Soft collections is the collection approach usually chosen when done from within the office setting. When these efforts have failed, the physician may choose to turn collection efforts over to an outside collection agency.

When claim inquiries and follow-up have failed, the office should proceed to file a complaint with the state insurance commissioner. The complaint may be initiated by the physician, the patient, or both. Such complaints could result in:

- Payment of the claim in question
- Financial penalties for the insurance company
- Insurance company's loss of its license to practice insurance (in that state)

REVIEW QUESTIONS

1. List three excuses given by patients for failure to pay at the time services are rendered.

   _____

   _____

   _____

2. Explain the function and importance of a co-insurance amount due list.

   _____

   _____

3. Collection efforts done in the office are called _____ collections.

4. List three helpful hints when sending out patient-due statements.

   _____

   _____

   _____

5. Practices may turn to a _____ _____ when soft collection efforts have failed.

6. Name the agency in charge of controlling and regulating insurance companies.

   _____

7. Name two types of complaints that can be filed against an insurance company.

   _____

   _____

8. List three possible results of filing a complaint against an insurance company.

_____

_____

_____

9. Define the following key terms.
   a. post-dated check

   _____

   b. soft collections

   _____

   c. write off

   _____

   d. collection agency

   _____

   e. Department of Insurance

   _____

   f. state insurance commissioner

   _____

Appendix I
Case Studies for the CMS-1500 Form

1

Registration form — top portion

STEVEN SPRING, M.D.

0909 Route 68 • Point Pleasant, NJ 08742 • (732) 004-0090
Tax ID# 11-9923989
NPI# 0101010101

Case Study

PATIENT INFORMATION:

Name:	Marcus Marks
Social Security #:	000-01-0011
Address:	0762 Apricot Lane
City:	Point Pleasant
State:	NJ
Zip Code:	08742
Home Telephone:	(732) 003-0976
Date of Birth:	07-12-1969
Gender:	Male
Occupation:	Welder
Employer:	XYZ Welding Inc
Employer Telephone:	(732) 004-2791
Spouse:	Mary Marks
Spouse's Social Security #:	000-02-2222
Spouse's Employer:	Dal-Mart
Spouse's Date of Birth:	08-22-1970

INSURANCE INFORMATION:

Patient Number:	Marma000
Place of Service:	Office
Primary Insurance Plan:	Prudential
Primary Insurance Plan ID #:	XYZ2790017
Group #: (FECA)	6642
Primary Policyholder:	Marcus Marks
Policyholder Date of Birth:	07-12-1969
Relationship to Patient:	Self
Secondary Insurance Plan:	
Secondary Insurance Plan ID #:	
Secondary Policyholder:	

Patient Status   ☒ Married   ☐ Divorced   ☐ Single   ☐ Student   ☐ Other

---

Service & Procedure Why?

DIAGNOSIS INFORMATION

Diagnosis	Code	Diagnosis	Code
1. Hyperlipidemia	272.4	5.	
2.		6.	
3.		7.	
4.		8.	

PROCEDURE INFORMATION

CPT

Description of Procedure or Service	Date	Code	Charge
1. Level 3 office visit - est patient	04-11-YYYY	99213	$65.00
2.			
3.			
4.			
5.			
6.			

SPECIAL NOTES:

Case Study 1

2

STEVEN SPRING, M.D.

0909 Route 68 • Point Pleasant, NJ 08742 • (732) 004-0090

Tax ID# 11-9923989

NPI# 0101010101

Case Study

PATIENT INFORMATION:		INSURANCE INFORMATION:	
Name:	Melissa Marks	Patient Number:	Marme000
Social Security #:	111-11-2222	Place of Service:	Office
Address:	0762 Apricot Lane	Primary Insurance Plan:	Prudential
City:	Point Pleasant	Primary Insurance Plan ID #:	XYZ2790017
State:	NJ	Group #:	6642
Zip Code:	08742	Primary Policyholder:	Marcus Marks
Home Telephone:	(732) 003-0976	Policyholder Date of Birth:	07-12-1969
Date of Birth:	01-16-1990	Relationship to Patient:	Parent
Gender:	Female	Secondary Insurance Plan:	
Occupation:	Student	Secondary Insurance Plan ID #:	
Employer:		Secondary Policyholder:	
Employer Telephone:			
Spouse:			
Spouse's Social Security #:			
Spouse's Employer:			
Spouse's Date of Birth:			

Patient Status	☐ Married	☐ Divorced	☒ Single	☒ Student	☐ Other

DIAGNOSIS INFORMATION

	Diagnosis	Code		Diagnosis	Code
1.	Acne	706.1	5.		
2.			6.		
3.			7.		
4.			8.		

PROCEDURE INFORMATION

	Description of Procedure or Service	Date	Code	Charge
1.	Level 2 office visit - new patient	05-02-YYYY	99202	$85.00
2.				
3.				
4.				
5.				
6.				

SPECIAL NOTES:

Pt was referred to dermatologist Claire Clearing, M.D.

Case Study 2

99202   level II non patient code

3

CLAIRE CLEARING, M.D.

0579 Bridge Ave • Point Pleasant, NJ 08742 • (732) 009-5555
Tax ID# 11-8256989
NPI# 0044002299

Case Study

PATIENT INFORMATION:		INSURANCE INFORMATION:	
Name:	Melissa Marks	Patient Number:	Marme000
Social Security #:	111-11-2222	Place of Service:	Office
Address:	0762 Apricot Lane	Primary Insurance Plan:	Prudential
City:	Point Pleasant	Primary Insurance Plan ID #:	XYZ2790017
State:	NJ	Group #:	6642
Zip Code:	08742	Primary Policyholder:	Marcus Marks
Home Telephone:	(732) 003-0976	Policyholder Date of Birth:	07-12-1969
Date of Birth:	01-16-1990	Relationship to Patient:	Parent
Gender:	Female		
Occupation:	Student	Secondary Insurance Plan:	
Employer:		Secondary Insurance Plan ID #:	
Employer Telephone:			
Spouse:		Secondary Policyholder:	
Spouse's Social Security #:			
Spouse's Employer:			
Spouse's Date of Birth:			

Patient Status	☐ Married	☐ Divorced	☒ Single	☒ Student	☐ Other

DIAGNOSIS INFORMATION

	Diagnosis	Code		Diagnosis	Code
1.	Acne	706.1	5.		
2.			6.		
3.			7.		
4.			8.		

PROCEDURE INFORMATION

	Description of Procedure or Service	Date	Code	Charge
1.	Level 2 office consultation	05-12-YYYY	99242	$125.00
2.				
3.				
4.				
5.				
6.				

SPECIAL NOTES:
Referred by Steven Spring, M.D., NPI# 0101010101.

Case Study 3

4

GARY GRAY, M.D.

0222 Route 70 • Brick, NJ 08723 • (732) 555-0000
Tax ID# 11-4311999
NPI# 9988001122

Case Study

PATIENT INFORMATION:

Name:	Yvonne Yager
Social Security #:	500-00-0000
Address:	030 Mango Court
City:	Brick
State:	NJ
Zip Code:	08724
Home Telephone:	(732) 008-8401
Date of Birth:	04-18-1930
Gender:	Female
Occupation:	Retired
Employer:	
Employer Telephone:	
Spouse:	
Spouse's Social Security #:	
Spouse's Employer:	
Spouse's Date of Birth:	

INSURANCE INFORMATION:

Patient Number:	Yagyv000
Place of Service:	Office
Primary Insurance Plan:	Medicare
Primary Insurance Plan ID #:	500-50-0000A
Group #:	
Primary Policyholder:	Yvonne Yager
Policyholder Date of Birth:	04-18-1930
Relationship to Patient:	Self
Secondary Insurance Plan:	AARP
Secondary Insurance Plan ID #:	114Z2397G
Secondary Policyholder:	Yvonne Yager

Patient Status   ☐ Married   ☐ Divorced   ☒ Single   ☐ Student   ☐ Other

DIAGNOSIS INFORMATION

Diagnosis	Code		Diagnosis	Code
1. Fatigue	780.79	5.		
2. Anemia	285.9	6.		
3.		7.		
4.		8.		

PROCEDURE INFORMATION

Description of Procedure or Service	Date	Code	Charge
1. Level 3 office visit - est patient	03-01-YYYY	99213	$65.00
2. Urinalysis	03-01-YYYY	81002	$20.00
3. Vitamin B-12 injection	03-01-YYYY	J3420	$15.00
4.			
5.			
6.			

SPECIAL NOTES:

Vitamin B-12 - up to 1000mcg.

Case Study 4

5

JUNEY JONES, M.D.

Case Study

0995 Hooper Ave • Toms River, NJ 08755 • (732) 999-5555

Tax ID# 11-99556789

NPI# 0077660055

PATIENT INFORMATION:

Name:	Sierra Shrewd
Social Security #:	999-00-8899
Address:	0512 Mango Road
City:	Asbury Park
State:	NJ
Zip Code:	00040
Home Telephone:	(732) 999-1111
Date of Birth:	05-17-1966
Gender:	Female
Occupation:	Teacher
Employer:	St. Anne's
Employer Telephone:	(732) 888-0000
Spouse:	
Spouse's Social Security #:	
Spouse's Employer:	
Spouse's Date of Birth:	

INSURANCE INFORMATION:

Patient Number:	Shrsi000
Place of Service:	Office
Primary Insurance Plan:	Oxford
Primary Insurance Plan ID #:	4497601
Group #:	P6239
Primary Policyholder:	Sierra Shrewd
Policyholder Date of Birth:	05-17-1966
Relationship to Patient:	Self
Secondary Insurance Plan:	
Secondary Insurance Plan ID #:	
Secondary Policyholder:	

Patient Status	☐ Married	☒ Divorced	☐ Single	☐ Student	☐ Other

---

DIAGNOSIS INFORMATION

Diagnosis	Code	Diagnosis	Code
1. Irregular periods	626.4	5.	
2. Fatigue	780.79	6.	
3. Hyperlipidemia	272.4	7.	
4.		8.	

PROCEDURE INFORMATION

Description of Procedure or Service	Date	Code	Charge
1. Level 4 office visit - est patient	04-11-YYYY	99214	$75.00
2. Venipuncture	04-11-YYYY	36415	$30.00
3.			
4.			
5.			
6.			

SPECIAL NOTES:

Juney Jones, M.D., is part of: Hooper Medical Group, NPI# 0606010188, Tax ID# 22-9988779. Pt referred to Hooper OB/GYN.

Case Study 5

6

HOOPER OB/GYN
0401 Hooper Ave • Toms River, NJ 08755 • (732) 000-2200
Tax ID# 22-0011289
NPI# 1000290001

Case Study

PATIENT INFORMATION:

Name:	Sierra Shrewd
Social Security #:	999-00-8899
Address:	0512 Mango Road
City:	Asbury Park
State:	NJ
Zip Code:	00040
Home Telephone:	(732) 999-1111
Date of Birth:	05-17-1966
Gender:	Female
Occupation:	Teacher
Employer:	St. Anne's
Employer Telephone:	(732) 888-0000
Spouse:	
Spouse's Social Security #:	
Spouse's Employer:	
Spouse's Date of Birth:	

INSURANCE INFORMATION:

Patient Number:	Shrsi000
Place of Service:	Office
Primary Insurance Plan:	Oxford
Primary Insurance Plan ID #:	4497601
Group #:	P6239
Primary Policyholder:	Sierra Shrewd
Policyholder Date of Birth:	05-17-1966
Relationship to Patient:	Self
Secondary Insurance Plan:	
Secondary Insurance Plan ID #:	
Secondary Policyholder:	

Patient Status	☐ Married	☒ Divorced	☐ Single	☐ Student	☐ Other

DIAGNOSIS INFORMATION

	Diagnosis	Code		Diagnosis	Code
1.	Irregular periods	626.4	5.		
2.			6.		
3.			7.		
4.			8.		

PROCEDURE INFORMATION

	Description of Procedure or Service	Date	Code	Charge
1.	Level 3 office consultation	04-19-YYYY	99243	$150.00
2.				
3.				
4.				
5.				
6.				

SPECIAL NOTES:
Pt was seen by Mindy Mable, M.D., NPI# 0707566500.

Case Study 6

7 – HW for 11/12

HOOPER OB/GYN

0401 Hooper Ave • Toms River, NJ 08755 • (732) 000-2200
Tax ID# 22-0011289
NPI# 1000290001

Case Study

PATIENT INFORMATION:		INSURANCE INFORMATION:	
Name:	Sierra Shrewd	Patient Number:	Shrsi000
Social Security #:	999-00-8899	Place of Service:	Out-patient hospital
Address:	0512 Mango Road	Primary Insurance Plan:	Oxford
City:	Asbury Park	Primary Insurance Plan ID #:	4497601
State:	NJ	Group #:	P6239
Zip Code:	00040		
Home Telephone:	(732) 999-1111	Primary Policyholder:	Sierra Shrewd
Date of Birth:	05-17-1966	Policyholder Date of Birth:	05-17-1966
Gender:	Female	Relationship to Patient:	Self
Occupation:	Teacher		
Employer:	St. Anne's	Secondary Insurance Plan:	
Employer Telephone:	(732) 888-0000	Secondary Insurance Plan ID #:	
Spouse:		Secondary Insurance Plan ID #:	
Spouse's Social Security #:		Secondary Policyholder:	
Spouse's Employer:			
Spouse's Date of Birth:			

Patient Status ☐ Married ☒ Divorced ☐ Single ☐ Student ☐ Other

DIAGNOSIS INFORMATION

Diagnosis	Code	Diagnosis	Code
1. Irregular periods	626.4	5.	
2.		6.	
3.		7.	
4.		8.	

PROCEDURE INFORMATION

Description of Procedure or Service	Date	Code	Charge
1. Dilation and curettage	04-26-YYYY	58120	$750.00
2.			
3.			
4.			
5.			
6.			

SPECIAL NOTES:

Performing physician Mindy Mable, M.D., NPI# 0707566500,
Hooper Medical Center, 011 Hospital Drive, Toms River, NJ 08755,
Facility NPI# 9900000011.

Case Study 7

CATHY CRANE, M.D.
0626 Route 88 • Point Pleasant, NJ 08742 • (732) 001-6793
Tax ID# 11-4455798
NPI# 8007006000

Case Study

PATIENT INFORMATION:

Name:	Diane Dells
Social Security #:	000-47-0000
Address:	032 Ridge Trail
City:	Brick
State:	NJ
Zip Code:	08723
Home Telephone:	(732) 050-9927
Date of Birth:	03-24-1963
Gender:	Female
Occupation:	Secretary
Employer:	The Office Place
Employer Telephone:	(732) 090-2299
Spouse:	David Dells
Spouse's Social Security #:	000-66-0066
Spouse's Employer:	Telecom
Spouse's Date of Birth:	07-01-1961

INSURANCE INFORMATION:

Patient Number:	Deldi000
Place of Service:	Office
Primary Insurance Plan:	Connecticut General
Primary Insurance Plan ID #:	279322XZ27
Group #:	930001
Primary Policyholder:	Diane Dells
Policyholder Date of Birth:	03-24-1963
Relationship to Patient:	Self
Secondary Insurance Plan:	Aetna
Secondary Insurance Plan ID #:	273BA9264
Secondary Policyholder:	David Dells

Patient Status ☒ Married ☐ Divorced ☐ Single ☐ Student ☐ Other

DIAGNOSIS INFORMATION

	Diagnosis	Code		Diagnosis	Code
1.	Mass, breast	611.72	5.		
2.			6.		
3.			7.		
4.			8.		

PROCEDURE INFORMATION

	Description of Procedure or Service	Date	Code	Charge
1.	Level 3 office visit - new patient	03-16-YYYY	99203	$100.00
2.				
3.				
4.				
5.				
6.				

SPECIAL NOTES:
Pt referred to Dr. Lisa Lane who is part of XYZ Medical Group.

Case Study 8

LISA LANE, M.D.
0797 Route 88 • Point Pleasant, NJ 08742 • (732) 000-1792
Tax ID# 11-9955333
NPI# 6005004001

Case Study

PATIENT INFORMATION:		INSURANCE INFORMATION:	
Name:	Diane Dells	Patient Number:	Deldi000
Social Security #:	000-47-0000	Place of Service:	Office
Address:	032 Ridge Trail	Primary Insurance Plan:	Connecticut General
City:	Brick	Primary Insurance Plan ID #:	279322XZ27
State:	NJ	Group #:	930001
Zip Code:	08723	Primary Policyholder:	Diane Dells
Home Telephone:	(732) 050-9927	Policyholder Date of Birth:	03-24-1963
Date of Birth:	03-24-1963	Relationship to Patient:	Self
Gender:	Female	Secondary Insurance Plan:	Aetna
Occupation:	Secretary	Secondary Insurance Plan ID #:	273BA9264
Employer:	The Office Place	Secondary Policyholder:	David Dells
Employer Telephone:	(732) 090-2299		
Spouse:	David Dells		
Spouse's Social Security #:	000-66-0066		
Spouse's Employer:	Telecom		
Spouse's Date of Birth:	07-01-1961		

Patient Status	☒ Married	☐ Divorced	☐ Single	☐ Student	☐ Other

DIAGNOSIS INFORMATION

Diagnosis	Code	Diagnosis	Code
1. Mass, breast	611.72	5.	
2.		6.	
3.		7.	
4.		8.	

PROCEDURE INFORMATION

Description of Procedure or Service	Date	Code	Charge
1. Level 4 office consultation	03-29-YYYY	99244	$175.00
2.			
3.			
4.			
5.			
6.			

SPECIAL NOTES:
Physician is part of: XYZ Medical Group, Tax ID# 22-9346789, NPI# 0004400330.
Pt referred by: Cathy Crane, M.D., NPI# 8007006000.

Case Study 9

LINDA LEGGY, M.D.
0424 Route 88 • Brick, NJ 08724 • (732) 000-0977
Tax ID# 11-8844697
NPI# 0411021100

Case Study

PATIENT INFORMATION:

Name:	Fiona Flags
Social Security #:	010-10-0110
Address:	030 Maple Drive
City:	West Long Branch
State:	NJ
Zip Code:	07764
Home Telephone:	(732) 090-0120
Date of Birth:	07-12-1938
Gender:	Female
Occupation:	Retired
Employer:	
Employer Telephone:	
Spouse:	
Spouse's Social Security #:	
Spouse's Employer:	
Spouse's Date of Birth:	

INSURANCE INFORMATION:

Patient Number:	Fiofl000
Place of Service:	In-patient hospital
Primary Insurance Plan:	Medicare
Primary Insurance Plan ID #:	010-10-0110A
Group #:	
Primary Policyholder:	Fiona Flags
Policyholder Date of Birth:	07-12-1938
Relationship to Patient:	Self
Secondary Insurance Plan:	
Secondary Insurance Plan ID #:	
Secondary Policyholder:	

Patient Status   ☐ Married   ☐ Divorced   ☒ Single   ☐ Student   ☐ Other

DIAGNOSIS INFORMATION

Diagnosis	Code	Diagnosis	Code
1. Pneumonia	486	5.	
2.		6.	
3.		7.	
4.		8.	

PROCEDURE INFORMATION

Description of Procedure or Service	Date	Code	Charge
1. Initial hospital care - level 3	03-15-YYYY	99223	$175.00
2. Subsequent hospital care - level 2	03-16-YYYY	99232	$115.00
3.			
4.			
5.			
6.			

SPECIAL NOTES:
Linda Leggy, M.D., requests a consult from Peggy Peters, M.D., Community Central Hospital, 0599 Third Avenue, Howell, NJ 07701, Facility NPI# 0009207777.

Case Study 10

PEGGY PETERS, M.D.
0799 Broadway Ave • Long Branch, NJ 07740 • (732) 333-5555
Tax ID# 11-3344555
NPI# 0411332200

Case Study

PATIENT INFORMATION:

Name:	Fiona Flags
Social Security #:	010-10-0110
Address:	030 Maple Drive
City:	West Long Branch
State:	NJ
Zip Code:	07764
Home Telephone:	(732) 090-0120
Date of Birth:	07-12-1938
Gender:	Female
Occupation:	Retired
Employer:	
Employer Telephone:	
Spouse:	
Spouse's Social Security #:	
Spouse's Employer:	
Spouse's Date of Birth:	

INSURANCE INFORMATION:

Patient Number:	Fiof1000
Place of Service:	In-patient hospital
Primary Insurance Plan:	Medicare
Primary Insurance Plan ID #:	010-10-0110A
Group #:	
Primary Policyholder:	Fiona Flags
Policyholder Date of Birth:	07-12-1938
Relationship to Patient:	Self
Secondary Insurance Plan:	
Secondary Insurance Plan ID #:	
Secondary Policyholder:	

Patient Status	☐ Married	☐ Divorced	☒ Single	☐ Student	☐ Other

DIAGNOSIS INFORMATION

Diagnosis	Code	Diagnosis	Code
1. Pneumonia	486	5.	
2.		6.	
3.		7.	
4.		8.	

PROCEDURE INFORMATION

Description of Procedure or Service	Date	Code	Charge
1. Initial in-patient consultation - level 3	03-15-YYYY	99253	$225.00
2. Pneumocentesis, puncture of lung for aspiration	03-16-YYYY	32420	$675.00
3.			
4.			
5.			
6.			

SPECIAL NOTES:
Referring physician: Linda Leggy, M.D., NPI# 0411021100.
Community Central Hospital, 0599 Third Avenue, Howell, NJ 07701,
Facility NPI# 0009207777.

Case Study 11

ELLEN EMBERS, D.O.

076 Lakeridge Road • Manchester, NJ 00034 • (732) 111-4710

Tax ID# 11-9811223

NPI# 0132130000

Case Study

PATIENT INFORMATION:

Name:	Julie Jasper
Social Security #:	000-88-0008
Address:	0411 Haskill Road
City:	Manchester
State:	NJ
Zip Code:	00034
Home Telephone:	(732) 555-9959
Date of Birth:	04-09-1932
Gender:	Female
Occupation:	Retired
Employer:	
Employer Telephone:	
Spouse:	
Spouse's Social Security #:	
Spouse's Employer:	
Spouse's Date of Birth:	

INSURANCE INFORMATION:

Patient Number:	Jasju000
Place of Service:	Nursing facility
Primary Insurance Plan:	CIGNA Medicare
Primary Insurance Plan ID #:	422QME0008
Group #:	CM99326
Primary Policyholder:	Julie Jasper
Policyholder Date of Birth:	04-09-1932
Relationship to Patient:	Self
Secondary Insurance Plan:	
Secondary Insurance Plan ID #:	
Secondary Policyholder:	

Patient Status ☐ Married ☐ Divorced ☒ Single ☐ Student ☐ Other

DIAGNOSIS INFORMATION

Diagnosis	Code	Diagnosis	Code
1. Alzheimer's	331.0	5.	
2.		6.	
3.		7.	
4.		8.	

PROCEDURE INFORMATION

Description of Procedure or Service	Date	Code	Charge
1. Initial nursing facility care - level 2	05-17-YYYY	99305	$150.00
2. Subsequent nursing facility care - level 2	05-18-YYYY	99308	$130.00
3.			
4.			
5.			
6.			

SPECIAL NOTES:

Ocean Senior Care Village, 066 Route 1, Lake Hurst, NJ 02222, Facility NPI# 0210304050.

Case Study 12

PATRICIA PLATINUM, M.D.
010 Cedar Bridge Lane • Brick, NJ 08723 • (732) 333-4444
Tax ID# 11-8181811
NPI# 1002003000

Case Study

PATIENT INFORMATION:

Name:	John Johnson
Social Security #:	009-08-0007
Address:	0418 Lucy Court
City:	Brick
State:	NJ
Zip Code:	08723
Home Telephone:	(732) 555-7777
Date of Birth:	04-01-1935
Gender:	Male
Occupation:	Retired
Employer:	
Employer Telephone:	
Spouse:	
Spouse's Social Security #:	
Spouse's Employer:	
Spouse's Date of Birth:	

INSURANCE INFORMATION:

Patient Number:	Johjo000
Place of Service:	Office
Primary Insurance Plan:	Medicare
Primary Insurance Plan ID #:	009-08-0007A
Group #:	
Primary Policyholder:	John Johnson
Policyholder Date of Birth:	04-01-1935
Relationship to Patient:	Self
Secondary Insurance Plan:	Blue Cross/Blue Shield
Secondary Insurance Plan ID #:	009-08-0007BB
Secondary Policyholder:	John Johnson

Patient Status   ☐ Married   ☐ Divorced   ☒ Single   ☐ Student   ☐ Other

DIAGNOSIS INFORMATION

Diagnosis	Code	Diagnosis	Code
1. Irritable bowel syndrome	564.1	5.	
2.		6.	
3.		7.	
4.		8.	

PROCEDURE INFORMATION

Description of Procedure or Service	Date	Code	Charge
1. Level 3 office visit - est patient	02-09-YYYY	99213	$65.00
2.			
3.			
4.			
5.			
6.			

SPECIAL NOTES:
Pt referred to Gary Gold, D.O., NPI# 9008007000.

Case Study 13

GARY GOLD, D.O.

020 Chambers Rd • Brick, NJ 08724 • (732) 444-6666
Tax ID# 11-6677119
NPI# 9008007000

Case Study

PATIENT INFORMATION:

Name:	John Johnson
Social Security #:	009-08-0007
Address:	0418 Lucy Court
City:	Brick
State:	NJ
Zip Code:	08723
Home Telephone:	(732) 555-7777
Date of Birth:	04-01-1935
Gender:	Male
Occupation:	Retired
Employer:	
Employer Telephone:	
Spouse:	
Spouse's Social Security #:	
Spouse's Employer:	
Spouse's Date of Birth:	

INSURANCE INFORMATION:

Patient Number:	Johjo000
Place of Service:	Office
Primary Insurance Plan:	Medicare
Primary Insurance Plan ID #:	009-08-0007A
Group #:	
Primary Policyholder:	John Johnson
Policyholder Date of Birth:	04-01-1935
Relationship to Patient:	Self
Secondary Insurance Plan:	Blue Cross/Blue Shield
Secondary Insurance Plan ID #:	009-08-0007BB
Secondary Policyholder:	John Johnson

Patient Status ☐ Married ☐ Divorced ☒ Single ☐ Student ☐ Other

DIAGNOSIS INFORMATION

	Diagnosis	Code		Diagnosis	Code
1.	Irritable bowel syndrome	564.1	5.		
2.			6.		
3.			7.		
4.			8.		

PROCEDURE INFORMATION

	Description of Procedure or Service	Date	Code	Charge
1.	Level 4 office consultation	02-17-YYYY	99244	$175.00
2.				
3.				
4.				
5.				
6.				

SPECIAL NOTES:

Pt referred by Patricia Platinum, M.D., NPI# 1002003000.
Pt scheduled for colonoscopy on 02-25-YYYY.

Case Study 14

GARY GOLD, D.O.
020 Chambers Rd • Brick, NJ 08724 • (732) 444-6666
Tax ID# 11-6677119
NPI# 9008007000

Case Study

PATIENT INFORMATION:

Name:	John Johnson
Social Security #:	009-08-0007
Address:	0418 Lucy Court
City:	Brick
State:	NJ
Zip Code:	08723
Home Telephone:	(732) 555-7777
Date of Birth:	04-01-1935
Gender:	Male
Occupation:	Retired
Employer:	
Employer Telephone:	
Spouse:	
Spouse's Social Security #:	
Spouse's Employer:	
Spouse's Date of Birth:	

INSURANCE INFORMATION:

Patient Number:	Johjo000
Place of Service:	Out-patient hospital
Primary Insurance Plan:	Medicare
Primary Insurance Plan ID #:	009-08-0007A
Group #:	
Primary Policyholder:	John Johnson
Policyholder Date of Birth:	04-01-1935
Relationship to Patient:	Self
Secondary Insurance Plan:	Blue Cross/Blue Shield
Secondary Insurance Plan ID #:	009-08-0007BB
Secondary Policyholder:	John Johnson

Patient Status ☐ Married ☐ Divorced ☒ Single ☐ Student ☐ Other

DIAGNOSIS INFORMATION

	Diagnosis	Code		Diagnosis	Code
1.	IBS	564.1	5.		
2.	Polyps, colon	211.3	6.		
3.			7.		
4.			8.		

PROCEDURE INFORMATION

	Description of Procedure or Service	Date	Code	Charge
1.	Colonoscopy	02-25-YYYY	45378	$800.00
2.				
3.				
4.				
5.				
6.				

SPECIAL NOTES:

Hooper Medical Center, 011 Hospital Drive, Toms River, NJ 08755,
Facility NPI# 9900000011.

Case Study 15

JUNEY JONES, M.D.

0995 Hooper Ave • Toms River, NJ 08755 • (732) 999-5555
Tax ID# 11-99556789
NPI# 0077660055

Case Study

PATIENT INFORMATION:

Name:	Theresa Lewis
Social Security #:	944-00-0000
Address:	0490 Gary Lane
City:	Brick
State:	NJ
Zip Code:	08724
Home Telephone:	(732) 999-1111
Date of Birth:	06-08-1940
Gender:	Female
Occupation:	
Employer:	
Employer Telephone:	
Spouse:	Steve Lewis
Spouse's Social Security #:	866-00-0000
Spouse's Employer:	ABC Electronics
Spouse's Date of Birth:	05-30-1939

INSURANCE INFORMATION:

Patient Number:	Lewth000
Place of Service:	Office
Primary Insurance Plan:	Aetna
Primary Insurance Plan ID #:	729QR44731
Group #:	666426
Primary Policyholder:	Steve Lewis
Policyholder Date of Birth:	05-30-1939
Relationship to Patient:	Spouse
Secondary Insurance Plan:	
Secondary Insurance Plan ID #:	
Secondary Policyholder:	

Patient Status   ☒ Married   ☐ Divorced   ☐ Single   ☐ Student   ☐ Other

DIAGNOSIS INFORMATION

	Diagnosis	Code		Diagnosis	Code
1.	Rash	782.1	5.		
2.			6.		
3.			7.		
4.			8.		

PROCEDURE INFORMATION

	Description of Procedure or Service	Date	Code	Charge
1.	Level 4 office visit - est patient	04-21-YYYY	99214	$75.00
2.				
3.				
4.				
5.				
6.				

SPECIAL NOTES:

Pt referred to dermatologist Nancy Nibbles, M.D., NPI# 8108108108.

Case Study 16

NANCY NIBBLES, M.D.

04629 Brick Road • Brick, NJ 08724 • (732) 999-2299
Tax ID# 11-3434343
NPI# 8108108108

Case Study

PATIENT INFORMATION:

Name:	Theresa Lewis
Social Security #:	944-00-0000
Address:	0490 Gary Lane
City:	Brick
State:	NJ
Zip Code:	08724
Home Telephone:	(732) 999-1111
Date of Birth:	06-08-1940
Gender:	Female
Occupation:	
Employer:	
Employer Telephone:	
Spouse:	Steve Lewis
Spouse's Social Security #:	866-00-0000
Spouse's Employer:	ABC Electronics
Spouse's Date of Birth:	05-30-1939

INSURANCE INFORMATION:

Patient Number:	Lewth000
Place of Service:	Office
Primary Insurance Plan:	Aetna
Primary Insurance Plan ID #:	729QR44731
Group #:	666426
Primary Policyholder:	Steve Lewis
Policyholder Date of Birth:	05-30-1939
Relationship to Patient:	Spouse
Secondary Insurance Plan:	
Secondary Insurance Plan ID #:	
Secondary Policyholder:	

Patient Status   ☒ Married   ☐ Divorced   ☐ Single   ☐ Student   ☐ Other

DIAGNOSIS INFORMATION

Diagnosis	Code	Diagnosis	Code
1. Rash	782.1	5.	
2. Dermatitis	692.9	6.	
3.		7.	
4.		8.	

PROCEDURE INFORMATION

Description of Procedure or Service	Date	Code	Charge
1. Level 2 office consultation	05-02-YYYY	99242	$125.00
2.			
3.			
4.			
5.			
6.			

SPECIAL NOTES:

Pt was referred by Juney Jones, M.D., NPI# 0077660055.

Case Study 17

STEVEN SPRING, M.D.

0909 Route 68 • Point Pleasant, NJ 08742 • (732) 004-0090
Tax ID# 11-9923989
NPI# 0101010101

Case Study

PATIENT INFORMATION:

Name:	Carole Cramer
Social Security #:	999-22-9992
Address:	0463 Brook Lane
City:	Brick
State:	NJ
Zip Code:	08739
Home Telephone:	(732) 444-4454
Date of Birth:	09-22-1934
Gender:	Female
Occupation:	Retired
Employer:	
Employer Telephone:	
Spouse:	
Spouse's Social Security #:	
Spouse's Employer:	
Spouse's Date of Birth:	

INSURANCE INFORMATION:

Patient Number:	Craca000
Place of Service:	Office
Primary Insurance Plan:	Medicare
Primary Insurance Plan ID #:	999-22-9992A
Group #:	
Primary Policyholder:	Carole Cramer
Policyholder Date of Birth:	09-22-1934
Relationship to Patient:	Self
Secondary Insurance Plan:	
Secondary Insurance Plan ID #:	
Secondary Policyholder:	

Patient Status   ☐ Married   ☒ Divorced   ☐ Single   ☐ Student   ☐ Other

DIAGNOSIS INFORMATION

Diagnosis	Code	Diagnosis	Code
1. Asthma	493.90	5.	
2. Back pain	724.5	6.	
3.		7.	
4.		8.	

PROCEDURE INFORMATION

Description of Procedure or Service	Date	Code	Charge
1. Nebulizer treatment	04-19-YYYY	00664	$65.00
2. Level 2 office visit - est patient	04-19-YYYY	99212	$55.00
3.			
4.			
5.			
6.			

SPECIAL NOTES:

Pt comes in monthly for her asthma condition. She usually receives a nebulizer treatment on these visits. On her visit for 04-19-YYYY, she mentions a separate ailment (back pain) unrelated to her asthma.

Case Study 18

VICTOR VENICE, M.D.

0479 Ridge Road • Piscataway, NJ 08754 • (732) 909-9090
Tax ID# 11-3457899
NPI# 0020030049

Case Study

PATIENT INFORMATION:		INSURANCE INFORMATION:	
Name:	Megan Miles	Patient Number:	Milme000
Social Security #:	000-42-9300	Place of Service:	Office
Address:	47 Greenleaf Dr	Primary Insurance Plan:	Oxford
City:	Edison	Primary Insurance Plan ID #:	4692201
State:	NJ	Group #:	P7693
Zip Code:	08817		
Home Telephone:	(732) 400-3001	Primary Policyholder:	Michael Miles
Date of Birth:	06-28-2002	Policyholder Date of Birth:	01-28-1964
Gender:	Female	Relationship to Patient:	Parent
Occupation:		Secondary Insurance Plan:	
Employer:			
Employer Telephone:		Secondary Insurance Plan ID #:	
Spouse:			
Spouse's Social Security #:		Secondary Policyholder:	
Spouse's Employer:			
Spouse's Date of Birth:			

Patient Status	☐ Married	☐ Divorced	☒ Single	☐ Student	☐ Other

DIAGNOSIS INFORMATION

Diagnosis	Code	Diagnosis	Code
1. Pneumonia	486	5.	
2.		6.	
3.		7.	
4.		8.	

PROCEDURE INFORMATION

Description of Procedure or Service	Date	Code	Charge
1. Radiologic exam, chest, single view	01-16-YYYY	71010	$200.00
2.			
3.			
4.			
5.			
6.			

SPECIAL NOTES:

Dr. Venice is a radiologist. He is billing for reading and interpreting the patient's chest x-ray.

LOUISE LANCE, M.D.
092 Route 88 • Brick, NJ 08724 • (732) 555-1655
Tax ID# 11-9345789
NPI# 4040400101

Case Study

PATIENT INFORMATION:

Name:	Alyssa Allers
Social Security #:	002-00-3000
Address:	041 Cherry Rd
City:	Brick
State:	NJ
Zip Code:	08723
Home Telephone:	(732) 222-2222
Date of Birth:	05-22-1973
Gender:	Female
Occupation:	Cashier
Employer:	KBM Toys
Employer Telephone:	(732) 444-5555
Spouse:	Larry Allers
Spouse's Social Security #:	067-00-0067
Spouse's Employer:	Exxon
Spouse's Date of Birth:	04-17-1972

INSURANCE INFORMATION:

Patient Number:	Alla1000
Place of Service:	Office
Primary Insurance Plan:	Prudential
Primary Insurance Plan ID #:	P6799234802
Group #:	999367
Primary Policyholder:	Larry Allers
Policyholder Date of Birth:	04-17-1972
Relationship to Patient:	Spouse
Secondary Insurance Plan:	
Secondary Insurance Plan ID #:	
Secondary Policyholder:	

Patient Status ☒ Married ☐ Divorced ☐ Single ☐ Student ☐ Other

---

DIAGNOSIS INFORMATION

Diagnosis	Code	Diagnosis	Code
1. Skin tag	701.9	5.	
2.		6.	
3.		7.	
4.		8.	

PROCEDURE INFORMATION

Description of Procedure or Service	Date	Code	Charge
1. Removal of skin tags, up to 15	02-28-YYYY	11200	$75.00
2.			
3.			
4.			
5.			
6.			

SPECIAL NOTES:
Site of removal was upper left eyelid.

Case Study 20

BEATRICE BOWE, M.D.

091 Chambers Rd • Brick, NJ 08724 • (732) 555-7755
Tax ID# 11-2399888
NPI# 0000055555

Case Study

PATIENT INFORMATION:

Name:	Steven Scally
Social Security #:	000-99-3344
Address:	04127 Blackhorse Lane
City:	Point Pleasant
State:	NJ
Zip Code:	08742
Home Telephone:	(732) 400-5000
Date of Birth:	01-22-1936
Gender:	Male
Occupation:	Retired
Employer:	
Employer Telephone:	
Spouse:	
Spouse's Social Security #:	
Spouse's Employer:	
Spouse's Date of Birth:	

INSURANCE INFORMATION:

Patient Number:	Scast000
Place of Service:	Office
Primary Insurance Plan:	Medicare
Primary Insurance Plan ID #:	000-99-3344A
Group #:	
Primary Policyholder:	Steven Scally
Policyholder Date of Birth:	01-22-1936
Relationship to Patient:	Self
Secondary Insurance Plan:	
Secondary Insurance Plan ID #:	
Secondary Policyholder:	

Patient Status ☐ Married ☐ Divorced ☒ Single ☐ Student ☐ Other

DIAGNOSIS INFORMATION

Diagnosis	Code		Diagnosis	Code
1. Shoulder pain	719.41	5.		
2. Preventative influenza	V04.81	6.		
3.		7.		
4.		8.		

PROCEDURE INFORMATION

Description of Procedure or Service	Date	Code	Charge
1. Level 3 office visit - est patient	05-19-YYYY	99213	$65.00
2. Influenza vaccine	05-19-YYYY	90658	$30.00
3. Administration of influenza vaccine	05-19-YYYY	G0008	$25.00
4.			
5.			
6.			

SPECIAL NOTES:

Pt comes in for his annual flu vaccine. While in the exam room, patient mentions a separate ailment - he has been experiencing recent shoulder pain.

GARY GRAY, M.D.
0222 Route 70 • Brick, NJ 08723 • (732) 555-0000
Tax ID# 11-4311999
NPI# 9988001122

Case Study

PATIENT INFORMATION:

Name:	Linda Lowe
Social Security #:	909-09-9090
Address:	069 Peach Blvd
City:	Toms River
State:	NJ
Zip Code:	08755
Home Telephone:	(732) 888-5555
Date of Birth:	02-13-1933
Gender:	Female
Occupation:	Retired
Employer:	
Employer Telephone:	
Spouse:	
Spouse's Social Security #:	
Spouse's Employer:	
Spouse's Date of Birth:	

INSURANCE INFORMATION:

Patient Number:	Lowli000
Place of Service:	Nursing facility
Primary Insurance Plan:	Medicare
Primary Insurance Plan ID #:	909-09-9090A
Group #:	
Primary Policyholder:	Linda Lowe
Policyholder Date of Birth:	02-13-1933
Relationship to Patient:	Self
Secondary Insurance Plan:	
Secondary Insurance Plan ID #:	
Secondary Policyholder:	

Patient Status ☐ Married ☐ Divorced ☒ Single ☐ Student ☐ Other

DIAGNOSIS INFORMATION

Diagnosis	Code	Diagnosis	Code
1. Dementia	294.8	5.	
2.		6.	
3.		7.	
4.		8.	

PROCEDURE INFORMATION

Description of Procedure or Service	Date	Code	Charge
1. Subsequent nursing facility care - level 2	05-18-YYYY	99308	$130.00
2. Nursing facility discharge (more than 30 mins)	05-19-YYYY	99316	$110.00
3.			
4.			
5.			
6.			

SPECIAL NOTES:

Ocean City Senior Care Home, 0223 Ocean Rd, Ocean City, NJ 00204,
Facility NPI# 0201020300.

SAL SILVER, M.D.
00039 Route 70 • Brick, NJ 08724 • (732) 469-0009
Tax ID# 11-4239900
NPI# 6003000700

Case Study

PATIENT INFORMATION:		INSURANCE INFORMATION:	
Name:	Chelsea Chaney	Patient Number:	Chach000
Social Security #:	090-92-0092	Place of Service:	In-patient hospital
Address:	0437 Kitty Court	Primary Insurance Plan:	CIGNA
City:	Howell	Primary Insurance Plan ID #:	CC392678501
State:	NJ	Group #:	923923
Zip Code:	07701		
Home Telephone:	(732) 501-0005	Primary Policyholder:	Cherie Chaney
Date of Birth:	02-28-1991	Policyholder Date of Birth:	03-18-1966
Gender:	Female	Relationship to Patient:	Parent
Occupation:			
Employer:		Secondary Insurance Plan:	
Employer Telephone:		Secondary Insurance Plan ID #:	
Spouse:		Secondary Policyholder:	
Spouse's Social Security #:			
Spouse's Employer:			
Spouse's Date of Birth:			

Patient Status	☐ Married	☐ Divorced	☒ Single	☐ Student	☐ Other

DIAGNOSIS INFORMATION

Diagnosis	Code	Diagnosis	Code
1. Hepatic failure	572.8	5.	
2.		6.	
3.		7.	
4.		8.	

PROCEDURE INFORMATION

Description of Procedure or Service	Date	Code	Charge
1. Initial in-patient hospital care - level 3	02-01-YYYY	99223	$175.00
2. Critical care services (30 - 74 mins)	02-01-YYYY	99291	$250.00
3. Critical care services (ea add'l 30 mins)	02-01-YYYY	99292	$225.00
4. Critical care services (ea add'l 30 mins)	02-01-YYYY	99292	$225.00
5.			
6.			

SPECIAL NOTES:
Physician spent a total of two hours dedicated to the critical care service of patient on 02-01-YYYY. Hooper Medial Center, 011 Hospital Drive, Toms River, NJ 08755, Facility NPI# 9900000011.

Case Study 23

GRETA GREEN, M.D.

01102 Neptune Blvd • Neptune, NJ 07070 • (732) 009-0049
Tax ID# 11-3499988
NPI# 3004005000

Case Study

PATIENT INFORMATION:

Name:	Frank Fender
Social Security #:	011-00-2121
Address:	0937 Kathy Court
City:	Brick
State:	NJ
Zip Code:	08724
Home Telephone:	(732) 505-0000
Date of Birth:	02-22-1932
Gender:	Male
Occupation:	Retired
Employer:	
Employer Telephone:	
Spouse:	
Spouse's Social Security #:	
Spouse's Employer:	
Spouse's Date of Birth:	

INSURANCE INFORMATION:

Patient Number:	Fenfr000
Place of Service:	Office
Primary Insurance Plan:	Medicare
Primary Insurance Plan ID #:	011-00-2121A
Group #:	
Primary Policyholder:	Frank Fender
Policyholder Date of Birth:	02-22-1932
Relationship to Patient:	Self
Secondary Insurance Plan:	
Secondary Insurance Plan ID #:	
Secondary Policyholder:	

Patient Status	☐ Married	☐ Divorced	☒ Single	☐ Student	☐ Other

DIAGNOSIS INFORMATION

	Diagnosis	Code		Diagnosis	Code
1.	Pain, finger	729.5	5.		
2.			6.		
3.			7.		
4.			8.		

PROCEDURE INFORMATION

	Description of Procedure or Service	Date	Code	Charge
1.	Arthrocentesis, small joint	07-22-YYYY	20600	$105.00
2.	Depo-medrol - up to 40 mg	07-22-YYYY	J1030	$40.00
3.				
4.				
5.				
6.				

SPECIAL NOTES:

Site of procedure is right hand, third digit.

Case Study 24

GRETA GREEN, M.D.

01102 Neptune Blvd • Neptune, NJ 07070 • (732) 009-0049

Tax ID# 11-3499988

NPI# 3004005000

Case Study

PATIENT INFORMATION:

Name:	Helen Hurley
Social Security #:	002-00-0220
Address:	00973 Lakewood Road
City:	Neptune
State:	NJ
Zip Code:	07070
Home Telephone:	(732) 001-0222
Date of Birth:	04-01-1933
Gender:	Female
Occupation:	Retired
Employer:	
Employer Telephone:	
Spouse:	
Spouse's Social Security #:	
Spouse's Employer:	
Spouse's Date of Birth:	

INSURANCE INFORMATION:

Patient Number:	Hurhe000
Place of Service:	Office
Primary Insurance Plan:	Medicare
Primary Insurance Plan ID #:	002-00-0220A
Group #:	
Primary Policyholder:	Helen Hurley
Policyholder Date of Birth:	04-01-1933
Relationship to Patient:	Self
Secondary Insurance Plan:	
Secondary Insurance Plan ID #:	
Secondary Policyholder:	

Patient Status	☐ Married	☐ Divorced	☒ Single	☐ Student	☐ Other

DIAGNOSIS INFORMATION

	Diagnosis	Code		Diagnosis	Code
1.	Cyst, skin	706.2	5.		
2.			6.		
3.			7.		
4.			8.		

PROCEDURE INFORMATION

	Description of Procedure or Service	Date	Code	Charge
1.	Incision and drainage of cyst	04-27-YYYY	10060	$110.00
2.				
3.				
4.				
5.				
6.				

SPECIAL NOTES:

Site of procedure is left hand, thumb.

Case Study 25

Appendix II
Forms

BLANK CMS-1500 FORM

Figure App-1 is provided to make copies for completing the case studies in Appendix I.

E&M CODEBUILDER

Figure App-2 contains guidelines used by the provider in determining the level of evaluation and management service to be coded for provider reimbursement.

EVALUATION AND MANAGEMENT CODES

Figure App-3 lists commonly used codes found on the superbill/encounter form in the physician's office. Refer to this list for selecting the codes needed to complete the case-study exercises in Appendix I.

ADVANCE BENEFICIARY NOTICE (ABN) FORM

Figure App-4 is the form used when a service or procedure is expected to be denied by Medicare. The patient has an option of checking "yes" or "no" as to receiving the service or procedure. If the patient checks "yes" and signs the form, the patient is agreeing to pay the physician for the service or procedure if it is denied.

NOTICE OF EXCLUSIONS FROM MEDICARE BENEFITS (NEMB) FORM

Figure App-5 is the form used when a service or procedure is *not* a benefit covered by Medicare. By signing this form, the patient is agreeing to pay the physician for the service or procedure.

CMS OVERPAYMENT/REFUND FORM

Figure App-6 is the form completed by the physician's office when Medicare has erroneously sent an overpayment to the physician. The form is sent along with a refund check to Medicare for the overpayment.

REQUEST FOR OPINION/CONSULT

Figure App-7 is a sample of a form that may be used when an attending physician is requesting an opinion or consult from another physician regarding a patient.

REFUSAL TO AUTHORIZE PAYMENT

Figure App-8 is a sample form letter from an insurance company to a physician stating a refusal to authorize payment on a procedure or service.

INFORMED REFUSAL

Figure App-9 is a sample form letter written to the patient informing the patient that the insurance company has refused to authorize payment on a procedure or service.

CODE OF CONDUCT

Figure App-10 contains sample guidelines, rules, and restrictions that may be used for employees in the medical office. They detail the conduct and ethics expected from employees in regard to Medicare and Medicaid and patient privacy.

THE UB-04 FORM

The UB-04 form (Figure App-11) is used when billing for a facility. Examples might include:

- Hospital
- Nursing home
- Ambulatory surgical center

Guidelines and codes for billing on a UB-04 form are different from those used on a CMS-1500 form. To learn more about the UB-04, visit www.nubc.org.

1500

HEALTH INSURANCE CLAIM FORM

APPROVED BY NATIONAL UNIFORM CLAIM COMMITTEE 08/05

◻◻ PICA

PICA ◻◻

CARRIER

1. MEDICARE ◻ (Medicare #)   MEDICAID ◻ (Medicaid #)   TRICARE CHAMPUS ◻ (Sponsor's SSN)   CHAMPVA ◻ (Member ID#)   GROUP HEALTH PLAN ◻ (SSN or ID)   FECA BLK LUNG ◻ (SSN)   OTHER ◻ (ID)

1a. INSURED'S I.D. NUMBER   (For Program in Item 1)

2. PATIENT'S NAME (Last Name, First Name, Middle Initial)

3. PATIENT'S BIRTH DATE   MM ┊ DD ┊ YY   SEX   M ◻   F ◻

4. INSURED'S NAME (Last Name, First Name, Middle Initial)

5. PATIENT'S ADDRESS (No., Street)

6. PATIENT RELATIONSHIP TO INSURED   Self ◻   Spouse ◻   Child ◻   Other ◻

7. INSURED'S ADDRESS (No., Street)

CITY   STATE

8. PATIENT STATUS   Single ◻   Married ◻   Other ◻

CITY   STATE

ZIP CODE   TELEPHONE (Include Area Code) ( )

Employed ◻   Full-Time Student ◻   Part-Time Student ◻

ZIP CODE   TELEPHONE (Include Area Code) ( )

9. OTHER INSURED'S NAME (Last Name, First Name, Middle Initial)

10. IS PATIENT'S CONDITION RELATED TO:

11. INSURED'S POLICY GROUP OR FECA NUMBER

a. OTHER INSURED'S POLICY OR GROUP NUMBER

a. EMPLOYMENT? (Current or Previous)   ◻ YES   ◻ NO

a. INSURED'S DATE OF BIRTH   MM ┊ DD ┊ YY   SEX   M ◻   F ◻

b. OTHER INSURED'S DATE OF BIRTH   MM ┊ DD ┊ YY   SEX   M ◻   F ◻

b. AUTO ACCIDENT?   PLACE (State)   ◻ YES   ◻ NO

b. EMPLOYER'S NAME OR SCHOOL NAME

c. EMPLOYER'S NAME OR SCHOOL NAME

c. OTHER ACCIDENT?   ◻ YES   ◻ NO

c. INSURANCE PLAN NAME OR PROGRAM NAME

d. INSURANCE PLAN NAME OR PROGRAM NAME

10d. RESERVED FOR LOCAL USE

d. IS THERE ANOTHER HEALTH BENEFIT PLAN?   ◻ YES   ◻ NO   *If yes*, return to and complete item 9 a-d.

PATIENT AND INSURED INFORMATION

READ BACK OF FORM BEFORE COMPLETING & SIGNING THIS FORM.

12. PATIENT'S OR AUTHORIZED PERSON'S SIGNATURE I authorize the release of any medical or other information necessary to process this claim. I also request payment of government benefits either to myself or to the party who accepts assignment below.

SIGNED _____ DATE _____

13. INSURED'S OR AUTHORIZED PERSON'S SIGNATURE I authorize payment of medical benefits to the undersigned physician or supplier for services described below.

SIGNED _____

14. DATE OF CURRENT: MM ┊ DD ┊ YY ◄ ILLNESS (First symptom) OR INJURY (Accident) OR PREGNANCY(LMP)

15. IF PATIENT HAS HAD SAME OR SIMILAR ILLNESS. GIVE FIRST DATE MM ┊ DD ┊ YY

16. DATES PATIENT UNABLE TO WORK IN CURRENT OCCUPATION   MM ┊ DD ┊ YY   FROM   TO   MM ┊ DD ┊ YY

17. NAME OF REFERRING PROVIDER OR OTHER SOURCE

17a.

17b. NPI

18. HOSPITALIZATION DATES RELATED TO CURRENT SERVICES   MM ┊ DD ┊ YY   FROM   TO   MM ┊ DD ┊ YY

19. RESERVED FOR LOCAL USE

20. OUTSIDE LAB?   ◻ YES   ◻ NO $ CHARGES

21. DIAGNOSIS OR NATURE OF ILLNESS OR INJURY (Relate Items 1, 2, 3 or 4 to Item 24E by Line)

1. ┗___ . ___   3. ┗___ . ___

2. ┗___ . ___   4. ┗___ . ___

22. MEDICAID RESUBMISSION CODE   ORIGINAL REF. NO.

23. PRIOR AUTHORIZATION NUMBER

24. A. DATE(S) OF SERVICE						B. PLACE OF SERVICE	C. EMG	D. PROCEDURES, SERVICES, OR SUPPLIES (Explain Unusual Circumstances)		E. DIAGNOSIS POINTER	F. $ CHARGES	G. DAYS OR UNITS	H. EPSDT Family Plan	I. ID. QUAL.	J. RENDERING PROVIDER ID. #
From			To					CPT/HCPCS	MODIFIER						
MM	DD	YY	MM	DD	YY										
1															NPI
2															NPI
3															NPI
4															NPI
5															NPI
6															NPI

25. FEDERAL TAX I.D. NUMBER   SSN ◻ EIN ◻

26. PATIENT'S ACCOUNT NO.

27. ACCEPT ASSIGNMENT? (For govt. claims, see back)   ◻ YES   ◻ NO

28. TOTAL CHARGE $

29. AMOUNT PAID $

30. BALANCE DUE $

31. SIGNATURE OF PHYSICIAN OR SUPPLIER INCLUDING DEGREES OR CREDENTIALS (I certify that the statements on the reverse apply to this bill and are made a part thereof.)

SIGNED _____ DATE _____

32. SERVICE FACILITY LOCATION INFORMATION

a. NPI   b.

33. BILLING PROVIDER INFO & PH # ( )

a. NPI   b.

PHYSICIAN OR SUPPLIER INFORMATION

NUCC Instruction Manual available at: www.nucc.org

APPROVED OMB-0938-0999 FORM CMS-1500 (08/05)

Figure App-1 Blank CMS-1500 form.

E&M CodeBuilder

SELECTING THE LEVEL OF HISTORY

HISTORY OF PRESENT ILLNESS (HPI) (place a check mark next to each documented HPI element)

_____ **Location** (of pain/discomfort; is pain diffuse/localized, unilateral/bilateral, does it radiate or refer)

_____ **Quality** (a description of the quality of the symptom [e.g., is pain described as sharp/dull/throbbing/stabbing/constant/intermittent/acute or chronic/stable/improving or worsening])

_____ **Severity** (use of self-assessment scale to measure subjective levels, 1–10, or comparison of pain quantitatively with previously experienced pain)

_____ **Timing** (establishing onset of pain and a rough chronology of pain development [e.g., migraine occurring mornings])

_____ **Context** (where is the patient and what is he doing when pain begins; is patient at rest or involved in an activity; is pain aggravated or relieved, or does it recur with a specific activity; has situational stress or some other factor been present preceding or accompanying the pain)

_____ **Modifying factors** (what has patient attempted to do to relieve pain [e.g., heat vs. cold—does it relieve or exacerbate pain; what makes the pain worse; have over-the-counter drugs been attempted—with what results])

_____ **Associated signs/symptoms** (clinician's impressions formulated during the interview may lead to questioning about additional sensations or feelings [e.g., diaphoresis associated with indigestion or chest pain, blurred vision accompanying a headache, etc.])

_____ **Total Score** (add the check marks and record the total; then place a check mark next to the history type below)

_____ BRIEF HISTORY (1–3 elements)   _____ EXTENDED HISTORY (4 or more elements)

REVIEW OF SYSTEMS (ROS) (place a check mark next to each documented ROS elements)

_____ Constitutional symptoms (e.g., fever, weight loss, etc.)   _____ Genitourinary

_____ Eyes   _____ Musculoskeletal

_____ Ears, nose, mouth, throat   _____ Allergic/Immunologic

_____ Cardiovascular   _____ Hematologic/Lymphatic

_____ Respiratory   _____ Neurological

_____ Gastrointestinal   _____ Psychiatric

_____ Integumentary (including skin and breast)   _____ Endocrine

_____ **Total Score** (add the check marks and record the total; then place a check mark next to the ROS type below)

_____ NONE

_____ PROBLEM-PERTINENT (1 body system documented)

_____ EXTENDED (2–9 body systems documented)

_____ COMPLETE (all body systems documented)

PAST, FAMILY, AND/OR SOCIAL HISTORY (PFSH) (place a check mark next to each documented PFSH element)

_____ Past history (patient's past experience with illnesses, operations, injuries, and treatments)

_____ Family history (review of medical events in the patient's family, including diseases that may be hereditary or place the patient at risk)

_____ Social history (an age-appropriate review of past and current activities)

_____ **Total Score** (add the check marks and record the total; then place a check mark next to the PFSH type below)

_____ NONE

_____ PERTINENT (1 history area documented)

_____ COMPLETE (2 or all 3 history areas documented)

Figure App-2 E&M CodeBuilder.

Circle the type of HPI, ROS, and PFSH and then select the appropriate level of history				
History of Present Illness	Brief	Brief	Extended	Extended
Review of Systems	None	Problem-pertinent	Extended	Complete
Past, Family, Social History	None	None	Pertinent	Complete
Select Level of History	**Problem-focused**	**Expanded problem-focused**	**Detailed**	**Comprehensive**

SELECTING THE LEVEL OF EXAMINATION

GENERAL MULTISYSTEM EXAM (refer to the general multisystem examination requirements in the HCFA *Guidelines for Evaluation and Management Services*. Place a tally mark for each bulleted item documented for each organ system/body area for up to the total number of allowed items [e.g., up to 2 marks can be made for the Neck exam])

_____ Constitutional (2)
_____ Eyes (3)
_____ Ears, nose, mouth, and throat (6)
_____ Neck (2)
_____ Respiratory (4)
_____ Cardiovascular (7)
_____ Chest (Breasts) (2)

_____ Gastrointestinal (5)
_____ Genitourinary (Male: 3; Female: 6)
_____ Lymphatic (4)
_____ Musculoskeletal (6)
_____ Skin (2)
_____ Neurological (3)
_____ Psychiatric (4)

_____ **Total Score** (add the tally marks and record the total; then place a check mark next to the exam type below)

_____ PROBLEM-FOCUSED EXAMINATION (1–5 elements identified by a bullet)
_____ EXPANDED PROBLEM-FOCUSED EXAMINATION (at least 6 elements identified by a bullet)
_____ DETAILED EXAMINATION (at least 2 elements identified by a bullet from each of 6 organ systems/body areas, *or* at least 12 elements identified by a bullet in two or more areas/systems)
_____ COMPREHENSIVE EXAMINATION (perform all elements identified by a bullet in at least 9 organ systems or body areas and document at least 2 elements identified by a bullet from each of 9 organ systems/body areas)

SINGLE ORGAN SYSTEM EXAMINATION (refer to the single organ system examination documentation requirements in the HCFA *Guidelines for Evaluation and Management Services*; place a check next to the appropriate exam type below)

_____ PROBLEM-FOCUSED EXAMINATION (1–5 elements identified by a bullet)
_____ EXPANDED PROBLEM-FOCUSED EXAMINATION (at least 6 elements identified by a bullet)
_____ DETAILED EXAMINATION (at least 12 elements identified by a bullet; NOTE: for eye and psychiatric examinations, at least 9 elements in each box with a shaded border and at least 1 element in each box with an shaded or unshaded border is documented)
_____ COMPREHENSIVE EXAMINATION (all elements identified by a bullet; document every element in each box with a shaded border and at least 1 element in each box with an unshaded box)

Select the appropriate level of medical decision making based upon the following criteria:			
Number of diagnoses or management options	*Amount/complexity of data to be reviewed*	*Risk of complications and/or morbidity/mortality*	*Medical decision making*
Minimal	Minimal or none	Minimal	Straightforward
Limited	Limited	Low	Low complexity
Multiple	Moderate	Moderate	Moderate complexity
Extensive	Extensive	High	High complexity

Figure App-2 (Continued).

Select the E/M code based on selection of level of history, examination, and medical decision making:					
History	Problem-focused	Expanded problem-focused	Expanded problem-focused	Detailed	Comprehensive
Examination	Problem-focused	Expanded problem-focused	Expanded problem-focused	Detailed	Comprehensive
Medical decision making	Straightforward	Low complexity	Moderate complexity	Moderate complexity	High complexity
Go to the appropriate E&M category and select the code based upon the information above					

Figure App-2 (Continued).

Office Visit Codes

New Patient	Established Patient
99201	99211
99202	99212
99203	99213
99204	99214
99205	99215

Office Consultation

New and Established Patients

99241
99242
99243
99244
99245

Inpatient Hospital Codes

Attending/Admitting Physician

Initial Visit	*Subsequent/Follow-up Visit*
99221	99231
99222	99232
99223	99233

Consulting Physician

Initial Visit	*Subsequent/Follow-up Visit*
99251	99231
99252	99232
99253	99233
99254	
99255	

Hospital Discharge

99238 30 minutes or under
99239 more than 30 minutes

ICU/Critical Care

99291 30 to 74 minutes
99292 each additional 30 minutes

Nursing Facility Services Codes

New and Established Patients

Initial Visit	*Subsequent/Follow-up*	*Discharge*
99304	99307	99315 (30 minutes or less)
99305	99308	99316 (more than 30 minutes)
99306	99309	
	99310	

Figure App-3 Evaluation and management codes.

Patient's Name: _____   Medicare # (HICN): _____

ADVANCE BENEFICIARY NOTICE (ABN)

NOTE: You need to make a choice about receiving these health care items or services.

We expect that Medicare will not pay for the item(s) or service(s) that are described below. Medicare does not pay for all of your health care costs. Medicare only pays for covered items and services when Medicare rules are met. The fact that Medicare may not pay for a particular item or service does not mean that you should not receive it. There may be a good reason your doctor recommended it. Right now, in your case, **Medicare probably will not pay for —**

Items or Services:

Because:

The purpose of this form is to help you make an informed choice about whether or not you want to receive these items or services, knowing that you might have to pay for them yourself. Before you make a decision about your options, you should **read this entire notice carefully.**

- Ask us to explain, if you don't understand why Medicare probably won't pay.
- Ask us how much these items or services will cost you (**Estimated Cost: $_____**), in case you have to pay for them yourself or through other insurance.

PLEASE CHOOSE **ONE** OPTION. CHECK **ONE** BOX. **SIGN & DATE** YOUR CHOICE.

☐ **Option 1. YES. I want to receive these items or services.**

I understand that Medicare will not decide whether to pay unless I receive these items or services. Please submit my claim to Medicare. I understand that you may bill me for items or services and that I may have to pay the bill while Medicare is making its decision. If Medicare does pay, you will refund to me any payments I made to you that are due to me. If Medicare denies payment, I agree to be personally and fully responsible for payment. That is, I will pay personally, either out of pocket or through any other insurance that I have. I understand I can appeal Medicare's decision.

☐ **Option 2. NO. I have decided not to receive these items or services.**

I will not receive these items or services. I understand that you will not be able to submit a claim to Medicare and that I will not be able to appeal your opinion that Medicare won't pay.

_____   _____
Date   **Signature of patient or person acting on patient's behalf**

NOTE: **Your health information will be kept confidential.** Any information that we collect about you on this form will be kept confidential in our offices. If a claim is submitted to Medicare, your health information on this form may be shared with Medicare. Your health information which Medicare sees will be kept confidential by Medicare.

OMB Approval No. 0938-0566   Form No. CMS-R-131-G   (June 2002)

Figure App-4 Advance Beneficiary Notice (ABN) form.

NOTICE OF EXCLUSIONS FROM MEDICARE BENEFITS (NEMB)

There are items and services for which Medicare <u>will not pay.</u>

- Medicare does **not** pay for all of your health care costs. Medicare only pays for covered benefits. **Some items and services are not Medicare benefits and Medicare will not pay for them.**

- When you receive an item or service that is **not** a Medicare benefit, **you are responsible to pay for it,** personally or through any other insurance that you may have.

  The purpose of this notice is to help you make an informed choice about whether or not you want to receive these items or services, knowing that you will have to pay for them yourself. **Before you make a decision, you should read this entire notice carefully.**
  Ask us to explain, if you don't understand why Medicare won't pay.
  Ask us how much these items or services will cost you (**Estimated Cost: $_____**).

Medicare will not pay for: _____
_____;

☐ **1. Because it does not meet the definition of any Medicare benefit.**

☐ **2. Because of the following exclusion * from Medicare benefits:**

☐ Personal comfort items.	☐ Routine physicals and most tests for screening.
☐ Most shots (vaccinations).	☐ Routine eye care, eyeglasses and examinations.
☐ Hearing aids and hearing examinations.	☐ Cosmetic surgery.
☐ Most outpatient prescription drugs.	☐ Dental care and dentures (in most cases).
☐ Orthopedic shoes and foot supports (orthotics).	☐ Routine foot care and flat foot care.
☐ Health care received outside of the USA.	☐ Services by immediate relatives.
☐ Services required as a result of war.	☐ Services under a physician's private contract.

☐ Services paid for by a governmental entity that is not Medicare.
☐ Services for which the patient has no legal obligation to pay.
☐ Home health services furnished under a plan of care, if the agency does not submit the claim.
☐ Items and services excluded under the Assisted Suicide Funding Restriction Act of 1997.
☐ Items or services furnished in a competitive acquisition area by any entity that does not have a contract with the Department of Health and Human Services (except in a case of urgent need).
☐ Physicians' services performed by a physician assistant, midwife, psychologist, or nurse anesthetist, when furnished to an inpatient, unless they are furnished under arrangements by the hospital.
☐ Items and services furnished to an individual who is a resident of a skilled nursing facility (a SNF) or of a part of a facility that includes a SNF, unless they are furnished under arrangements by the SNF.
☐ Services of an assistant at surgery without prior approval from the peer review organization.
☐ Outpatient occupational and physical therapy services furnished incident to a physician's services.

* **This is only a general summary of exclusions from Medicare benefits. It is not a legal document. The official Medicare program provisions are contained in relevant laws, regulations, and rulings.**

Figure App-5 Notice of Exclusions from Medicare Benefits (NEMB) form.

CMS
CENTERS for MEDICARE & MEDICAID SERVICES

MEDICARE
Part B Carrier

Please send any overpayment refunds to:

For NY: Empire Medicare Services
Accounting Department
P.O. Box 4776
Syracuse, NY 13221-4776

For NJ: Empire Medicare Services
Cashier
P.O. Box 69216
Harrisburg, PA 17106-9216

TO BE COMPLETED BY MEDICARE CONTRACTOR

Date: _____

Contractor Deposit Control # _____   Date of Deposit:_____

Contractor Contact Name:_____   Phone Number: _____

Contractor Address:_____

Contractor Fax Number: _____

TO BE COMPLETED BY PROVIDER/PHYSICIAN/SUPPLIER, OR OTHER ENTITY

Please complete and forward to Medicare Contractor. This form, or a similar document containing the following information, should accompany every voluntary refund so that receipt of check is properly recorded and applied.

PROVIDER/PHYSICIAN/SUPPLIER OR OTHER ENTITY NAME: _____

ADDRESS:_____

PROVIDER/PHYSICIAN/SUPPLIER #:_____   TAX ID #:_____

CONTACT PERSON: _____   PHONE #:_____

AMOUNT OF CHECK: $_____   CHECK #: _____   CHECK DATE: _____

REFUND INFORMATION

For each claim, provide the following:

Patient Name_____Date of Service _____HIC#_____

Medicare Claim Number _____   Claim Amount Refunded $_____

Reason Code for Claim Adjustment: _____   (Select reason code from list below. Use one reason per claim.)

(Please list all claim numbers involved. Attach separate sheet, if necessary.)

Note: If Specific Patient/HIC/Claim #/Claim Amount data not available for all claims due to Statistical Sampling, please indicate methodology and formula used to determine amount and reason for overpayment:

Note: If specific patient/HIC/Claim # information is not provided, no appeal rights can be afforded with respect to this refund. Providers/physicians/suppliers, and other entities who are submitting a refund under the OIG's Self-Disclosure Protocol are not afforded appeal rights as stated in the signed agreement presented by the OIG.

For Institutional Facilities Only:

Cost Report Year(s) _____

(If multiple cost report years are involved, provide a breakdown by amount and corresponding cost report year.)

For OIG Reporting Requirements:

Do you have a Corporate Integrity Agreement with OIG? _____Yes   _____No

Are you a participant in the OIG Self-Disclosure Protocol? _____Yes   _____No

---

Reason Codes:

Billing/Clerical Error	**MSP/Other Payer Involvement**	**Miscellaneous**
01 - Corrected Date of Service	07 - MSP Group Health Plan Insurance	12 - Insufficient Documentation
02 - Duplicate	08 - MSP No Fault Insurance	13 - Patient enrolled in an HMO
03 - Corrected CPT Code	09 - MSP Liability Insurance	14 - Services Not Rendered
04 - Not Our Patient(s)	10 - MSP, Workers' Comp.	15 - Medical Necessity
05 - Modifier Added/Removed	(Including Black Lung)	16 - Other (Please Specify)
06 - Billed in Error	11 - Veterans Administration	_____

PROVIDER/PHYSICIAN/SUPPLIER OR AUTHORIZED REPRESENTATIVE NAME (PRINTED)

_____

TITLE/POSITION

_____   _____

SIGNATURE   DATE   MC2843 Rev. 07/01/2004

Figure App-6 CMS Overpayment/Refund form.

PRACTICE NAME
Practice Street Address
Suite X
Practice City, State Zip
Practice Phone Number

REQUEST FOR OPINION

Consultation request from: Doctor "A"
Doctor "B"
Doctor "C"

To: Consultant's Name: _____

Specialty: _____

Re: Patient Name: _____

Date: _____

Please provide an opinion and consult for the above-named patient. This patient is being sent to you for the following reasons:

_____

_____

_____

_____

_____

_____

_____

We understand that you may initiate treatment or perform medically necessary diagnostics for this patient. We look forward to your opinion and plan of care:

_____

Practice Name
"A", MD
"B", DO
"C", MD

Figure App-7 Request for opinion/consult.

Sample Letter
Refusal to Authorize Payment

Chairperson
Utilization Review Committee

Dear _____ ,

On ____(DATE)____ , I prescribed _____(TEST/PROCEDURE)_____ for _____(PATIENT'S NAME)_____ .

On ____(DATE)____ , you refused to authorize payment for that _____(TEST/PROCEDURE)_____ . I find that I must take issue with your determination for the following reasons:

(List reasons and if applicable, include any prior examples where a payer
approved this recommendation and/or examples of how this
test/procedure was effective before.)

In my medical judgment, a _____(TEST/PROCEDURE)_____ is a very important part of my overall

care of ___(PATIENT'S NAME)___ . ___(PATIENT'S NAME)___ suffers from ___(DESCRIBE CONDITION)___ .

The _____(TEST/PROCEDURE)_____ is necessary to ___(DESCRIBE WHY NECESSARY)___ .

Failure to perform the _____(TEST/PROCEDURE)_____ could result in the following problems:

(DESCRIBE PROBLEMS)

For these reasons, I urge you to reconsider your refusal to authorize payment for the procedure I have prescribed.

By copy of this letter to _____(PATIENT'S NAME)_____ , I am reiterating my suggestion that

he/she obtain the ___(TEST/PROCEDURE)___ , despite your refusal to authorize payment, for the

reasons I have set forth in this letter and in prior discussions with _____(PATIENT'S NAME)_____ .

Yours truly,

(YOUR NAME)

cc: (PATIENT'S NAME)

Figure App-8 Refusal to authorize payment (sample letter).

Sample Letter
Informed Refusal

Patient Name
Patient Address

Dear _____ ,

On _____(DATE)_____ , I prescribed _____(TEST/PROCEDURE)_____ . On ____(DATE)____ ,

_____(NAME OF PPO, IPA, HMO)_____ refused to authorize payment for same. On that basis, you

have informed me of your decision to forego the _____(TEST/PROCEDURE)_____ I have prescribed.

I expressed my concerns regarding your decision during our discussion on _____(DATE)_____ about

the potential ramifications of your refusal to undergo the _____(TEST/PROCEDURE)_____ .

I recommend you appeal the _____(NAME OF PPO, IPA, HMO)_____ denial of benefits and

reconsider your decision to forego the _____(TEST/PROCEDURE)_____ in light of the potential
consequences of your refusal. My staff can assist you with the appeal.

Please call _____(NAME OF STAFF PERSON)_____ if you would like our assistance.

Should you wish to discuss this further, please do not hesitate to contact me.

Sincerely yours,

(YOUR NAME)

Figure App-9 Informed refusal (sample letter).

[Practice Name]

CODE OF CONDUCT

I. INTRODUCTION

The medical practice of *[practice name]* will hereinafter be referred to as *[practice name]*.
     This Code of Conduct sets forth *[practice name]*'s *Principles* and *Standards* for all *[practice name]* employees as those Principles and Standards specifically relate to *[practice name]*'s compliance efforts pursuant to federal laws, rules, and standards of the Medicare/Medicaid programs. The Principles articulate the policies of *[practice name]* and the Standards are intended to provide additional guidance to persons functioning in managerial or administrative capacities. The Principles set forth in this Code of Conduct shall be distributed to all physicians and employees. The Code of Conduct will be updated as necessary; *[practice name]* will distribute any change or update by sending each employee an individual copy. All employees are responsible to ensure that their behavior and activities are consistent with this Code of Conduct.

II. PURPOSE

This Code of Conduct has been adopted by the *[practice name],* Inc. Board of Directors to provide standards by which employees of *[practice name]* will conduct themselves in order to protect and promote corporation-wide integrity and to enhance *[practice name]*'s ability to achieve *[practice name]*'s mission.

III. LEGAL COMPLIANCE

A. Principle

[Practice name] will strive to ensure that all activity by or on behalf of the professional corporation is in compliance with applicable federal and state laws and regulations, as they specifically relate to the prohibitions against the filing of false or fraudulent claims with Medicare, Medicaid, or other federally funded health care programs. All employees of *[practice name]* are expected to support the professional corporation in its commitment.

B. Standards

The following standards are intended to provide guidance to management and employees in administrative positions to assist them in their obligation to comply with applicable laws. These standards are neither exclusive nor complete. Employees are required to comply with all applicable laws, whether or not specifically addressed in this Code of Conduct. If questions regarding the existence, interpretation, or application of any law arise, they should be directed to *[practice name]*'s Compliance Officer or *[practice name]*'s respective Accounts Manager, who shall refer all legal issues to *[practice name]*'s outside legal counsel.

1. **Antitrust.** All employees must comply with applicable antitrust and similar laws that regulate competition. Examples of conduct prohibited by the laws include: (1) agreements to fix prices, bid rigging, and collusion (including price sharing) with competitors; (2) boycotts, certain exclusive dealing and price discrimination agreements; and (3) unfair trade practices, including bribery, misappropriation of trade secrets, deception, intimidation, and similar unfair practices. *[Practice name]*

Figure App-10 Code of Conduct.

employees in managerial or administrative positions are expected to seek advice from *[practice name]*'s Compliance Officer, who shall refer the issue to *[practice name]*'s outside legal counsel when confronted with business decisions involving a risk of violation of the antitrust laws.

2. **Fraud and Abuse.** *[Practice name]* expects its employees to refrain from conduct that may violate the fraud and abuse laws. These laws prohibit (1) direct, indirect, or disguised payments in exchange for the referral of patients; (2) the submission of false, fraudulent, or misleading claims to any government entity, including claims for services not rendered, claims that characterize the service as different from the service actually rendered, or claims that do not otherwise comply with applicable program or contractual requirements; and (3) making false representations to any person or entity in order to gain or retain participation in a program or to obtain payment for any service. (For additional guidance, please refer to the *[practice name]* Fraud and Abuse Compliance Policy and the *[practice name]* Corporate Compliance Plan.)

3. **Discrimination.** *[Practice name]* believes that the fair and equitable treatment of employees, patients, and other persons is critical to fulfilling its vision and goals. It is a policy of *[practice name]* to treat patients without regard to the race, color, religion, sex, ethnic origin, age, or disability of such person, or any other classification prohibited by law. It is a policy of *[practice name]* to recruit, hire, train, promote, assign, transfer, lay off, recall, and terminate employees based on their own ability, achievement, experience, and conduct, without regard to race, color, religion, sex, ethnic origin, age, or disability, or any other classification prohibited by law. No form of harassment or discrimination on the basis of sex, race, color, disability, age, religion, ethnic origin, or disability, or any other classification prohibited by law will be permitted. Each allegation of harassment or discrimination will be promptly investigated.

4. **Stark.** All employees must comply with applicable Stark regulations and similar laws that regulate self-referral and compensation. Examples of provisions included in these laws are: (1) agreements for "kickbacks" between doctors and providers; (2) supervision by referring physicians of those providing designated health services to qualify for the in-office ancillary service exception; (3) managed care exemptions; (4) exception when no alternative provider is available; (5) reporting of provider financial relationships and those of their immediate families; and (6) a list of designated health services that are covered by the self-referral ban. *[Practice name]* employees in managerial or administrative positions are expected to seek advice from *[practice name]*'s Compliance Officer, who shall refer the issue to *[practice name]*'s outside legal counsel when confronted with business decisions involving a risk of violation of the self-referral and compensation laws.

5. **OSHA.** All employees must comply with *[practice name]*'s OSHA Policy Manual.

6. **ADA.** *[Practice name]* and *[practice name]*'s employees will comply with the Americans with Disabilities Act (ADA). The ADA prohibits discrimination on the basis of disability in employment. It also prohibits discrimination on the basis of disability for goods and services provided to *[practice name]* patients. Each allegation of discrimination will be promptly investigated.

IV. BUSINESS ETHICS

A. Principle

In furtherance of *[practice name]*'s commitment to the highest standards of business ethics and integrity, employees shall strive to accurately and honestly represent *[practice name]* and shall strive not to engage in any activity or scheme intended to defraud anyone of money, property, or honest services. Furthermore, any *[practice name]*

Figure App-10 (Continued).

employee who becomes aware of any potential violation of the federal fraud and abuse laws shall have the primary obligation to report such potential wrongdoing to the professional corporation.

B. Standards

The standards set forth below are designed to provide guidance to ensure that *[practice name]*'s business activities reflect the highest standards of business ethics and integrity. Employee conduct not specifically addressed by these standards must be consistent with *[practice name]*'s Principle with respect to business ethics.

1. **Honest Communication.** *[Practice name]* requires candor and honesty from its employees in the performance of their responsibilities and in communication with *[practice name]*'s Compliance Officer. No employee shall make false or misleading statements to any patient, person, or entity doing business with *[practice name]* about other patients, persons, or entities doing business or competing with *[practice name]*, or about the products or services of *[practice name]* or its competitors.

2. **Misappropriation of Proprietary Information.** *[Practice name]* employees shall not misappropriate confidential or proprietary information belonging to another person or entity nor utilize any publication, document, computer program, information, or product in violation of a third party's interest in such product. All *[practice name]* employees are responsible to ensure that they do not improperly copy, for their own use, documents or computer programs in violation of applicable copyright laws or licensing agreements. Employees shall not utilize confidential business information obtained from competitors, including customer lists, price lists, contracts, or other information, in violation of a covenant not to compete, prior employment agreements, or in any other manner likely to provide an unfair competitive advantage to *[practice name]*.

3. **Fraud and Abuse.** *[Practice name]* expects its employees to refrain from conduct that may violate the fraud and abuse laws. These laws prohibit: (1) direct, indirect, or disguised payments in exchange for the referral of patients; (2) the submission of false, fraudulent, or misleading claims to any government entity, including claims for services not rendered, claims that characterize the service as different from the service actually rendered, or claims that do not otherwise comply with applicable program or contractual requirements; and (3) making false representations to any person or entity in order to gain or retain participation in a program or to obtain payment for any service. (For additional guidance, please refer to the *[practice name]* Fraud and Abuse Compliance Policy and the *[practice name]* Corporate Compliance Plan.) If a *[practice name]* employee becomes aware of any wrongdoing under the standards set forth in the *[practice name]* Compliance Program, whether committed by that employee or by someone else, that employee is obligated to report such wrongdoing to *[practice name]* in a manner procedurally consistent and in accordance with the *[practice name]* Corporate Compliance Plan and any and all written *[practice name]* compliance policies.

V. CONFIDENTIALITY

A. Principle

[Practice name] employees shall strive to maintain the confidentiality of patients and other confidential information in accordance with applicable legal and ethical standards.

Figure App-10 (Continued).

B. Standards

[Practice name] and its employees are in possession of and have access to a broad variety of confidential, sensitive, and proprietary information, the inappropriate release of which could be injurious to individuals, *[practice name]* business partners, and *[practice name]* itself. Every *[practice name]* employee has an obligation to actively protect and safeguard confidential, sensitive, and proprietary information in a manner designed to prevent the unauthorized disclosure of information.

1. **Patient Information.** All *[practice name]* employees have an obligation to conduct themselves in accordance with the principle of maintaining the confidentiality of patient information in accordance with all applicable laws and regulations. Employees shall refrain from revealing any personal or confidential information concerning patients unless supported by legitimate business or patient care purposes. If questions arise regarding an obligation to maintain the confidentiality of information or the appropriateness of releasing information, employees should seek guidance from *[practice name]* management or *[practice name]*'s Compliance Officer.

2. **Proprietary Information.** Information, ideas, and intellectual property assets of *[practice name]* are important to the corporation's success. Information pertaining to *[practice name]*'s competitive position or business strategies, payment and reimbursement information, and information relating to negotiations with employees or third parties should be protected and shared only with employees having a need to know such information in order to perform their job responsibilities. Employees should exercise care to ensure that intellectual property rights, including patents, trademarks, copyrights, and software, are carefully maintained and managed to preserve and protect the value of the intellectual property.

3. **Personnel Actions/Decisions.** Salary, benefit, and other personal information relating to employees shall be treated as confidential. Personnel files, payroll information, disciplinary matters, and similar information shall be maintained in a manner designed to ensure confidentiality in accordance with applicable laws. Employees will exercise due care to prevent the release or sharing of information beyond those persons who may need such information to fulfill their job functions.

VI. ADMINISTRATION AND APPLICATION OF THIS CODE OF CONDUCT

[Practice name] expects each person to whom this Code of Conduct applies to abide by the Principles and Standards set forth herein and to conduct the business and affairs of *[practice name]* in a manner consistent with the general statement of principles set forth herein.

Failure to abide by this Code of Conduct or the guidelines for behavior that the Code of Conduct represents may lead to disciplinary action. For alleged violations of the Code of Conduct, *[practice name]* will weigh relevant facts and circumstances, including, but not limited to, the extent to which the behavior was contrary to the express language or general intent of the Code of Conduct, the egregiousness of the behavior, the employee's history with the corporation, and other factors that *[practice name]* deems relevant. Discipline for failure to abide by the Code of Conduct may, in *[practice name]*'s discretion, range from oral correction to termination.

Nothing in this Code of Conduct is intended to nor shall be construed as providing any additional employment or contract rights to employees or other persons.

Although *[practice name]* will generally attempt to communicate changes concurrent with or prior to the implementation of such changes, *[practice name]* reserves the right to modify, amend, or alter the Code of Conduct without notice to any person or employee.

Figure App-10 (Continued).

Figure App-11 UB-04 form.

Appendix III
Commonly Used Acronyms in Medical Billing and Coding

AAPC	American Academy of Professional Coders
ABN	Advance Beneficiary Notice
AHIMA	American Health Information Management Association
AMA	American Medical Association
AMBA	American Medical Billing Association
BA	body area
BLK LUNG	black lung
C	comprehensive
CBCS	Certified Billing and Coding Specialist
CC	chief complaint
CCA	Certified Coding Associate
CCS	Certified Coding Specialist
CCSPB	Certified Coding Specialist, Physician Based
CCYY	year: indicates entry of two digits each for century and year
CHAMPUS	Civilian Health and Medical Program of the Uniformed Services
CHAMPVA	Civilian Health and Medical Program of the Department of Veterans Affairs
CLIA	Clinical Laboratory Improvement Amendments
CMRS	Certified Medical Reimbursement Specialist
CMS	Centers for Medicare and Medicaid Services
COB	coordination of benefits
CPT	*Current Procedural Terminology*
D	detailed
DD	day: indicates entry of two digits for the day
DHHS	Department of Health and Human Services
DME	durable medical equipment
Dx	diagnosis
E&M	evaluation and management
EDI	electronic data interchange

EFT	electronic funds transfer
EIN	Employer Identification Number
EMG	emergency
EOB	explanation of benefits
EP	established patient
EPF	expanded problem-focused
EPSDT	early and periodic screening, diagnosis, and treatment
ERA	electronic remittance advice
EX	exam
F	female
FECA	Federal Employees' Compensation Act
GTIN	Global Trade Item number
H	high
HCFA	Health Care Financing Administration
HCPCS	Healthcare Common Procedure Coding System
HIBCC	Health Industry Business Communications Council
HIC	health insurance claim
HIPAA	Health Insurance Portability and Accountability Act of 1996
HMO	health maintenance organization
HPI	history of present illness
HX	history
ICD-9-CM	*Internal Classification of Diseases, 9th Revision, Clinical Modification*
ICN	internal control number
ID or I.D.	identification
INFO	information
IP	inpatient
IPPE	initial preventive (preventative) physical examination
L	low
LMP	last menstrual period
M	male
M	moderate
MCO	managed care organization
MDM	medical decision making
MFS	Medicare fee schedule
MM	month: indicates entry of two digits for the month
NCQA	National Committee for Quality Assurance
NDC	National Drug Codes
NEBA	National Electronic Biller Alliance
NEMB	Notice of Exclusion from Medicare Benefits
NHA	National Healthcareer Association
No.	number
NONPAR	nonparticipating provider
NP	new patient
NPI	National Provider Identification

NUCC	National Uniform Claim Committee
NUCC-DS	National Uniform Claim Committee Data Set
OCR	optical character reader (*or* recognition)
OMB	Office of Management and Budget
OP	outpatient
OS	organ system
OZ	product number (Health Care Uniform Code Council)
PAR	participating provider
PCP	primary care provider
PF	problem-focused
PFSH	past family and social history
PH	phone number
PIN	provider identification number
POS	point of service
PPMP	physician-performed microsurgery procedures
PPO	preferred provider organization
QUAL	qualifier
REF	reference
ROS	review of systems
Rx	prescription
SF	straightforward
SOF	signature on file
SPR	standard paper remittance
SSN	Social Security number
UCR	usual and customary rate
UPC	Universal Product Code
UPIN	unique provider identification number
USIN	universal supplier identification number
VP	vendor product number
YY	year: indicates entry of two digits for the year (see also CCYY)

Appendix IV
Medicare Part B
Carriers by State

Note: Please remember that this information is subject to change. You can obtain the most current information online at http://www.cms.hhs.gov

Alabama (Regional Office: Atlanta)
Part B—Blue Cross and Blue Shield of Alabama

Alabama office:
MSID-F00005
450 Riverchase Parkway East
Birmingham, AL 35244
PO Box 830139
Birmingham, AL 35283-1039
almedicare@bcbsal.org

Alaska (Regional Office: Seattle)
Part B—Noridian Mutual Insurance Company
Noridian Mutual Insurance Company
4305 13th Avenue, S.W.
Fargo, ND 58103

Arizona (Regional Office: San Francisco)
Part B—Noridian Mutual Insurance Company
Noridian Mutual Insurance Company
4305 13th Avenue, S.W.
Fargo, ND 58103

Arkansas (Regional Office: Dallas)
Part B—Arkansas Blue Cross and Blue Shield, A Mutual Insurance Company

Mailing address: AR Medicare Services Operations
Medicare Services
PO Box 1418
Little Rock, AR. 72203
www.arkmedicare.com

California (Regional Office: San Francisco)
Part B—National Heritage Insurance Company
National Heritage Insurance Company
402 Otterson Drive
Chico, CA 95928
www.medicarenhic.com

Colorado (Regional Office: Denver)
Part B—Noridian Mutual Insurance Company
Noridian Mutual Insurance Company
4305 13th Avenue, S.W.
Fargo, ND 58103

Connecticut (Regional Office: Boston)
Part B—First Coast Service Options, Inc. (First Coast Service Options)

Mailing address for claims and correspondence (Connecticut—Part B Only):
First Coast Service Options, Inc.
PO Box 9000
Meriden, CT 06540

Delaware (Regional Office: Philadelphia)
Part B—TrailBlazer Health Enterprises, LLC

Mailing address:
TrailBlazer Health Enterprises, LLC
PO Box 660156
Dallas, TX 75266-0156

Street address:
TrailBlazer Health Enterprises, LLC
8330 LBJ Freeway
Executive Center 3
Dallas, TX 75243
www.trailblazerhealth.com

District of Columbia (Regional Office: Philadelphia)
Part B—TrailBlazer Health Enterprises, LLC
TrailBlazer Health Enterprises, LLC
PO Box 660156
Dallas, TX 75266-0156
www.trailblazerhealth.com

Florida (Regional Office: Atlanta)
Part B—First Coast Service Options, Inc. (First Coast Service Options)

Mailing address for Part B claims:
First Coast Service Options, Inc. (Florida)
PO Box 2525
Jacksonville, FL 32231-0048

Mailing address for correspondence:
First Coast Service Options, Inc. (Florida)
PO Box 2360
Jacksonville, FL 32231-0048

Georgia (Regional Office: Atlanta)
Part B—Blue Cross and Blue Shield of Alabama
Blue Cross and Blue Shield of Alabama
PO Box 830139
Birmingham, AL 35283-1039

Hawaii (Regional Office: San Francisco)
Part B—Noridian Mutual Insurance Company
Noridian Mutual Insurance Company
4305 13th Avenue, S.W.
Fargo, ND 58103

Idaho (Regional Office: Seattle)
Part B—Connecticut General Life Insurance Company (CGLIC), a CIGNA Company
Connecticut General Life Insurance Company
Hartford, CT 06152
www.cignamedicare.com

Illinois (Regional Office: Chicago)
Part B—Wisconsin Physicians Service
Administration
PO Box 8190
Madison, WI 53708

Illinois claims:
Administration
PO Box 1030
Marion, IL 62959

Indiana (Regional Office: Chicago)
Part B—AdminaStar Federal, Inc.
Adminastar Federal, Inc.
8115 Knue Road
Indianapolis, IN 46250
www.adminastar.com

Iowa (Regional Office: Kansas City)
Part B—Noridian Mutual Insurance Company
Noridian Mutual Insurance Company
4305 13th Avenue, S.W.
Fargo, ND 58103

Kansas (Regional Office: Kansas City)
Part B—Blue Cross and Blue Shield of Kansas, Inc.
Blue Cross and Blue Shield of Kansas, Inc.
PO Box 239
Topeka, KS 66601
bc.medicare@bcbsks.com

Kentucky (Regional Office: Atlanta)
Part B—AdminaStar Federal, Inc.
Adminastar Federal, Inc.
8115 Knue Road
Indianapolis, IN 46250
www.adminastar.com

Louisiana (Regional Office: Dallas)
Part B—Arkansas Blue Cross and Blue Shield, A Mutual Insurance Company

Louisiana Part B operations:
Pinnacle Medicare Services—Louisiana Correspondence
PO Box 8066
Little Rock, AR 72203-8066
www.lamedicare.com

Maine (Regional Office: Boston)
Part B—National Heritage Insurance Company
National Heritage Insurance Company
402 Otterson Drive
Chico, CA 95928
www.medicarenhic.com

Maryland (Regional Office: Philadelphia)
Part B—TrailBlazer Health Enterprises, LLC
TrailBlazer Health Enterprises, LLC
PO Box 660156
Dallas, TX 75266-0156
www.trailblazerhealth.com

Massachusetts (Regional Office: Boston)
Part B—National Heritage Insurance Company
National Heritage Insurance Company
402 Otterson Drive
Chico, CA 95928
www.medicarenhic.com

Michigan (Regional Office: Chicago)
Part B—Wisconsin Physicians Service

Wisconsin claims:
Wisconsin Physicians Service Insurance Corporation
PO Box 1787
Madison, WI 53701

Minnesota (Regional Office: Chicago)
Part B—Wisconsin Physicians Service

Minnesota claims:
Wisconsin Physicians Service Insurance Corporation
8120 Penn Avenue South
Bloomington, MN 55431

Mississippi (Regional Office: Atlanta)
Part B—Blue Cross and Blue Shield of Alabama
Blue Cross and Blue Shield of Alabama
PO Box 22545
Jackson, MS 39225-2545
msmedicare@cahabag.com

Missouri (Regional Office: Kansas City)
Part B—Blue Cross and Blue Shield of Kansas, Inc. (Western Missouri)
Blue Cross and Blue Shield of Kansas, Inc.
PO Box 239
Topeka, KS 66601
bc.medicare@bcbsks.com

Part B—Arkansas Blue Cross and Blue Shield, A Mutual Insurance Company
    (Eastern Missouri)
Arkansas Blue Cross and Blue Shield
Eastern Missouri Part B Satellite Office
12755 Olive Street
St. Louis, MO 63141
www.momedicare.com

Montana (Regional Office: Denver)
Part B—Blue Cross and Blue Shield of Montana, Inc.
Blue Cross and Blue Shield of Montana, Inc. (Part B)
PO Box 4310
2501 Beltview
Helena, MT 59604
thubbard@bcbsmt.com

Nebraska (Regional Office: Kansas City)
Part B—Blue Cross and Blue Shield of Kansas, Inc.
Blue Cross and Blue Shield of Kansas, Inc.
PO Box 239
Topeka, KS 66601
bc.medicare@bcbsks.com

Nevada (Regional Office: San Francisco)
Part B—Noridian Mutual Insurance Company
Noridian Mutual Insurance Company
4305 13th Avenue, S.W.
Fargo, ND 58103

New Hampshire (Regional Office: Boston/San Francisco)
Part B—National Heritage Insurance Company
National Heritage Insurance Company
402 Otterson Drive
Chico, CA 95928
www.medicarenhic.com

New Jersey (Regional Office: New York)
Part B—National Government Services
National Government Services
PO Box 69201
Harrisburg, PA 17106-9201

New Mexico (Regional Office: Dallas)
Part B—Arkansas Blue Cross and Blue Shield, A Mutual Insurance Company
Arkansas Blue Cross and Blue Shield
Oklahoma/New Mexico Part B Operations
701 NW 63rd
Oklahoma City, OK 73116
www.oknmmedicare.com

New York (Regional Office: New York)
Part B—HealthNow New York Inc.; Empire HealthChoice Assurance, Inc.; Group Health Incorporated
HealthNow New York Inc.
PO Box 80
Buffalo, NY 14240-0080
www.umd.nycpic.com

National Government Services
PO Box 69201
Harrisburg, PA 17106-9201

Group Health Incorporated
25 Broadway
New York, NY 10004

North Carolina (Regional Office: Atlanta)
Part B—Connecticut General Life Insurance Company (CGLIC), a CIGNA Company
Connecticut General Life Insurance Company
Hartford, CT 06152
cignapartb@cigna.com
cignadmerc@cigna.com
www.cignamedicare.com

North Dakota (Regional Office: Denver)
Part B—Noridian Mutual Insurance Company
Noridian Mutual Insurance Company
4305 13th Avenue, S.W.
Fargo, ND 58103

Ohio (Regional Office: Chicago)
Part B—Blue Cross and Blue Shield of South Carolina (d/b/a Palmetto GBA)

Operations offices:
Blue Cross and Blue Shield of South Carolina
PO Box 100190
Columbia, SC 29202-3190

Overnight mail:
Blue Cross and Blue Shield of South Carolina
2300 Springdale Drive
Building One
Camden, SC 29020

Oklahoma (Regional Office: Dallas)
Part B—Arkansas Blue Cross and Blue Shield, A Mutual Insurance Company
Arkansas Blue Cross and Blue Shield
Oklahoma/New Mexico Part B Operations
701 NW 63rd
Oklahoma City, OK 73116
www.oknmmedicare.com

Oregon (Regional Office: Seattle)
Part B—Noridian Mutual Insurance Company
Noridian Mutual Insurance Company
4305 13th Avenue, S.W.
Fargo, ND 58103

Pennsylvania (Regional Office: Philadelphia)
Part B—Highmark, Inc. (d/b/a HGSAdministrators)
Highmark, Inc.
PO Box 890065
Camp Hill, PA 17089-0065

Express mail:
Highmark, Inc.
1800 Center Street
Camp Hill, PA 17089
www.hgsa.com

Puerto Rico (Regional Office: New York)
Part B—Triple-S, Inc.
Triple-S, Inc.
Box 71391
San Juan, PR 00936-1391
mortiz@triples-med.org
www.triples-med.org

Rhode Island (Regional Office: Boston)
Part B—Pinnacle Medicare Services

Operations offices:
Pinnacle Medicare Services
PO Box 3470
Little Rock, AR 72203-3470

South Carolina (Regional Office: Atlanta)
Part B—Blue Cross and Blue Shield of South Carolina (d/b/a Palmetto GBA)

Operations offices:
Blue Cross and Blue Shield of South Carolina
PO Box 100190
Columbia, SC 29202-3190

Overnight mail:
Blue Cross and Blue Shield of South Carolina
2300 Springdale Drive
Building One
Camden, SC 29020

South Dakota (Regional Office: Denver)
Part B—Noridian Mutual Insurance Company
Noridian Mutual Insurance Company
4305 13th Avenue, S.W.
Fargo, ND 58103

Tennessee (Regional Office: Atlanta)
Part B—Connecticut General Life Insurance Company (CGLIC), a CIGNA Company
Connecticut General Life Insurance Company
Hartford, Connecticut 06152
cignapartb@cigna.com
cignadmerc@cigna.com
www.cignamedicare.com

Texas (Regional Office: Dallas)
Part B—TrailBlazer Health Enterprises, LLC
TrailBlazer Health Enterprises, LLC
PO Box 660156
Dallas, TX 75266-0156
tb.mail@trailblazerhealth.com

U.S. Virgin Islands (Regional Office: New York)
Part B—Triple-S, Inc.
Triple-S, Inc.
Box 71391
San Juan, PR 00936-1391
mortiz@triples-med.org
www.triples-med.org

Utah (Regional Office: Denver)
Part B—Blue Cross and Blue Shield of Utah
Regence Blue Cross and Blue Shield of Utah
PO Box 30269
Salt Lake City, UT 84130-0269
ut.medicaregeneral@regence.com

Vermont (Regional Office: Boston/San Francisco)
Part B—National Heritage Insurance Company
National Heritage Insurance Company
402 Otterson Drive
Chico, CA 95928
www.medicarenhic.com

Virginia (Regional Office: Philadelphia)
Part B—TrailBlazer Health Enterprises, LLC
TrailBlazer Health Enterprises, LLC
PO Box 660156
Dallas, TX 75266-0156
tb.mail@trailblazerhealth.com

Washington (Regional Office: Seattle)
Part B—Noridian Mutual Insurance Company
Noridian Mutual Insurance Company
4305 13th Avenue, S.W.
Fargo, ND 58103

West Virginia (Regional Office: Philadelphia)
Part B—Blue Cross and Blue Shield of South Carolina (d/b/a Palmetto GBA)

Operations offices:
Blue Cross and Blue Shield of South Carolina
PO Box 100190
Columbia, SC 29202-3190

Overnight mail:
Blue Cross and Blue Shield of South Carolina
2300 Springdale Drive
Building One
Camden, SC 29020

Wisconsin (Regional Office: Chicago)
Part B—Wisconsin Physicians Service Insurance Corporation

Wisconsin claims:
Wisconsin Physicians Service Insurance Corporation
PO Box 1787
Madison, WI 53701

Wyoming (Regional Office: Denver)
Part B—Noridian Mutual Insurance Company
Noridian Mutual Insurance Company
4305 13th Avenue, S.W.
Fargo, ND 58103

Appendix V
Insurance Commissioners by State

Note: Please remember that this information is subject to change. You can obtain the most current information online at http://www.naic.org

Alabama

Walter Bell, Commissioner
Alabama Department of Insurance
201 Monroe Street, Suite 1700
Montgomery, AL 36104
http://www.aldoi.gov

Alaska

Linda Hall, Director
Alaska Division of Insurance
550 West 7th Avenue, Suite 1560
Anchorage, AK 99501-3567
http://www.dced.state.ak.us

Arizona

Christina Urias, Director
Arizona Department of Insurance
2910 North 44th Street, Suite 210
Phoenix, AZ 85018-7256
http://www.id.state.az.us

Arkansas

Julie Benafield Bowman, Commissioner
Arkansas Department of Insurance
1200 West 3rd Street
Little Rock, AR 72201-1904
http://insurance.arkansas.gov

California

Steve Poizner, Commissioner
California Department of Insurance
300 Capitol Mall, Suite 1700
Sacramento, CA 95814
http://www.insurance.ca.gov

Colorado

Marcy Morrison, Commissioner
Colorado Division of Insurance
1560 Broadway, Suite 850
Denver, CO 80202
http://www.dora.state.co.us

Connecticut

Susan F. Cogswell, Commissioner
Connecticut Department of Insurance
PO Box 816
Hartford, CT 06142-0816
http://www.ct.gov

Delaware

Matt Denn, Commissioner
Delaware Department of Insurance
Rodney Building
841 Silver Lake Boulevard
Dover, DE 19904
http://www.state.de.us

District of Columbia

Thomas E. Hampton, Acting Commissioner
Department of Insurance, Securities Regulation and Banking
Government of the District of Columbia
810 First Street, N.E., Suite 701
Washington, DC 20002
http://disr.washingtondc.gov

Florida

Kevin McCarty, Commissioner
Office of Insurance Regulation
Florida Department of Financial Services
State of Florida
200 East Gaines Street, Room 101A
Tallahassee, FL 32399-0301
http://www.floir.com

Georgia

John Oxendine, Commissioner
Georgia Department of Insurance
2 Martin Luther King, Jr. Drive
Floyd Memorial Building
704 West Tower
Atlanta, GA 30334
http://www.gainsurance.org

Hawaii

J.P. Schmidt, Commissioner
Hawaii Insurance Division
Department of Commerce & Consumer Affairs
PO Box 3614
Honolulu, HI 96811-3614
http://www.hawaii.gov

Idaho

William W. Deal, Director
Idaho Department of Insurance
700 West State Street, 3rd Floor
Boise, ID 83720-0043
http://www.doi.idaho.gov

Illinois

Michael McRaith, Director
Department of Financial and Professional Regulation
Illinois Division of Insurance
100 West Randolph Street, Suite 9-301
Chicago, IL 60601-3251
http://www.idfpr.com

Indiana

Jim Atterholt, Commissioner
Indiana Department of Insurance
311 W. Washington Street, Suite 300
Indianapolis, IN 46204-2787
http://www.ai.org

Iowa

Susan Voss, Commissioner
Division of Insurance
State of Iowa
330 E. Maple Street
Des Moines, IA 50319
http://www.iid.state.ia.us

Kansas

Sandy Praeger, Commissioner
Kansas Department of Insurance
420 S.W. 9th Street
Topeka, KS 66612-1678
http://www.ksinsurance.org

Kentucky

Julie Mix McPeak, Executive Director
Kentucky Office of Insurance
PO Box 517
Frankfort, KY 40602-0517
http://doi.ppr.ky.gov

Louisiana

James J. Donelon, Commissioner
Louisiana Department of Insurance
PO Box 94214
Baton Rouge, LA 70804-9214
http://www.ldi.state.la.us

Maine

Eric A. Cioppa, Acting Superintendent
Maine Bureau of Insurance
Department of Professional & Financial Regulation
State Office Building, Station 34
Augusta, ME 04333-0034
http://www.state.me.us

Maryland

R. Steven Orr, Commissioner
Maryland Insurance Administration
525 St. Paul Place
Baltimore, MD 21202-2272
http://www.mdinsurance.state.md.us

Massachusetts

Julie Bowler, Commissioner
Division of Insurance
Commonwealth of Massachusetts
One South Station, 5th Floor
Boston, MA 02110
Phone: 617.521.7794
Fax: 617.521.7758
http://www.mass.gov/doi/

Michigan

Linda Watters, Commissioner
Office of Financial and Insurance Services
Attn: Office of the Commissioner
PO Box 30220
Lansing, MI 48909
http://www.michigan.gov

Minnesota

Glenn Wilson, Commissioner
Minnesota Department of Commerce
85 7th Place East, Suite 500
St. Paul, MN 55101-2198
http://www.state.mn.us

Mississippi

George Dale, Commissioner
Mississippi Insurance Department
PO Box 79
Jackson, MS 39205
http://www.doi.state.ms.us

Missouri

Douglas Ommen, Director
Missouri Department of Insurance
301 West High Street, Suite 530
Jefferson City, MO 65102
http://www.insurance.mo.gov

Montana

John Morrison, Commissioner
Montana Department of Insurance
840 Helena Avenue
Helena, MT 59601
http://sao.mt.gov

Nebraska

L. Tim Wagner, Director
Nebraska Department of Insurance
Terminal Building, Suite 400
941 "O" Street
Lincoln, NE 68508
http://www.doi.ne.gov

Nevada

Alice Molasky-Arman, Commissioner
Nevada Division of Insurance
788 Fairview Drive, Suite 300
Carson City, NV 89701-5753
http://doi.state.nv.us

New Hampshire

Roger A. Sevigny, Commissioner
New Hampshire Insurance Department
21 South Fruit Street, Suite 14
Concord, NH 03301
http://www.state.nh.us/insurance

New Jersey

Steven M. Goldman, Commissioner
New Jersey Department of Insurance
20 West State Street CN325
Trenton, NJ 08625
http://www.state.nj.us

New Mexico

Morris J. Chavez, Superintendent
New Mexico Department of Insurance
PO Drawer 1269
Santa Fe, NM 87504-1269
http://www.nmprc.state.nm.us

New York
Eric R. Dinallo, Acting Superintendent
New York Department of Insurance
25 Beaver Street
New York, NY 10004-2319

or

New York Department of Insurance
One Commerce Plaza, Suite 1700
Albany, NY 12257
http://www.ins.state.ny.us

North Carolina

Jim Long, Commissioner
Department of Insurance
State of North Carolina
1201 Mail Service Center
Raleigh, NC 27699-1201
http://www.ncdoi.com

North Dakota

Jim Poolman, Commissioner
North Dakota Department of Insurance
600 East Boulevard
Bismarck, ND 58505-0320
http://www.state.nd.us/ndins

Ohio

Mary Jo Hudson, Director
Ohio Department of Insurance
2100 Stella Court
Columbus, OH 43215-1067
http://www.ohioinsurance.gov

Oklahoma

Kim Holland, Commissioner
Oklahoma Department of Insurance
2401 NW 23rd St., Suite 28
Oklahoma City, OK 73107
http://www.oid.state.ok.us

Oregon

Joel Ario, Insurance Administrator
Oregon Insurance Division
PO Box 14480
Salem, OR 97309-0405
http://www.cbs.state.or.us

Pennsylvania

Randy Rohrbaugh, Acting Commissioner
Pennsylvania Insurance Department
1326 Strawberry Square, 13th Floor
Harrisburg, PA 17120
http://www.ins.state.pa.us

Puerto Rico

Dorelisse Juarbe Jimenez, Commissioner
Puerto Rico Department of Insurance
PO Box 8330—Fernandez Juncos Station
Santurce, PR 00910-8330
http://www.gobierno.pr/GPRPortal

Rhode Island

Joseph Torti, III, Superintendent
Rhode Island Insurance Division
Department of Business Regulation

233 Richmond Street, Suite 233
Providence, RI 02903-4233
http://www.dbr.state.ri.us

South Carolina

Scott H. Richardson, Director
South Carolina Department of Insurance
PO Box 100105
Columbia, SC 29202-3105
https://www.doi.sc.gov

South Dakota

Merle Scheiber, Director
South Dakota Division of Insurance
Department of Revenue and Regulation
445 East Capitol Avenue, 1st Floor
Pierre, SD 57501-3185
http://www.state.sd.us/drr2/reg/insurance

Tennessee

Leslie A. Newman, Commissioner
Tennessee Department of Commerce & Insurance
Davy Crockett Tower, 5th Floor
500 James Robertson Parkway
Nashville, TN 37243-0565
http://www.state.tn.us

Texas

Mike Geeslin, Commissioner
Texas Department of Insurance
PO Box 149104
Austin, TX 78714-9104
http://www.tdi.state.tx.us

Utah

D. Kent Michie, Commissioner
Utah Department of Insurance
3110 State Office Building
Salt Lake City, UT 84114-1201
http://www.insurance.utah.gov

Vermont

Paulette J. Thabault, Commissioner
Vermont Division of Insurance
Department of Banking, Insurance & Securities
89 Main Street, Drawer 20
Montpelier, VT 05620-3101
http://www.bishca.state.vt.us/

Virgin Islands

Gregory R. Francis, Lieutenant Governor/Commissioner
Attn: Deverita Sturdivant
#18 Kongens Gade, Charlotte Amalie
St. Thomas, VI 00802

Division of Banking & Insurance
1131 King Street, Suite 101
Christiansted
St. Croix, VI 00820
http://www.ltg.gov.vi

Virginia

Alfred W. Gross, Commissioner
State Corporation Commission
Bureau of Insurance
Commonwealth of Virginia
PO Box 1157
Richmond, VA 23218
http://www.scc.virginia.gov

Washington

Mike Kreidler, Commissioner
Washington State
Office of the Insurance Commissioner
PO Box 40255
Olympia, WA 98504-0255
http://www.insurance.wa.gov

West Virginia

Jane L. Cline, Commissioner
West Virginia Department of Insurance
PO Box 50540
Charleston, WV 25305-0540
http://www.wvinsurance.gov

Wisconsin

Sean Dilweg, Commissioner
Office of the Commissioner of Insurance
State of Wisconsin
PO Box 7873
Madison, WI 53707-7873
http://oci.wi.gov

Wyoming
Ken Vines, Commissioner
Wyoming Department of Insurance
Herschler Building
122 West 25th Street, 3rd East
Cheyenne, WY 82002-0440
http://insurance.state.wy.us

Glossary

accounts receivable   monies owed to a physician for his or her services.

admit   term used when the physician admits the patient into the hospital.

admit/discharge sheet   a sheet generated by the hospital listing all patient information, including demographics and insurance information.

age   grow old.

allowed amount   the dollar amount an insurance company deems fair for a specific service or procedure.

appeal   a procedure used when the payer denies a service the patient thinks is needed or refuses to pay for care that the patient has already received.

audit   a formal examination of an individual's or organization's accounts.

authorization   a patient's signed approval.

batch   a set of claims.

beneficiary   term used for a patient who has Medicare coverage.

CAP   Claims Assistance Professional; a title used by members of the Alliance of Claims Assistance Professionals.

capitated   system in which a physician is prepaid monthly for members enrolled in an HMO with which the physician has contracted. The payment is made to the physician regardless of whether the physician sees no patients or all the patients in this plan.

capitated rate   a rate determined by the HMO for reimbursement for medical services when the physician is capitated with that plan.

capitation check   a monthly check the physician receives from the HMO plan.

capitation list   a list of patients enrolled in a particular HMO plan with which the physician is capitated.

carrier   a company that has contracted with CMS to pay Part B claims.

cash flow   a stream of cash (income) used for disbursements.

CBCS   Certified Billing and Coding Specialist; a certification offered by the National Healthcareer Association.

Centers for Medicare and Medicaid Services (CMS)   a government agency that oversees the Medicare and Medicaid programs.

certification   a professional status or level earned by successful completion of an examination; a person who is certified may subsequently list the designated credentials after her or his name.

CHP   Certified in Healthcare Privacy; a certification offered by the American Health Information Management Association.

CHRS Certified Healthcare Reimbursement Specialist; a certification offered by the National Electronic Billers Alliance.

claim attachment additional information submitted with the health insurance claim (e.g., progress notes).

clean describes a claim with no errors.

clearinghouse an entity that forwards claims to insurance payers electronically.

CMRS Certified Medical Reimbursement Specialist; a certification offered by the American Medical Billing Association.

coder the person whose job it is to assign CPT, HCPCS, and ICD-9 codes on the superbill, based on the physician's documentation.

codes assigned letters, numbers, or a combination of both used to report procedures, services, supplies, durable medical equipment, and diagnoses.

co-insurance a percentage the patient is responsible to pay of the cost of medical services. This is associated with indemnity, traditional, and commercial health insurance plans.

collection agency an agency retained by the practice for the purpose of collecting debts.

commercial another term for indemnity or traditional health insurance plans.

consult term used when a physician calls upon another physician to evaluate and make an assessment on a patient in the hospital setting.

consulting physician the physician called upon to provide a consultation regarding a patient who is in the hospital.

continuing education unit (CEU) a level of measurement of noncredited education.

contract an agreement between two or more parties.

co-payment a flat fee the patient pays each time for medical services. This is associated with managed care plans.

coverage existence and scope of existing health insurance.

CPT codes used to report services and procedures. These are level I codes under HCPCS.

CPT modifier a two-character numeric descriptor used only with CPT codes.

critical care direct delivery by a physician of medical care for a critically ill or critically injured patient.

decipher to interpret the meaning of.

deductible the amount the patient is responsible to pay before any reimbursement is issued by the insurance company. This is usually associated with indemnity, traditional, or commercial plans.

demographics statistical information on a patient.

denied refused to grant (as in payment for the claim).

Department of Insurance the governmental agency in charge of controlling and regulating insurance companies.

dependents persons covered under the policyholder's plan.

diagnosis (plural: diagnoses) the conclusion reached about a patient's ailment by thorough review of the patient's history, examination, and review of laboratory data.

disability insurance insurance providing income to a policyholder who is disabled and cannot work.

discharge the patient's release from the hospital.

discount a reduced fee.

documentation the process of recording information in the medical chart, or the materials in a medical chart.

E codes codes used to describe external causes of injury, poisoning, or other adverse reactions affecting the patient's health.

electronic claims submission the process of submitting health insurance claims via computer modem.

electronic data interchange (EDI) a mutual exchange of data via computer modem.

electronic funds transfer (EFT) payment method in which funds are deposited directly into the physician's bank account.

electronically via a computer modem.

eligibility category a category listing requirements for a person to be covered by a specific plan.

emergency room visits an encounter in the emergency room.

employee a person employed who is covered under an employer's group health plan.

employee/significant other (E/S) coverage health insurance covering the employee and the employee's significant other.

encounter form another name for the superbill.

encrypted information that is converted into code for security purposes.

established patient a patient who has been seen in the past 36 months.

explanation of benefits (EOB) the form sent to a physician or patient detailing benefits paid or denied by the insurance company.

family coverage health insurance coverage for the individual employee, the employee's spouse, and the employee's children.

fee for service a payment system in which the physician is paid a specific amount for each service performed.

fee schedule a list of allowed amounts for all services and procedures payable by the insurance company.

file an element of data storage.

fiscal agent a company that contracts with CMS to pay Medicaid claims.

follow-up the process of checking the status of a claim.

follow-up visit subsequent visit made by the physician following an admission.

government plan a health insurance plan funded by the government.

group number the number on the identification card that identifies the patient's employer group health plan.

guarantor information information on the person financially responsible for the patient's account.

HCPCS a coding system used to report procedures, services, supplies, medicine, and durable medical equipment. Comprised of CPT (level I) and national (level II) codes.

HCPCS modifier a two-character alphabetic or alphanumeric descriptor used with both CPT level I and level II national codes.

HCPCS national codes alphanumeric codes used to identify categories not included in HCPCS level I codes. These codes are considered level II codes.

health insurance a contract between the subscriber and the insurance company to pay for medical care and preventive services.

health insurance identification card card given to subscriber as proof of insurance.

health maintenance organization (HMO) a prepaid medical service plan that provides services to plan members.

HIPAA the Health Insurance Portability and Accountability Act of 1996, a law that stipulates patients' privacy rights regarding their PHI.

home visit a visit made by the physician to the patient's home.

hospital billing sheet form used by the physician to record hospital codes for inpatient visits.

husband/wife (H/W) coverage health insurance covering both the husband and wife.

ICD-9-CM *International Classification of Diseases, 9th Revision, Clinical Modification.* The ICD-9 codes are used to report diagnoses, signs, and symptoms of a patient.

identification number the number listed on the identification card that identifies the patient to the insurance company.

in network medical care sought from participating providers within a managed care plan.

indemnity plan a type of insurance plan in which reimbursement is made at 80 percent of the allowed amount. The patient is then responsible to pay the remaining 20 percent.

indigent impoverished; needy.

individual the one and only person covered under a health insurance plan.

initial hospital care the first hospital inpatient encounter with a patient by the admitting physician.

inpatient a patient who has been admitted to a hospital.

insurance adjustment the dollar amount adjusted off the patient's account reflecting the difference between the fee for services billed and the allowed amount determined by the insurance company.

insurance aging report report showing monies owed to the physician from insurance companies.

insured another term for policyholder or subscriber.

intelligence-free does not carry information about health care providers, such as the state in which they practice or their specialization.

intermediate care facility an institution that provides health-related care and services to individuals who do not require the degree of care and treatment that a hospital or nursing facility is designed to provide.

Internet-based medical billing the process of submitting health claims through a Web site on the Internet.

legacy number an identification number assigned to a physician that identifies the physician to payers.

long-term care facility a facility that provides medical services and assistance to patients over an extended period of time, and is designed to meet the medical, personal, and social needs of the patient.

maintaining keeping current.

managed care plan a health insurance plan that includes financing, management, and delivery of health care services.

manual claims submission the process of submitting health insurance claims via mail. The claim may be either handwritten or printed from the computer.

Medicaid a government plan for financially indigent people.

medical biller the person responsible for submitting a provider's charges to the appropriate party.

medical billing company an offsite company hired to process medical bills for the physician.

medical chart a confidential document that contains detailed and comprehensive information on the individual patient and the care given to that patient.

medical discount card a card listing the patient's name and verifying that the patient can receive a discount on services, if the provider's office participates.

Medicare a government health insurance plan primarily covering persons aged 65 and older.

Medicare managed care plan a plan offered by managed care companies to replace Original Medicare as the patient's health insurance.

Medigap supplemental insurance for patients with Medicare as their primary. These plans may pick up the Medicare deductible and co-insurance.

military treatment facility (MTF) a place where Tricare members receive medical treatment.

modifier a two-character alphabetic, numeric, or alphanumeric descriptor used to signify that a procedure or service has been altered by an unusual or specific circumstance, although the code itself has not changed. Additional use includes referencing a specific body site.

National Provider Identifier (NPI) a 10-digit, intelligence-free, numeric identifier.

new patient a patient who has never been seen before, or who has not been seen in the past 36 months.

noncovered service or procedure not listed as a covered benefit in the payer's master benefit list.

nursing facility a facility that provides continuous medical supervision via 24-hour-a-day nursing care and related services, in addition to food, shelter, and personal care.

nursing home visit a visit made by the physician to a patient who resides in a nursing home.

office visit an encounter in the physician's office.

Original Medicare the Medicare plan in which reimbursement for most services and procedures is paid at 80 percent of the allowed amount.

out of network medical care sought from nonparticipating providers; those providers who have not contracted with specific managed care plans.

out of pocket the patient's share of the cost of health care services. This can include co-payment, co-insurance, or a deductible.

outpatient services performed at a facility where the patient stays less than 24 hours and is not admitted to the facility; also, the term for the patient receiving such services.

outsource send work offsite.

outstanding not yet paid.

overhead a business expense.

parent/child coverage health insurance coverage for a parent and child.

participates the physician has signed a contract with the insurance company.

patient aging report report showing monies owed to the physician from patients (patient balances due).

patient registration form a form used to gather all patient information, including demographics and insurance information.

payer synonym for insurance company.

PHI protected health information.

physician-based pertaining only to a physician.

plan type a specific name assigned by the insurance company designating a specific plan for that type of insurance. For example, Oxford has a "liberty" plan.

point-of-service (POS) plan a health insurance plan in which the patient pays a co-payment when staying in network.

policyholder the person who has (carries) the health insurance.

post-dated check a check dated for the future.

posting the act of making an entry in the patient's account.

preferred provider network (PPN) a group of civilian medical providers that has contracted with Tricare.

preferred provider organization (PPO) this type of plan offers discounts to insurance company clients in exchange for more members.

prescription drugs medications prescribed by a physician (or other licensed prescriber).

primary the insurance plan that is billed first for medical services.

primary care provider (PCP) a physician (or other health care provider) who is responsible for a patient's main health care.

rebill to resubmit a claim.

referral permission from the primary care physician to seek services from a specialist for an evaluation, testing, and/or treatment. Managed care plans require this.

referred patient is sent to a specialist for evaluation and testing.

rejected refused to accept.

secondary the insurance plan that is billed after the primary has paid or denied payment.

self-pay a patient with no health insurance who must pay out of pocket for medical care.

sickness insurance insurance purchased in the early 1900s to provide income replacement in the event of illness.

soft collections mailing patient-due statements or calling patients to remind them of their past-due balances.

specialist physician who concentrates on a particular area of medicine (for example, cardiology or gastroenterology).

state insurance commissioner the appointed official in charge of each state's Department of Insurance.

subscriber another term for policyholder.

subsequent hospital care care provided to a patient (per day) following the initial hospital care.

superbill a form listing CPT, HCPCS, and ICD-9 codes used to record services performed for the patient and the patient's diagnosis(es) for a given visit.

supplemental another name for secondary insurance. A supplemental plan usually picks up the patient's deductible and/or co-insurance.

traditional another term for indemnity or commercial health insurance plans.

Tricare Extra a Tricare plan available only to retired military service members and their families. This plan is not available overseas.

Tricare Prime the only Tricare plan offering coverage for active-duty service members. Retired members may also select this plan.

Tricare Standard a Tricare plan available only to retired military service members and their families. This plan is available both in the United States and overseas.

unauthorized   authorization or approval not obtained prior to treatment.

V codes   ICD-9 codes assigned for preventive medicine services and for reasons other than disease or injuries.

write off   to adjust the dollar amount due from the patient or insurance company to reflect a zero balance due on the claim in question, or sometimes the patient's entire balance. The amount adjusted is called a *write-off*.

Index

A

ACAP (Alliance of Claims Assistance Professionals), 3–4
Accounts receivable
  defined, 1
  follow-up, claims, 117
  maintaining, 115, 118
  rebilling, 117
Acronyms, list of common, 181–183
Active duty military, 13–14
Admit sheet, 38
  sample form, blank, 39
Admitting physicians, 79, 83
ADN (Advance Beneficiary Notice) form, blank, 163, 169
Advance Beneficiary Notice (ABN) form, blank, 163, 169
Age, 115
Aging reports. *See* insurance aging reports
AHIMA (American Health Information Management Association), 3
Alliance of Claims Assistance Professionals (ACAP), 3–4
Allowed amount, 10
AMA (American Medical Association), 22
AMBA (American Medical Billing Association), 2–3
American Health Information Management Association (AHIMA), 3
American Medical Association (AMA), 22
American Medical Billing Association (AMBA), 2–3
American National Standards Institute (ANSI), 88
ANSI (American National Standards Institute), 88
Appeal, 107
Appealed claims, 107–114
  defined, 107
  of denied claims, 109
  sample appeal letter for "place of service" denial, 112
  sample failure to preauthorize treatment letter, 111
  sample letter, appeal for "not medically necessary" denial, 111
  sample letter, appeal for "place of service" denial, 112
  sample Medicare Part B claim inquiry/appeal request form, blank, 110
Audit, 25
Authorization, 37
Authorization to release protected health information (PHI), 35–37

B

Batch, 88
Beneficiary, 9
Billing. *See also* medical billing
  electronic claims submission, 87–88
  established patients, 62

frequency of, 40
hospital billing sheet form, 38–39
Internet-based medical billing, 87–88, 90
manual claims submission, 87
new patients, 61
office services and procedures, 61–71
rebilling, 115, 117
Blank forms. *See specific topics and forms*

C

CAP (Claims Assistance Professional), 3–4
Capitated, 12
Capitated rate, 12
Capitation check, 12
Capitation list, 12
Carrier, 11
Case study
  sample admitting physician critical care services form, completed, 83
  sample admitting physician services form, completed, 79
  sample CMS-1500 form, blank, 69
  sample CMS-1500 new patient form, completed, 67
  sample consulting physician services form, completed, 81
  sample consult visit form, completed, 70
  sample established patient form, completed, 68
  sample form, blank, 64
  sample form, completed, 79
  sample new patient form, completed, 66
  sample nursing facility form, completed, 85
Cash flow, 118
CBCS (Certified Billing and Coding Specialist), 3
Centers for Medicare and Medicaid Services (CMS), 10. *See also* CMS-1500 form
Certification, medical billing, 2, 4
Certified Billing and Coding Specialist (CBCS), 3
Certified Healthcare Reimbursement Specialist (CHRS), 3
Certified in Healthcare Privacy (CHP), 3
Certified Medical Reimbursement Specialist (CMRS), 2–3
CEU (continuing education unit), 4
CHP (Certified in Healthcare Privacy), 3
CHRS (Certified Healthcare Reimbursement Specialist), 3
Claim cycle, flowchart, 89
Claims
  accounts receivable follow-up, 117
  appealed claims, 107–114
  attachment to, 87
  cycles of, 89
  denied claims, 105–114
  electronic claims submission, 87–91
  filing instructions, CMS-1500 form, 47–59

Claims—cont'd
  payment of, 95, 130–132
  rejected, 105
  unauthorized, 107
Claims Assistance Professional (CAP), 3–4
Clean, 88
Clearinghouse
  defined, 88
  denied claims, 105
  electronic data interchange (EDI), 88
  rejected claims, 105
  resubmitted, 105
CMRS (Certified Medical Reimbursement Specialist), 2–3
CMS. *See* Centers for Medicare and Medicaid Services (CMS)
CMS-1500 form, 45–60
  blocks 1-13: patient and insured information, 47–50
  blocks 14-33: provider of supplier information, 50–59
  carrier or payer block, 47–59
  claim filing instructions, 47–59
  introduction, 45–47
  sample form, blank, 46, 69, 71, 163, 165
  sample form, completed with errors, 106, 113
  sample new patient form, completed, 67
CMS (Centers for Medicare and Medicaid Services), 10. *See also* CMS-1500 form
Coder, 38
Codes, 21. *See also* Healthcare Common Procedure Coding System (HCPCS); ICD-9-CM coding; modifiers
Codes of Conduct, 164, 175–178
Co-insurance, 9
"Co-insurance amounts due" sample form, completed, 124
Collection agency
  defined, 124
  sample letter, courtesy past-due notice, 127
  sample letter, final notice, 129
  sample letter, second past-due notice, 128
Collections, 121–135
  co-insurance amount due list, 122
  need for, 121–126
  post-dated checks, 122
  sample patient-due statement, completed, 125
  sample time-of-treatment collection script, 122
  soft, 122
  state insurance commissioner, 121–135
  write offs, 124
Commercial, 10
Consult
  consultation codes, office services, 62–63
  defined, 38
  sample consulting physician services form, completed, 81
  sample consult visit form, completed, 70
  sample request form, blank, 164, 172
Consulting physicians, 74, 81
Continuing education unit (CEU), 4
Contract, 12
Co-payment, 9, 11
Coverage, 15
Coverage, health insurance, types, 15
CPT codes. *See also* Current Procedural Terminology (CPT)
  CPT/HCPCS codes, 16
  defined, 22
  level I and level II, 25
  manual, 22, 25
  modifiers, 22, 25–57
  office visits, 62
Critical care, 74
Current Procedural Terminology (CPT). *See also* CPT codes

  defined, 22
  manual for, 25
  modifiers, 22, 25–27

D
Data gathering, 61–63
Decipher, 93
Deductible, 9
Demographics, 35
Denied claims, 105–114
  appealing, 109
  described, 105, 107
  reasons for, 107
  responding to, 107–108
  sample CMS-1500, completed with errors, 106, 113
  sample EOB denial, completed, 114
  sample EOB for denied claim form, completed, 108
  sample letter, appeal for "not medically necessary" denial, 111
Department of Insurance, state, 126
Dependents, 15
Diagnosis, 25
Disability insurance, 8
Discharge, 75
Discharge sheet sample, blank, 39
Discount, 16
Disease index, ICD-9-CM coding manual, 32
Doctors. *See* physicians
Documentation, 38

E
E codes, ICD-9-CM coding, 32
EDI (electronic data interchange), 88
EFT. *See* electronic funds transfer (EFT)
Electronically transmitted, 99
Electronic claims submission, 87–91
  clearinghouse role, 88
  defined, 88
  and EDI, 88
  encrypted data, 88–89
  flowchart for, 89
  formats for, 88
  vs. "snail mail," 87
  submissions and benefits, 87–88
  via Internet and the Web, 87–88, 90
Electronic data interchange (EDI), 88
Electronic funds transfer (EFT), 93
  authorization agreement form, blank, 97–98
Eligibility category, 11
E&M Code Builders, 163, 166–167
Emergency room visits, 11
Employee, 15
Employee/significant other (E/S) coverage, 15
Encoder Pro software free trial, xxv–xxvi
Encounter forms, 37–38
Encrypted data, 88–89
EOB. *See* explanation of benefits (EOB)
ER (emergency room) visits, 11
E/S (employee/significant other coverage), 15
Established patients
  billing, 62
  defined, 35
  office visit codes, 62
Evaluation and management codes, 163, 168
Exams, for certification, 2–4
Explanation of benefits (EOB)
  deciphering, 93
  defined, 95

explanation of payment report, 95
Medicare remittance notice, 95
payments, 93–103
provider claim summary, 95
provider voucher, 95
remittance advice, 95
sample EFT authorization agreement form, blank, 97–98
sample EOB annotated form, blank, 94
sample EOB for denied claim form, completed, 108
sample EOB form, completed, 100–101
sample Medicare remittance notice, completed, 96, 103
standard paper remittance, 95
Explanation of payment report, 95

F

Family coverage, 15
Federal government
government plans, 9–10
Medicare, 10
ruling against insurance company, 132
Fee for service, 12
Fee schedule, 10
sample Medicare, completed, 123
File, 88
Filing instructions for claims, CMS-1500 form, 47–59
Fiscal agent, 11
Follow-up
claims, 115, 117
visit, 38
Forms. *See specific topics and forms*
Frequency of billing, 40

G

Government health insurance plans, 9–10
Group number, 9
Guarantor information, 35

H

HCPCS. *See* Healthcare Common Procedure Coding System (HCPCS)
Healthcare Common Procedure Coding System (HCPCS)
defined, 21
level II codes, 22, 24–25, 63
modifiers, 25, 28–31
national codes, 22
place of service code, 54–55
procedure-based coding system, 21
Health insurance
claim form instructions, 47–59
claim payment timing, 95, 130–132
coverage, 15
defined, 8
example of federal ruling against insurance company, 132
government plans, 9–10
identification card, 7–17
indemnity card, sample, 9
indemnity plan, 9
insurance adjustments, explanation of benefits (EOB), 95
Insurance aging report, 115–117, 119
managed care plans, 10–14
medical discount cards, 13, 15–16
for military service members, 13–14
traditional plans, 10
Tricare, 13–14
types of coverage, 15
types of plans, 9–14
Health Insurance Portability and Accountability Act (HIPAA), 37

Health maintenance organization (HMO), 11–12
HIPAA (Health Insurance Portability and Accountability Act), 37
HIPAA Release forms, 37
HMO (health maintenance organization), 11–12
Home visits, 38, 40
Hospital billing sheets, 38–39
sample blank, 38
sample completed, 38, 44
Husband/wife (H/W) coverage, 15
H/W (husband/wife) coverage, 15

I

ICD-9-CM coding
defined, 25
E codes, 32
manual for, 25, 32
V codes, 32
Volume 1 (tabular list), 31–32
Volume 2 (index to diseases), 31–32
Volume 3 (index to procedures and tabular list), 32
Identification card, health insurance, 7–17
Identification number, 9
Indemnity card, sample, 9
Indemnity health insurance plan, 9
Index
to diseases, ICD-9-CM, 31–32
to procedures, ICD-9-CM, 32
Indigent person, 11
Individual, 15
Information gathering, 61–63
Informed Refusal form, blank, 164, 174
Initial hospital care, 73
In network, 11
Inpatient, 73
Insurance adjustment, 95. *See also* health insurance
Insurance aging reports, 115–120
defined, 115
process, 115
reports, 115–120
sample, completed, 116–117, 119–120
Insurance commissioners, by state, 195–202
Insurance companies
example of federal ruling against insurance company, 132
state laws and regulations, 126
state laws on claim payment timing, 130–132
Insured persons, 9
Intelligence-free, 47
Intermediate care facility, 76
Internet-based medical billing, 87–88, 90
Interpret EOBs, 93

J

Job location, medical billers, 1

L

Legacy number, 47
Legal considerations
adjustments, explanation of benefits (EOB), 95
claim payment timing, 130–132
federal ruling against insurance company, 132
insurance companies, 126, 130–132
state laws and regulations, 126, 130–132
Level I and level II codes, CPT, 25
Level II codes, HCPCS, 22, 24–25, 63
Location, medical billers, 1
Long-term care facility, 76

M

Maintaining
    accounts receivable, 115, 118
    aging reports, 115
    defined, 118
    rebilling, 115
Managed care health insurance plans, 10–14
    described, 10–11
    HMOs, 11
    Medicaid managed care plans, 12–13
    Medicare Advantage, 12–13
    Medicare managed care plans, 12–13
    POS plans, 12
    PPOs, 11
Manual claims submission, 87, 89
Manuals
    CPT, 22, 25
    ICD-9-CM coding, 25, 32
Medicaid, 10
Medical billers, 1–4
    certification, 2
    defined, 1
    organizational memberships, 2–4
    work location, 1
Medical billing. *See also* billing; *specific topics*
    companies for, 1
    terms, 21
Medical chart, 37
Medical discount cards
    defined, 15
    vs. health identification card, 13, 15–16
    sample, 16
    savings chart, 16
Medicare
    defined, 10
    EOB remittance notice, 95
    Original, 12
    Part B, 110, 185–193
    sample "co-insurance amounts due," completed, 124
    sample fee schedule, 123
    sample managed care plan card, 13
    sample Medicare card, 10, 13
    sample Medicare patient's remittance notice, completed, 96
Medicare Advantage, 13
Medicare Part C (Advantage), 13
Medigap, 8
Military personnel, 13–14
Military treatment facility (MTF), 13
Modifiers
    CPT, 25–27
    defined, 22
    HCPCS, 25, 28–31
MTF (military treatment facility), 13

N

National Electronic Billers Alliance (NEBA), 3
National Healthcareer Association (NHA), 3
National Provider Identifier (NPI), 45
National Standard Format (NSF), 88
National Uniform Claim Committee (NUCC), 45
NEBA (National Electronic Billers Alliance), 3
NEMB (Notice of Exclusions from Medicare Benefits), 164, 170
New patients
    billing, 61
    defined, 35
    office visit codes, 61
NHA (National Healthcareer Association), 3

Noncovered persons, 107
Notice of Exclusions from Medicare Benefits (NEMB), 164, 170
NPI (National Provider Identifier), 45
NSF (National Standard Format), 88
NUCC (National Uniform Claim Committee), 45
Nursing facility, 76
Nursing home visit, 38, 40

O

Office services and procedures, 61–71
    See also case study
    consultation codes, 62–63
    data gathering, 61–63
    established patients, 62
    modifiers, determining usage, 63
    new patients, 63
    procedures, 63
    sample CMS-1500 form, blank, 69, 71
    sample CMS-1500 form, completed, 67
    sample consult visit form, completed, 70
    sample new patient form, completed, 66
Office visits, 61–62
Online. *See* Web sites
Organizational membership, medical billers, 2–4
    Certified Billing and Coding Specialist (CBCS), 3
    Certified Healthcare Reimbursement Specialist (CHRS), 3
    Certified in Healthcare Privacy (CHP), 3
    Certified Medical Reimbursement Specialist (CMRS), 2–3
    Claims Assistance Professional (CAP), 3–4
Original Medicare, 11–12. *See also* Medicare
Out of network, 11
Out of pocket, 13
Outpatient, 10
Outsource, 1
Outstanding, 115
Overhead, 118

P

Parent/child coverage, 15
Participants, 8
Patient registration form, 35–37
    defined, 35
    HIPPA release, 337
    PHI authorization, 35–37
    sample form, blank, 36
    sample form, completed, 42
Patients. *See also* insurance aging reports
    complaint initiated by, state insurance
        commissioner, 132–133
    patient-due statement, completed form, 125
Payer, 47
Payments
    of claims, 95
    electronic funds transfer (EFT), 95
    explanation of benefits (EOB), 93–103
    at time-of-treatment, 122
PCP (primary care provider), 11
PHI (protected health information), 35–37
Physician-based billing, 1
Physicians
    admitting, 79, 83
    complaint initiated by, to state insurance commissioner, 133
    consulting, 74, 81
    sample admitting physician critical care services form,
        completed, 83
    sample admitting physician services form, completed, 79

sample complaint initiated by, state insurance commissioner, 126, 133
sample consulting physician services form, completed, 81
Place of service codes, 54–55
Plan type, 9
Point-of-service (POS) plan, 13
Policyholder, 9
POS (point-of-service) plan, 13
Post-dated check, 122
Posting, 95
PPN (preferred provider network), 13
PPO (preferred provider organization), 12
Preferred provider network (PPN), 13
Preferred provider organization (PPO), 12
Prescription drugs, 11
Primary, 8
Primary care provider (PCP), 11
Protected health information (PHI), 35–37
Providers
    claim summary, EOB, 95
    voucher, EOB, 95

R
Rebilling, 115, 117
Referral, 13
Referred person, 62
Refusal to Authorize Payment form, blank, 164, 173
Rejected claims, 105. *See also* appealed claims; denied claims
Release forms
    HIPAA, 37
    PHI authorization, 35–37
Remittance advice, 95
Request for Opinion/Consult, blank, 164, 172
Retired military service, 14

S
Secondary, 8
Self-pay, 8
Sickness insurance, 8
Soft collections, 122
Software
    E&M Code Builders, 163, 166–167
    Encoder Pro free trial, xxv–xxvi
    student practice software guidelines, xix–xxiii
Specialist, 11, 62
Standard paper remittance, EOB, 95
State insurance commissioner, 121–135
    defined, 126
    listed by state, 195–202
    patient-initiated complaint, 132–133
    physician-initiated complaint, 126, 133

sample patient-initiated complaint, blank, 133
sample physician-initiated complaint, blank, 133
States and state laws. *See also* state insurance commissioner
    claim payment timing, 130–132
    Departments of Insurance, 126
    example of federal ruling against insurance company, 132
    government of, 9
    insurance companies, on claim payment timing, 130–132
    laws and regulations, 126
    Medicare Part B carriers, 185–193
    Medicare Part B carriers by, 185–193
Student practice software guidelines, xix–xxiii
Subscriber, 9
Subsequent hospital care, 74
Superbill, 16, 37–38
    sample form, blank, 37
Supplemental, 8

T
Tabular list, ICD-9-CM volume 1&3 coding, 31–32
Traditional health insurance plans, 10
Tricare, 13–14
Tricare Extra, 14
Tricare Prime, 13–14
Tricare Standard, 14

U
UB-04 form, blank, 164, 179
Unauthorized claims, 107

V
V codes, ICD-9-CM coding, 32
Visits
    emergency room visits, 11
    follow-up, 38
    home, 40
    nursing home, 40
    office, 61–62
Volume 1 (tabular list), ICD-9-CM coding, 31–32
Volume 2 (index to diseases), ICD-9-CM coding, 31–32
Volume 3 (index to procedures and tabular list), ICD-9-CM coding, 32

W
Web sites
    insurance commissioners by state, 195–202
    Internet-based medical billing, 87–88, 90
    Medicare Part B carriers by state, 185–193
    Web-based medical billing, 87–88, 90
Workplace, medical billers, 1
Write off, 124

Minimum System Requirements
- Operating system: Microsoft Windows 98 or later (including Windows ME, Windows NT, Windows 2000, Windows XP, Windows VISTA)
- Processor: Pentium PC 500 MHz or higher (750 MHz recommended)
- 64 MB of RAM (128 MB recommended)
- 32 MB free hard drive space
- Monitor screen resolution: 800 × 600 pixels
- Color depth: 16-bit color (thousands of colors)
- Mouse
- Printer: 16 MB memory recommended

Installing the Student Practice Software on Your Computer
1. Insert the CD-ROM into a CD-ROM drive.
2. Click **Start**, then click **Run**.
3. Enter **d:\Setup** and click **OK** (Note: replace d with your CD-ROM drive letter).
4. In a few moments, you will be welcomed to the installation program. Click **Next** to start the installation.
5. A dialog box will ask for the drive and directory where you want the program installed. To install the program in the default directory at c:\Program Files\Delmar\Medical Billing 101, click **Next**. If you want to change this, click **Browse**, and enter the directory and drive where you want the program to be installed.
6. Once the installation begins, it can be cancelled at any time by clicking **Cancel**.
7. A Delmar Medical Billing 101 icon will be added to the Start menu under Programs | Delmar Applications.
8. The install program will automatically complete the installation process. Click **OK** when you see the "Installation is Complete" message.

Removing the Student Practice Software from Your Computer
To remove the Medical Billing 101 program from your computer, follow this procedure:

1. First, exit the program before attempting to uninstall it.
2. On the Windows task bar choose **Start** > **Programs** > **Delmar Applications** > **Uninstall Medical Billing 101**.
3. A prompt will appear asking you to confirm that you want to delete the program. Click **Yes** to continue.
4. When the program uninstall procedure is completed, click **OK**.

ownership. The Licensed Content is protected by U.S., Canadian and other applicable copyright laws and by international treaties, including the Berne Convention and the Universal Copyright Convention. Nothing contained in this Agreement shall be construed as granting the End User any ownership rights in or to the Licensed Content.

3.2 Cengage Learning reserves the right at any time to withdraw from the Licensed Content any item or part of an item for which it no longer retains the right to publish, or which it has reasonable grounds to believe infringes copyright or is defamatory, unlawful, or otherwise objectionable.

4.0 PROTECTION AND SECURITY

4.1 The End User shall use its best efforts and take all reasonable steps to safeguard its copy of the Licensed Content to ensure that no unauthorized reproduction, publication, disclosure, modification, or distribution of the Licensed Content, in whole or in part, is made. To the extent that the End User becomes aware of any such unauthorized use of the Licensed Content, the End User shall immediately notify Cengage Learning. Notification of such violations may be made by sending an e-mail to Delmar.help@cengage.com.

5.0 MISUSE OF THE LICENSED PRODUCT

5.1 In the event that the End User uses the Licensed Content in violation of this Agreement, Cengage Learning shall have the option of electing liquidated damages, which shall include all profits generated by the End User's use of the Licensed Content plus interest computed at the maximum rate permitted by law and all legal fees and other expenses incurred by Cengage Learning in enforcing its rights, plus penalties.

6.0 FEDERAL GOVERNMENT CLIENTS

6.1 Except as expressly authorized by Cengage Learning, Federal Government clients obtain only the rights specified in this Agreement and no other rights. The Government acknowledges that (i) all software and related documentation incorporated in the Licensed Content is existing commercial computer software within the meaning of FAR 27.405(b)(2); and (2) all other data delivered in whatever form, is limited rights data within the meaning of FAR 27.401. The restrictions in this section are acceptable as consistent with the Government's need for software and other data under this Agreement.

7.0 DISCLAIMER OF WARRANTIES AND LIABILITIES

7.1 Although Cengage Learning believes the Licensed Content to be reliable, Cengage Learning does not guarantee or warrant (i) any information or materials contained in or produced by the Licensed Content, (ii) the accuracy, completeness or reliability of the Licensed Content, or (iii) that the Licensed Content is free from errors or other material defects. THE LICENSED PRODUCT IS PROVIDED "AS IS," WITHOUT ANY WARRANTY OF ANY KIND AND CENGAGE LEARNING DISCLAIMS ANY AND ALL WARRANTIES, EXPRESSED OR IMPLIED, INCLUDING, WITHOUT LIMITATION, WARRANTIES OF MERCHANTABILITY OR FITNESS FOR A PARTICULAR PURPOSE. IN NO EVENT SHALL CENGAGE LEARNING BE LIABLE FOR: INDIRECT, SPECIAL, PUNITIVE OR CONSEQUENTIAL DAMAGES INCLUDING FOR LOST PROFITS, LOST DATA, OR OTHERWISE. IN NO EVENT SHALL CENGAGE LEARNING'S AGGREGATE LIABILITY HEREUNDER, WHETHER ARISING IN CONTRACT, TORT, STRICT LIABILITY OR OTHERWISE, EXCEED THE AMOUNT OF FEES PAID BY THE END USER HEREUNDER FOR THE LICENSE OF THE LICENSED CONTENT.

8.0 GENERAL

8.1 <u>Entire Agreement</u>. This Agreement shall constitute the entire Agreement between the Parties and supercedes all prior Agreements and understandings oral or written relating to the subject matter hereof.

8.2 <u>Enhancements/Modifications of Licensed Content</u>. From time to time, and in Cengage Learning's sole discretion, Cengage Learning may advise the End User of updates, upgrades, enhancements and/or improvements to the Licensed Content, and may permit the End User to access and use, subject to the terms and conditions of this Agreement, such modifications, upon payment of prices as may be established by Cengage Learning.

8.3 <u>No Export</u>. The End User shall use the Licensed Content solely in the United States and shall not transfer or export, directly or indirectly, the Licensed Content outside the United States.

8.4 <u>Severability.</u> If any provision of this Agreement is invalid, illegal, or unenforceable under any applicable statute or rule of law, the provision shall be deemed omitted to the extent that it is invalid, illegal, or unenforceable. In such a case, the remainder of the Agreement shall be construed in a manner as to give greatest effect to the original intention of the parties hereto.

8.5 <u>Waiver</u>. The waiver of any right or failure of either party to exercise in any respect any right provided in this Agreement in any instance shall not be deemed to be a waiver of such right in the future or a waiver of any other right under this Agreement.

8.6 <u>Choice of Law/Venue</u>. This Agreement shall be interpreted, construed, and governed by and in accordance with the laws of the State of New York, applicable to contracts executed and to be wholly preformed therein, without regard to its principles governing conflicts of law. Each party agrees that any proceeding arising out of or relating to this Agreement or the breach or threatened breach of this Agreement may be commenced and prosecuted in a court in the State and County of New York. Each party consents and submits to the nonexclusive personal jurisdiction of any court in the State and County of New York in respect of any such proceeding.

8.7 <u>Acknowledgment</u>. By opening this package and/or by accessing the Licensed Content on this Web site, THE END USER ACKNOWLEDGES THAT IT HAS READ THIS AGREEMENT, UNDERSTANDS IT, AND AGREES TO BE BOUND BY ITS TERMS AND CONDITIONS. IF YOU DO NOT ACCEPT THESE TERMS AND CONDITIONS, YOU MUST NOT ACCESS THE LICENSED CONTENT AND RETURN THE LICENSED PRODUCT TO DELMAR LEARNING (WITHIN 30 CALENDAR DAYS OF THE END USER'S PURCHASE) WITH PROOF OF PAYMENT ACCEPTABLE TO CENGAGE LEARNING, FOR A CREDIT OR A REFUND. Should the End User have any questions/comments regarding this Agreement, please contact Cengage Learning at Delmar.help@cengage.com.